ROMAN GAUL

Fig. 1. The Tour d'Ordre, or Old Man of Boulogne,
a Roman lighthouse destroyed in 1544

ROMAN GAUL

by

OLWEN BROGAN, F.S.A.

with drawings by
EDGAR HOLLOWAY

LONDON
G. BELL AND SONS, LTD
1953

Printed in Great Britain by
Richard Clay and Company, Ltd., Bungay, Suffolk

PREFACE

THIS book does not attempt to instruct the expert, but only to serve as an introduction to students and travellers who may wish to get a general picture of Roman Gaul, its history and its chief monuments. The greatest difficulty in its composition has been to bring so large a subject within 250 pages, a very narrow cockpit to hold the vasty fields of France. Perhaps, however, this brief summary may be found useful by some who have not the time to make a deeper study of the subject; I should like to think that it might even persuade a few to share the pleasures of a hobby which affords a wonderful excuse for wandering about the beautiful land of France, and combining the interest of a study of the past with the enjoyments of the present.

An attempt to be consistent over place-names had to be abandoned. It is easy to start off with Narbo and Massilia, but obviously absurd to talk about the Arch of Arausio. Also, the names of many cities were changing in the later Empire, when Lutetia was becoming Paris and Samarobriva Amiens. So, in general, the classical names are used in the early, historical chapters, but modern names are used in the descriptive part. Both classical and modern place-names are to be found in the index.

I owe thanks to many scholars on both sides of the Channel. Most of all I am indebted to Monsieur P.-F. Fournier of Clermont-Ferrand, Professor I. A. Richmond and Mr. Russell Meiggs, for their kindness in reading the book, for making many helpful suggestions and for steering me clear of all manner of pitfalls.

I am very grateful to the many Directors and other officials of museums and other institutes who have allowed me to linger over their collections and helped me in so many ways, especially to M. R. Lantier of Saint

Germain-en-Laye, Drs. H. Eiden and W. Reusch of Trier, Dr. J. Breuer of Brussels Museum, M. J. Latour of Arles and Dr. G. Bersu of the Archaeological Institute of Frankfort-on-Main. My thanks for photographs and other illustrations, or for help in obtaining them, is due to M. L. Balsan (Rodez), Dr. H. Brunsting (Leyden), M. P. Cordonnier (Le Mans), M. P.-M. Duval (Ministry of Education, Paris), Dr. H. Eiden (Trier), M. P.-F. Fournier (Clermont-Ferrand), M. J. Harmand (Saint Germain-en-Laye), M. J. Latour (Arles), Dr. R. Laur-Belart (Basle), M. G. Matherat (Compiègne), Dr. H. von Petrikovits (Bonn), Mlle. Popovitch (Reims), Dr. W. Reusch (Trier), M. l'Abbé J. Sautel (Avignon), M. E. Thevenot (Neuilly), the Museums of Lyons, Berne and Bordeaux, and most particularly to M. M. Labrousse (Toulouse), who went all the way to Agassac to take the photograph which I am proud to have as fig. 48.

I have also to thank the Loeb Classical Library for permission to use a quotation from H. L. Jones's translation of Strabo (page 2), the N. V. Standaard-Boekhandel for fig. 28, and the City of Lyons for fig. 37b. Various figures have been based upon illustrations in other books, and thanks is due to the editors of *Gallia* for figs. 3, 12, and 14–17, to the Verein von Altertumsfreunden im Rheinlande for figs. 5 and 20 and the upper half of fig. 7, to Benno Schwabe & Co. for figs. 6, 30 and 34, to Editions A. & J. Picard & Cie. for the lower half of fig. 7, and figs. 17, 22 and 25, to the editors of the *Trierer Zeitschrift* for figs. 18, 19 and 32, and to the Römisch-Germanische Kommission for figs. 9, 11 and 35.

The chief sources of information, new and old, to which I am indebted, are shown in the bibliography. Lastly, I should like to add a word of thanks to the publishers and their artist for all the trouble they have taken and the help they have given.

O. B.

Cambridge,
  September 1952

CONTENTS

A WORD ON MEASUREMENTS

When we cross the Channel we exchange miles for kilometres and acres for hectares, so I have used the metric system throughout.

1 metre = 39·37 ins. or 3¼ feet
1 kilometre = 1093·6 yards (⅝ of a mile)
1 hectare = 2·47 acres

LIST OF ILLUSTRATIONS

PLATES BETWEEN PAGES 234 AND 235

I

GAUL AND THE REPUBLIC

No province of the Roman Empire has had a greater influence on the modern world than Gaul. Gaul was the bastion of the Mediterranean world against the barbarians, and during the first four centuries of our era it lay in the main stream of history. The fortunes of the Julian house were based on its hold on Gaul, and vanished when, in the year 69, a Gallic governor initiated the revolt against Nero. The family of Constantine rose to fame in Gaul, and under Constantius Trier became one of the imperial capitals. One of the last achievements of the Western Empire was the defeat of Attila the Hun on Gallic soil.

In Gaul the arts of peace developed over a long period. The great size of the land was to be a decisive factor in its destiny, for it could endure the infiltration of large numbers of northern wanderers and yet manage to preserve much of the framework of Roman society, its cities, ports, bishoprics, landed domains and roads. It thus carried over into the dark ages the shell of the old civilization on which men could gradually build, so that the Frankish peoples climbed more rapidly out of barbarism than did other nations, and the influence of the old Roman Empire was never entirely lost in western Europe.

Though we may mourn the bold, generous Gauls, with their great talents and their love of freedom, who were so ruthlessly subdued, we have to remember that they had shown very few signs of political wisdom. Their disunity was so great that there were always some among them ready to call in German or Roman to help them in

their quarrels. The coming of Rome gave cohesion to
Gaul and laid the foundations of modern France.

We are fortunate in being able to see Gaul through the
eyes of the ancients themselves. 'This land,' says
Pomponius Mela, 'is rich above all in corn and pastures
and pleasant with great and sacred forests.' Strabo, a
Greek geographer who lived in the time of Augustus,
draws attention to the mighty navigable rivers of Gaul, so
different from the seasonal torrents of his own world, and
to the fact that therefore 'the necessities of life are with
ease interchanged by everyone with everyone else and
the advantages which have risen therefrom are common
to all; but especially so at present, when being at leisure
from the weapons of war, the people are tilling the
country diligently and are devising for themselves civil
modes of life.'

A glance at the map of France shows the accuracy of
Strabo's description, with the Rhone corridor from the
south communicating so easily with the northern river
systems, while access to the south-west may be had from
Narbonne through the Toulouse gap and then down the
Garonne valley. The Loire and the Seine and their
tributaries provide magnificent waterways for the centre
and north-west, and farther over to the north-east is the
Rhine system. Another feature to bear in mind is the
size of Gaul. France is a large country—more than three
and a half times the size of England and Wales—and Gaul
was larger still, for it included the territory of Belgium,
the Rhineland and much of the Netherlands and Switzerland, as well as that of modern France. As we journey
by train or car or aeroplane over the broad wheatlands
of the north, or on the long trip from Paris to Marseilles,
we may spare a thought for Caesar's legionaries tramping
from end to end of this great land, and realize what an
immense achievement was the conquest and government
of such a vast area.

The wide rolling plains of the north and west contain
large areas of naturally open, easily worked soil, notably

in Picardy, Hainault, the Beauce. Similar soils occur in parts of the Garonne valley. Much of the land was still covered with forests, invaluable for the timber trade and as shelter for herds of swine; there was also ample pasture for the horses, cattle and sheep which contributed greatly to the wealth of Gaul. The mountain-blocks of the centre, the north-east and the south-east were not impenetrable, and included much good grazing and forest land; they also sheltered tracts of very fertile soil, such as the Limagne, the rich plain of the middle Allier.

It is difficult to say when the first Celtic peoples entered Gaul, but their spread seems roughly to coincide with the coming of the Iron Age to western Europe, a phase called the Hallstatt culture and dating from about 800 B.C. The culture which is specially associated with the Celts is, however, that of the second or La Tène period of the Iron Age. This begins about 450 B.C., from which time successive waves of new invaders made their way into Gaul and completed the ethnic pattern which the Romans were to find. As the Iron Age peoples moved forward they found other folks there before them. This pre-Celtic element persisted, and still persists, as a substratum all over France, but it was strongest in the south-west, among the Iberian ancestors of the Gascons, along the north side of the Pyrenees, and in the south-east, where, in the departments of Var and Alpes-Maritimes, the Ligurians long maintained themselves.

The last conquering Celts who pushed down the Rhone valley and south-west towards Spain found, besides Hallstatt folk, Ligurians and Iberians, the Greeks of Massilia. The Massiliotes had been established here since about 600 B.C., and had founded a number of colonies along the coast, including Agathe (Agde), Antipolis (Antibes) and Nicaea (Nice). The Greeks were constrained to look to their own safety, and built a number of strong points, including one recently excavated at Saint-Blaise near Fos, to keep watch on the new-comers. Accommodation was, however, soon reached and, judging by finds of Massiliote coins in the interior of Gaul, trade with the hinterland was re-established.

We do not know when the first Roman set foot in Gaul, but Rome and Massilia were long on friendly terms, having a common dread of the Gallic invader and a common hostility to the Carthaginian sailor. They formed an alliance as early as the fifth century B.C., and Massilia proved a useful ally during the Punic wars.

Hannibal made the Roman occupation of Gaul inevitable. His final defeat in 202 B.C. meant that Spain became a Roman province, and consequently Rome became increasingly interested in the affairs of Massilia, for the Greek city and its colonies were important ports of call on the route to Spain. For many years Rome was content merely to enjoy a right of way. This state of affairs came to an end through Ligurian piracy and Celtic unrest, which brought in the Roman legions and resulted in the ultimate overthrow of both Gauls and Greeks, for Massilia shared the usual tendency of Hellenistic cities to let the efficient Romans do police work which they should have done for themselves.

About 150 there seemed to be a chance of Celtic Gaul becoming united under the leadership of a single powerful tribe, the Arverni of the Massif Central, whose allies included the Allobroges of the Rhone Valley and their neighbours on the south-east, the Saluvii. The Saluvii were emboldened to attack Massiliote territory in 125. This move was bound to interest Rome because of its threat to her coastal communications, so she came willingly to the help of the Greeks, and in 125 Fulvius Flaccus led an army across the Alps. His successor in the command, C. Sextius Calvinus, defeated the Saluvii decisively (124), taking their stronghold at Entremont and building a Roman strong point at Aix-en-Provence in the valley below (123). This *castellum*, Aquae Sextiae, is thus the earliest Roman foundation in Gaul.

Opportunity for still heavier intervention in Gaul now

came, with the appeal of the Aedui of the Morvan and Nivernais for help against the Arverni, whose pretensions they resented. A year previously, Rome had flattered the Aedui by concluding a treaty of friendship with them, doubtless with an eye to possible developments. The Arverni, too, were ready for an opportunity of avenging the defeat of the Saluvii, so the stage was set for a major clash. The Arvernian king, Bituitus, made the mistake of allowing the Romans time to defeat his allies, the Allobroges, before he brought his host down into the Rhone valley, and his own inevitable defeat at the hands of Gnaeus Domitius Ahenobarbus, the ancestor of Nero, followed (121). Domitius then annexed all the former territory of the Allobroges, comprising the Rhone valley as far as Geneva and the arc of Mediterranean coastline between the Rhone and the Pyrenees. Bituitus was brought to Rome to march in his victor's triumph, and the handsome barbaric trappings of his arms and armour were long remembered. His no less flamboyant conqueror was also remembered for riding triumphantly about the conquered province on an elephant.

Rome had now a Transalpine province. She already had Gallic subjects in Cisalpine Gaul, the land between the Alps and the Po which had been subdued after the war with Hannibal. The Cisalpine Gauls had shown great capacity for rapid assimilation into Italian civilization, and by the time of Caesar they had become ready for admission to the Roman citizenship. The Transalpine Gauls were to show themselves equally apt pupils. The Celtic and Latin languages happened to be philologically close, within the Indo-European group, which helped to minimize the barrier between Gaul and Roman, but in any case Rome had no place for racial discrimination as such.

Rome signalized her arrival in Transalpine Gaul by founding a colony (118 B.C.) and building a road. The colony was Narbo Martius (Narbonne), the first citizen colony outside Italy. The road, the Via Domitia, was built over a track so ancient that it had become part of the legend of Heracles, who was said to have passed this way on his journey to the Hesperides. Mounting guard from time immemorial along this route, was a series of ancient strongholds (Ensérune, Montlaurès, Cayla). On all these *oppida* have been found pots from Rhodes of the sixth century B.C., then come fine Attic pieces and Phocaean pottery, then the Italiote and black Campanian ware of the third and second centuries. From their heights the inhabitants had looked down on the passing host of Hannibal, as they were now to see the Roman road-makers. These towns, however, did not long survive the conquest, as the population found it more pleasant to descend into the plain, but some of them were still occupied in the first century A.D.

Transalpine Gaul was an oddly shaped province, curving round from the Pyrenees to Geneva, and it was hemmed in on most sides by hostile or potentially hostile tribes. The Volcae Tectosages around Tolosa (Toulouse) were brought into alliance and persuaded to admit a Roman garrison into their chief town; out beyond the north-western frontier the Aedui maintained their alliance with Rome. Armed forces were maintained in the territory, and Cicero calls Narbo a watch-tower of the Roman people. When Caesar took over in 58 B.C. the province held one legion.

The new Roman province had scarcely been organized when the first Germanic invasion knocked on the door of European history. Wandering peoples, the Cimbri and Teutoni, displaced from their homes in the north, pressed into central and western Europe. The Cimbri came from northern Denmark, and seem to have been disturbed by inundations due to coast subsidence. The Teutoni were a neighbouring tribe. After reaching the Danube basin, where they defeated a Roman army (113 B.C.), the Germans turned and wandered about central Europe. In 109 they crossed the Rhine, and for ten years bands of them roamed at will through Gaul, terrorizing the inhabitants, but never able to find a place to settle. They were reinforced by Celtic elements, most prominent of which were the Tigurini of Helvetian stock. The Arvernian confederation had, as we have seen, fallen to pieces at a touch from Rome, and no tribe in central Gaul was strong enough to take the lead against the Germans. Only the Belgae in the north, Celts with an admixture of German blood, who had become established in the territory between Seine, Marne and Rhine a generation earlier, were able to put up a successful resistance.

It is not surprising that Gauls could not withstand these barbarians whom we find routing a succession of Roman armies. Marcus Junius Silanus was overwhelmed by the Cimbri somewhere north of the Province in 109; the Tigurini, marching to the south-west, were joined by the Volcae Tectosages, and together they defeated Cassius Longinus in 107, probably not far from Bordeaux, and his army was forced to march under the yoke. The interest of this battle, noteworthy as the only great battle on Gallic soil in which the Romans were defeated by the Celts, is overshadowed by the portentous events of the next few years. It had no immediate results. The Tigurini, after the manner of such invading hordes, moved away, and the Volcae, who had improved upon the occasion by capturing the Roman garrison of Tolosa, were left to the mercy of Quintus Servilius Caepio, who retook the town and carried off its temple treasure. The tale went round that this treasure was afterwards captured on its way to Massilia for shipment to Rome, and its fate was never known, though Caepio's enemies maintained that he had staged the attack in order to secure the booty for himself. If he did so, he did not long enjoy it, for in 105 he shared with Gnaeus Mallius Maximus the ignominy of the defeat of their two consular armies at Arausio (Orange) by the Cimbri and Teutoni.

The Germans did not follow up their victory. Instead, they moved out of Gallia Transalpina, but Rome was now aroused to the necessity for action, and Gaius Marius was

B

summoned from his African successes to take charge. In 104 and 103 he was in the Province restoring order and training his army rigorously. In 102 followed the crushing defeat at Aquae Sextiae of the Teutoni, who had re-entered the Province and were seeking to make their way into Italy. A year later Marius was to destroy the Cimbri, who had meanwhile returned to Noricum and entered Cisalpine Gaul from the north-east.

For ten years Roman and Gaul had been more concerned with the invasions than with each other. Now the way lay open for the development of the Roman Province. As ever, the army was the spearhead of the process of Romanization. Marius had occupied his army with public works, and left a monument of its labours in the canal from the neighbourhood of Arles to Fos, designed to avoid the difficulties of navigation of the Rhone mouth. After the end of the war this canal was bestowed on Massilia.

The story of Gallia Transalpina, like that of most Roman provinces under the Republic, is not a happy one. In the wake of the armies came the *publicani*—the tax-gatherers and money-lenders—all determined, as were governors and other high officials, to make their fortune as rapidly as possible, and the provincials were repeatedly driven to revolt. The Volcae Tectosages made a second attempt to regain their freedom before the end of the Cimbric war, but Sulla, acting as legate to Marius, captured their king Copillius, and Tolosa was incorporated in the Province. The Saluvii revolted in 90 and in 83. The Sertorian war, a by-product of the civil war between Sulla and Marius, convulsed Spain from 82 onwards. It had repercussions in Gaul, and Pompey had to cope with revolts there en route for his Spanish command in 77. Not until 72 did he finish with Sertorius, and in the intervening years, under the energetic but merciless government of the propraetor M. Fonteius (76–74), the Province felt the full rigours of Roman rule; it was compelled to provide cavalry for the Spanish campaign and also to supply large quantities of corn, whether the harvest was good or bad, to say nothing of enduring other forms of taxation.

We get a glimpse of the state of affairs there from Cicero's speech in defence of Fonteius, when the latter was impeached under the Extortion Laws on his return home. Cicero takes the line that the accusers had only recently been enemies of the state and that Fonteius was justified in his severity, but the burdens falling on the unlucky provincials are only too clearly shown, even allowing for rhetorical exaggeration, by such remarks as the following: 'All Gaul is filled with traders, is full of Roman citizens. No Gaul does any business without the aid of a Roman citizen; not a single sesterce in Gaul ever changes hands without being entered in the account-books of Roman citizens.' 'Let them [the accusers] produce out of the whole body of traders, of colonists, of publicans, of agriculturists, of graziers, but one witness [hostile to Fonteius]!' Transalpine Gaul was indeed being 'developed'. Although Fonteius evidently did his duty in building roads, this was another corvée for the inhabitants, and he lost no opportunity of raising money, his exactions on the wine-trade being specially felt. We can imagine the 'large and admirably appointed army of Gnaeus Pompeius that wintered in Gaul while Fonteius was governor' eating the provincials out of house and home and yet making large profits from them. The accusers of Fonteius came from all parts of the Province, but their efforts were clearly in vain, for both Roman Narbo and Greek Massilia rallied to the oppressor.

This gloomy picture is relieved by some brighter touches. Pompey, having finished with Sertorius, brought back into the upper valley of the Garonne a number of the Pyrenean supporters of the vanquished general. With one of his characteristically magnanimous gestures, he settled them in a new township of their own, the Civitas Convenarum, in the old native *oppidum* henceforth called Lugdunum Convenarum (Saint-Bertrand-de-Comminges). The new town was given the standard

municipal organization, and some of its leading citizens
evidently received Roman citizenship, taking the name of
Pompeius, as the frequent occurrence of the name in
funerary inscriptions of later years shows. Pompey
created Roman citizens elsewhere, such as the Vocontian
grandfather of Pompeius Trogus the historian; he also
had strong ties with Massilia, which owed to him certain
accretions of territory.

The families of generals who had been concerned in the
organization of Roman provinces generally maintained a
connection with the provincials, especially with such as
gained Roman citizenship through their good offices.
The Domitii kept in touch with Gaul, in memory of the
conqueror of the Allobroges. The Domitian house on
occasion helped individual provincials to assert their
rights. Domitii are found in Nîmes and elsewhere, and a
Gnaeus Domitius Afer from that city was consul in A.D. 39.
The Fabian family also maintained patronage of the
Gauls, and a Marcus Fabius was found to support the
Allobroges in their accusation of Fonteius.

Two poets of distinction in the first century B.C., an age
of great poets, came from Transalpine Gaul. They were
C. Cornelius Gallus and P. Terentius Varro Atacinus.
Gallus came from Forum Iulii and was probably the son
of a prominent Gaul who had done some service to Pompey or his legate C. Cornelius Lentulus and been rewarded
with the Roman citizenship. Gallus was not only a poet,
but a distinguished soldier and administrator whom
Augustus made his first Prefect of Egypt. Varro may have
been the son of a Roman colonist of Narbo, but it is not
impossible that he was a Celt.

Except for Glanum (p. 97) and the Via Domitia we
have as yet scarcely any buildings or monuments which
can be securely given a pre-Caesarian date. The trophy
which Pompey erected in the Pyrenees, probably on the
Col de Pertus, as a monument to his Spanish and Gaulish
exploits, has disappeared, and Republican buildings in
Saint-Bertrand-de-Comminges have not yet been identified.

Massilia had gained in lands and property, her commerce benefited from Pompey's suppression of piracy and from her control of the canal of Marius, but none the less she felt the result of the dislocations in Gaul and the rivalry of Narbonne. The coins of Massilia had hitherto circulated widely and been imitated in Gaul, but by now the Gauls increasingly received, used and imitated Roman money. Another factor in the growing Romanization of the Province was the number of Gauls who, willingly or unwillingly, had served in Roman armies, where their fine cavalry regiments were a valued arm. Gallia Transalpina would be an admirable base for Caesar's conquests.

The governors of the sixties, however, were worse than Fonteius, who at any rate had the excuse of the Spanish war for his extortions. Lucius Murena had in his train Publius Clodius, who made the most of his opportunities by forging wills and cheating legitimate heirs of their rights. The agents of Catilina were also busy fomenting trouble. The Allobroges tried again and sent another embassy to Rome. Despite the help of their patron Fabius Sanga, and despite the aid they gave to Cicero in unmasking the Catilinarian conspirators, their mission was a failure. In despair they took up arms once more, in 61. The whole Rhone valley flamed up, and before the governor could quell the rebellion he had to destroy Valentia (Valence) and the unidentified *oppidum* of Solonium. This broke all resistance, and the Allobroges settled down to their fate.

In outer Gaul, Gallia Comata or 'long-haired Gaul', as the Romans called it, the tribes continued to quarrel among themselves and within themselves. The kingship tended everywhere to disappear, and the Gallic society with which Caesar came into contact was almost feudal in structure; powerful, quarrelsome nobles and their large bands of followers increasingly depressed the lower classes, but nevertheless there were small but rising town centres like Avaricum (Bourges) or Cenabum (Orleans), where traders congregated and where Italian merchants were encouraged.

As we enter upon the second half-century of Roman Gaul there is fresh disturbance in the north caused by new German invaders. This time Ariovistus and his Suebi were making capital out of Gallic quarrels, in particular that between the Aedui and Sequani, who had an ancient bone of contention in the levy of tolls on the Saône traffic. The resentment of the Sequani found vent in a short-sighted invitation to Ariovistus to help them against the Aedui. Ariovistus agreed to come—on terms. He demanded a large slice of Sequanian territory in Alsace, and on this he settled a large band of his followers; they looked on the land and saw that it was good, and soon fresh multitudes were pressing across the Rhine in their wake and demanding more. Too late the Sequani realized what they had done and endeavoured to resist the Germans. For a second time the Aedui appealed for Roman help.

Here was a pretext for interference and, in view of what had happened in the case of the Cimbri, one to be weighed carefully; but nothing came of it at first. Ariovistus, alive to the state of affairs in Rome, took the precaution of sending an embassy to the Senate, which granted him recognition as King, and as Friend and Ally of the Roman people. This was in 59, when Caesar was Consul. Ariovistus was, nevertheless, indirectly responsible for bringing the legions into Gallia Comata. The Helvetii, the tribe occupying western Switzerland, were now feeling the strain of German pressure from across the Rhine and from Alsace, and decided that their old homeland was becoming untenable. It is the old story of folk migration: a tribe finds that for some reason beyond its control it is being squeezed out; it must either succumb or find somewhere else to go. So the long trek begins, the search for a place in which to settle and live undisturbed. Thus it had been with Cimbri; thus it would be with Visigoths and Burgundians; thus it was now with the Helvetii, who determined to move as far west as they could, into the land of the Santones (Saintonge). After prolonged preparation and negotiation with other Gallic tribes, they were ready to move out in the spring of 58, taking their families, their cattle and their waggons. Such a movement would inevitably cause trouble, and it would, moreover, leave their lands wide open for the Germans. News that they were starting, and that they intended to pass peacefully through Roman territory near Geneva, reached Caesar as he was preparing to set out for Cisalpine Gaul, of which, together with Transalpine Gaul, he had just become proconsul.

For Caesar a victorious war was essential, both politically and financially. He decided that the Helvetii provided the opportunity for which he had been waiting. He hurried to Geneva and made it plain that they would not be allowed to cross the Rhone. They made no attempt to do so, but turned north round the Jura and through the territory of the Sequani. Caesar, determined to stop them, hastily summoned all the forces he could muster and with six legions marched to intercept them. After a short and brilliant campaign he defeated them and compelled the survivors to get back to their homes—a grisly return, when we recall that no crops had been sown that spring and that they had deliberately burnt down their homesteads before leaving.

The aristocratic party among the Aedui welcomed Caesar to Bibracte, the chief *oppidum* of the tribe, and thanked him for his services to Gaul in preventing a migration which would have caused conflict. It was now, Caesar tells us, that the Gauls laid before him the state of affairs in the north-east and that he awoke to the real nature of the ambitions of Ariovistus. He marched forward to meet and defeat Ariovistus in Alsace, after which he installed his army in winter quarters at Vesontio (Besançon), in the territory of the Sequani. He had recognized that the destiny of Gaul lay with either the Romans or the Germans. From a mixture of motives, partly for the higher interests of the state, partly to feather his own nest, he was determined that it should be the Romans.

We cannot here follow in detail the familiar story of Caesar's War, except to comment upon the areas that fell to him in succession and to notice the extraordinary amount of marching and counter-marching that his legions performed, and their phenomenal powers of shovelling earth. Having crushed one enemy, Caesar would be beset with requests to give aid against another, and one campaign thus bred the next, until the whole country was conquered. On the Gallic side we can watch the awakening of tribe after tribe to the realization that the 'liberators' had come to stay, but at no time could inter-tribal jealousies be sufficiently forgotten to permit united action, and in this lies Caesar's chief justification.

The Belgae were quick to take up the challenge, and decided not to wait to be attacked, so they spent the winter of 58–57 in warlike preparations. One tribe among them, however, the Remi of Reims, was ready to play the part which the Aedui had played in central Gaul. When in 57 Caesar marched out from Vesontio, he was met by their envoys offering submission and begging for his aid against the Suessiones. He promptly concluded an alliance with them, to their mutual advantage; thereafter the Remi never wavered in their support of Caesar, and Caesar never let them down. He marched across their territory to the Aisne and into the land of the Bellovaci (Beauvais). The unwieldy Belgic host met the usual fate of barbarian hordes trying conclusions with a well-led Roman army, and despite further desperate and at times nearly successful resistance by the Nervii and Aduatuci, Caesar was everywhere victorious.

One of his legates, Publius Crassus, son of the Triumvir, had been sent to receive the submission of the tribes of Normandy and Brittany. By the spring the Veneti of the Morbihan, who were the chief seafarers of Gaul, controlling the British trade, had changed their mind. Rumours that Caesar had designs on Britain had perhaps got about, and the Veneti regarded his movements with suspicion. They seized the first chance of revolt, carrying with them many other tribes, and again both sides feverishly prepared for conflict, Caesar by building on the Loire the first Roman fleet destined to sail on the Atlantic. The two fleets met in 56 off Quiberon. The Romans countered the greater strength of the oaken vessels of the Veneti by cutting their rigging with hooks on the end of long poles, so that their sails collapsed and they could be outmanœuvred and boarded at will from the oar-propelled galleys. The break-up of Venetic sea-power, and the submission of the Morini of the Pas-de-Calais, left Caesar the mastery of the Channel and the opportunity for his British adventures of 55 and 54 B.C. Before these, however, he was called back to the Rhine, where more displaced German tribes had crossed over. After defeating them he decided to make a demonstration beyond the Rhine, and crossed the river in the Andernach region late in the year, after building his celebrated bridge.

When he returned from his second British expedition in 54, the north-eastern tribes, headed by Ambiorix, King of the Eburones, began a desperate revolt which lasted on into the following year and was one of the bitterest struggles of the whole war. The land of the Eburones, along the Meuse around Namur, was laid waste, but Ambiorix escaped Caesar's vengeance and disappeared into the fastnesses of the Ardennes.

The savage suppression of the revolt of Ambiorix and the rapacity of Caesar and his armies at last roused the leading tribes of central Gaul. The final trial of strength came in 52 B.C., when these peoples rose under Vercingetorix the Arvernian and taxed the uttermost resources of Caesar's genius. In the winter, while Caesar was in Cisalpine Gaul, representatives of the tribes met in the land of the Carnutes and plans for action were concerted. The revolt began by the massacre of the Roman business-men congregated in Cenabum, but Caesar by his speed and audacity circumvented the plan to prevent his rejoining his legions, which were in winter quarters in the north. Vercingetorix advocated a scorched-earth strategy, but the Bituriges would not sacrifice their town of Avaricum, which fell instead after a bitter siege. Caesar then followed Vercingetorix down into Auvergne and was repulsed from Gergovia, near Clermont-Ferrand, with considerable losses, including forty-six centurions. The effect of the defeat of the great proconsul himself was electric, and even the Aedui went over to Vercingetorix and seized Caesar's main depot at Noviodunum. Caesar hastened north to join Labienus, who had been sent to quell the Parisii of the middle Seine. Vercingetorix followed him, but after an unsuccessful cavalry encounter, committed the fatal error of allowing himself to be shut up in Alesia, near Dijon, where the final drama was played out amid a portentous display of siege-works and entrenchments not to be equalled again before the days of modern warfare. Messengers were sent out all over Gaul to bring help, while the garrison underwent the full horrors of blockade, but when the relieving force at last appeared Caesar was ready for it and its defeat was final. Vercingetorix surrendered, and languished for six years in captivity waiting to be paraded in Caesar's triumph, after which he suffered the usual fate of strangulation.

The winter of 52–51 was an uneasy one. Caesar remained in Gaul, in Bibracte, the hill-top capital of the Aedui, making some headway with the organization of his new province, but repeatedly called away to cope with incipient risings. Early in 51 he had a last desperate revolt of the Belgic Bellovaci to quell, followed by a campaign against Lucterius in the south-west, which culminated in the siege of Uxellodunum (Puy d'Issolu). For another year he remained in Gaul, trying by conciliation and clemency to undo the memories of earlier brutalities, until he set out for Italy in the autumn of 50. He did not enter Gallia Comata again, but he was in

Gallia Transalpina in 49, when he took Massilia, which had declared for its old patron Pompey.

The Romanization of Gaul had already been actively begun by Caesar and his lieutenants. When Caesar finally left the province, Decimus Junius Brutus was installed in command; under his able hand and that of first-class officers like Tiberius Claudius Nero and Aulus Hirtius peace was maintained even during the hazards of the Civil War. This was partly due to the exhaustion of the country, but partly also to the large recruitment of Gauls into Caesar's armies, which carried many of the more restless spirits abroad, and gave their kinsmen at home an interest in the success of Caesar's arms. Thus during the Civil War Gaul was one of Caesar's greatest assets. In addition to the renowned Gallic cavalry there was the yearly tribute of forty million sesterces which he had imposed on the vanquished.

THE SITES OF CAESAR'S BATTLES

Numerous sites have been identified with Caesar's campaigns, not always correctly. In France, as in Britain, any prehistoric earthwork is, as likely as not, called Caesar's Camp, but during the sixties of the last century, with the encouragement and the resources of the imperial antiquary, Napoleon III, great and often successful efforts were made to establish the real positions of Caesar's battlefields and marching camps. The results were embodied in an *Atlas* published with the Emperor's *Histoire de Jules César*. Since then successive generations of schoolboys have had their texts of the *Commentaries* illustrated with copies of the engravings in the *Atlas*. The most important of these still hold good, though others have been disproved. The outstanding achievement of Napoleon and his collaborators was the excavation of the great siege-works round Alesia. Pernet, who took part in the work, which began in 1861 and lasted six years, wrote a series of articles many years later (1906–1910), which describe clearly how the work went forward step

by step. The camps occupied by Caesar's troops varied
in size and were very irregular in shape. The entrenchments of some of them were still, according to Pernet,
distinguishable on the ground in 1862. One camp, on
the lower slopes of Mont Réa, was identified as that
which bore the brunt of the desperate efforts of the relieving force. This is where the greatest quantity of finds was
made, weapons of every kind and numerous bones of
men and horses, also a large number of Gallic and
Roman coins, none later than 52 B.C. in date.

The excavators found the ditches dug respectively to
hem in the besieged and to hold off the relieving force,
and, in addition, numbers of the ingenious obstacles,
such as the 'lily-pits' containing wooden spikes, which
Caesar describes. The chief finds are now in the museum
of Saint-Germain-en-Laye.

A more regularly proportioned camp was that constructed on the Oise at Mauchamp near Berry-au-Bac,
during Caesar's first campaign against the Bellovaci.
This was excavated in 1862, and five entrances were noted,
with their *claviculae*, the incurving extension of the rampart
which compelled anybody entering the camp to turn left
and so expose his right unshielded side to the defenders.
This area is now highly cultivated and has been bedevilled
with the trenches of the First World War and by the close
neighbourhood of a German aerodrome heavily bombed
in 1944; however the subsoil is chalk, and air-photographs
at the right season might yet reveal some traces of the
camp.

The large camp (35 hectares = 87 acres) at Orcet below
Gergovia, was also roughly rectangular. Colonel Stoffel
marked its boundaries by inscribed stones when the investigation was finished. A few trial trenches were dug
on the site in 1936, and these revealed the standard V-
shaped ditches in the position indicated. Other ditches
were uncovered on the site of Caesar's smaller camp on
the Roche Blanche, but the connecting ditch, running
through heavily cultivated ground, was not found in 1936.

An instance in which Napoleon's conclusions have been definitely disproved is the location of works constructed during the campaign of 51 against the Bellovaci. These, it now seems to be clear, were at Nointel near Clermont de l'Oise, and not, as shown in the *Atlas*, in the Forest of Compiègne.

The excavations recently carried out near Nointel have resulted in some of the most illuminating discoveries of earthworks of the Caesarian period yet made, and are scarcely less important than the Alesia lines themselves. The results therefore warrant a brief description for the benefit of those English readers to whom they have not as yet become familiar. As the excavator justly claims, here on the soil of France is a whole text-book of the art of castrametation as practised by its greatest master. Caesar occupied these heights long enough for the lines to be brought to perfection, and all the elements with which we are familiar, and some with which we are not, are present.

The site is at the west end of a low, wooded plateau, the Montagne de Nointel (100 m. above the valley), south-east of Clermont de l'Oise, protected on all sides by marshes. Hirtius in Book VIII of the *Bellum Gallicum*, is at pains to insist on the extra care with which Caesar fortified his camp, as the Bellovaci on the hill opposite were in great strength. The three main camps were enclosed within a larger one with specially formidable protective works. The outer enclosure, the *castra maiora* (100 hectares = 250 acres in size), follows the irregular crest of the northern slopes, but its other sides on the level top of the plateau are straight. It is pierced by a number of gateways whose *claviculae* show their Roman origin. Its central and eastern sectors were occupied by two large camps (22 hectares = 55 acres each) for the legions; in the northern sector is a small camp (1 hectare 60 = 4 acres) identified as that of the praetorian cohort, Caesar's bodyguard. The gateway of the last-named camp is specially well fortified. Three camps for auxiliary cohorts lie outside the main enclosure, to the east and south. One is of interest because a prehistoric earthwork was used for part of its defences. Many of these earthworks can still be traced on the ground (fig. 3).

Another feature of the system is a number of exterior lines—*brachia*—intended to facilitate defence of the position. They include advance works behind which

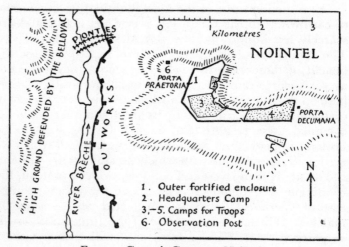

FIG. 3. Caesar's Camps at Nointel

artillery could operate, a dummy entrance which would lead the enemy into a trap, and protective screens to shield roadways.

Finally, a travelling earthwork was constructed at the foot of the hill on the west, and along it at regular intervals were *castella* with sides averaging 61 × 41 m. Another of these *castella* stands a little west of the *castra maiora*, on the best look-out point on that side of the hill. They are constructed as raised platforms protected by the deep ditches from which the earth was thrown up. A scale belonging to a Roman officer's armour was dug out of one of the ditches.

The excavations were conducted with great care, and

in many places the line of the palisade (the *vallum* proper) could be distinguished. The stakes of the *vallum* were set in the ground, or in a raised *agger* at intervals of 90 centimetres (3 Roman feet), and the space between them filled with wicker hurdles. Lines of the post-holes, packed with stones, with smaller holes between them for the uprights of the hurdles, have been found. The ditch in front was commonly further strengthened by chevaux de frise of sharp stakes, and the holes of many of these have also been discovered.

The works which led to the identification of the whole system were the *pontes*—the log-and-brushwood causeways which were carried across the marsh to enable the legions to advance against Clermont for the final battle. There are two of these, crossing the marshy valley of the Brèche, about 600 metres in length and 3·90 m. in breadth. One of them was discovered in the peat in the nineteenth century, but attempts to identify it with Caesar's wars were scoffed at, and not until 1935 were they vindicated. The *pontes* start alongside one another, then diverge slightly, and finally run parallel towards the hill opposite, being widened out to 9 and then 18 metres in the last third of their length, to give the soldiers a chance to get into formation to meet the enemy. They are based on fascines (bundles of brushwood), skewered down by long pickets. Above the fascines are layers of logs laid crossways and then lengthways, above which is wickerwork, and finally a bed of sand. The wood employed is mainly oak, but there is a good deal of alder.

The description in Hirtius implies that these *pontes* were laid rapidly just before the attack, but it must have taken a considerable time to collect and prepare the materials, and the large space of the *castra maiora* outside the actual camping areas provided ideal room and shelter for these purposes.

II

THE FRAMEWORK OF IMPERIAL GAUL

THE AUGUSTAN ORGANIZATION

AFTER Caesar's victory over the Pompeians a number of his legions were settled in colonies in the old Province. Tiberius Claudius Nero, father of the emperor Tiberius, superintended this operation. So Narbonne was reinforced with veterans of the famous X Legion, Baeterrae (Béziers) received men of the VII; the VIII was settled in the new town of Forum Iulii (Fréjus), the VI went to Arelate and the II to Arausio. Other cities including Vienna (Vienne) and Nemausus (Nîmes) were given the half-citizenship, or Latin rights, by which their magistrates became Roman citizens after holding office. Many leading Gauls who had supported Caesar were rewarded with the Roman citizenship and took the *nomen* of their patron—hence the large number of Julii one meets in Gaul a generation or two later. One such eminent family, owing its citizenship to Julius or Augustus, was that of Gnaeus Julius Agricola. In the newly conquered territory also there were to be colonies, the earliest we know of being Colonia Iulia Equestris (Nyon), on the Lake of Geneva, keeping guard over the country of the Helvetii. We find Lucius Munatius Plancus, Caesar's legate-designate at the time of his death, founding, in 44 and 43 B.C. respectively, the colonies of Lugudunum and Augusta Raurica. The former—Lyons—stood at the carfax of central France, at the confluence of Rhone and Saône, the latter, Augst, the earliest Roman foundation on the Rhine, commanded the route to Italy and the route from the territory of the as yet unsubdued Raeti. It can hardly be doubted that these colonies were laid out in furtherance of plans already formulated by the Dictator. Some of the colonists of Lyons were Roman citizens who had been expelled from Vienna by the Allobroges, which explains the subsequent hostility between the two cities. Plancus appears to have been a fine governor, and the peace enjoyed by Gaul during the wars of Octavian and Antony was due in large degree to the foundations laid by his conciliatory rule.

In 40 B.C. the Province came under the control of Octavian, who thenceforth ruled it through his legates. The importance he attached to Gaul is measured by the eminence of its governors, the first of whom was Agrippa (governor in 39–37 and in 19–17). Agrippa dealt with an Aquitanian revolt in 39–38, and at the opposite end of the land he brought the friendly German tribe of the Ubii over to the left bank of the Rhine and settled them in a new city, destined afterwards to be Cologne. Agrippa also took in hand the development of the administrative system which was to last so well, and he and Augustus must be given joint credit for laying the foundations of imperial Gaul.

Augustus went to Gaul in 27 B.C. to superintend in person the first stages of the taking of the census, a serious ordeal for Gaul and Gaul's masters. It is impossible to draw regular and equitable revenue from a territory without an adequate record of its resources, but the making of such a record is always resented by a primitive people which has no understanding of the mysteries of taxation. With the presence of the Imperator trouble was avoided, but the census was a complicated business which must have lasted over a matter of years. Not only were heads counted, but land holdings were recorded and the nature of the soil and the crops it bore: an equally rigorous examination of town property was made.

Meanwhile the organization of Gaul proceeded. There were four provinces in all: Gallia Transalpina, now called Gallia Narbonensis, and the three provinces—the 'Three Gauls'—into which Gallia Comata was divided: Gallia

c

Belgica, including the Belgic tribes north of the Seine; Gallia Lugudunensis, with the Celtic tribes of the centre; and Aquitania, in the formation of which ethnology was disregarded, for with the old Aquitani, the partly Iberian peoples between the Pyrenees and the Garonne, were now grouped the Celtic tribes between the Garonne and the Loire, including the Arverni, Santones, Pictones and Bituriges Cubi.

Gallia Narbonensis was left under the control of the Roman Senate, to be governed by proconsuls answerable to the Senate. This province was fast becoming strongly Latinized, a process hastened by the new colonies. The old tribal capitals like Nemausus, having received Latin rights, were governed according to Latin municipal usage, so that the whole of the province fell into line with Italy. Its proconsul, who held office for one year, was assisted by a financial official, his quaestor, and by an advisory staff. The district of the Maritime Alps was reserved under a separate authority, an equestrian prefect, who probably governed from Cemenelum (Cimiez).

The governor of each province of Gallia Comata was a legate of the emperor. At first, in the early days, one governor of high rank was often placed in control of all Gallia Comata, but this practice ceased after the recall of Germanicus in A.D. 16. A strip of land along the Rhine was then cut off as the two military zones of Germany under their own legates. The seats of government of the Gallic provinces were respectively Narbo; Durocortorum (Reims); Lugudunum; Burdigala (Bordeaux), perhaps in succession to Saintes. When the provinces of Upper and Lower Germany were finally created by Domitian, their governors resided at Moguntiacum (Mainz) and Colonia Agrippina (Cologne). Each governor was assisted by a council of assessors of his own choosing, generally men with legal or administrative experience. The finances of the provinces were in the hands of procurators appointed directly by the emperor, and responsible to him, and not to the legates, with whom they were not always on the best of terms. Lugudunensis and Aquitania were under one procurator, whose offices were at Lugudunum: the procurator of Belgica also administered the finances of the Germanies, and lived at Augusta Treverorum (Trier).

The basis of the organization of Roman Gaul was the old tribal unit, the *civitas*. The chief town of each *civitas* was the centre of its administration, which was carried out in the Roman fashion, the chief magistrates being two elected *duumvirs*, assisted by *aediles* and by a city council, in imitation of the Roman Senate.

The two chief burdens which fell upon ordinary provincials were taxation and military service. The latter was not a heavy one in the ordinary way: provincials were eligible for service in the auxiliary forces, which did not exceed a total strength of 150,000 men throughout the empire at any time during its first two centuries. The Gallic auxiliaries, especially the cavalry forces, were crack corps, and normally recruitment must have been on a voluntary basis. In times of special need, special levies were held. After his term of service in the auxiliaries a soldier, at least from the Principate of Claudius, was admitted to Roman citizenship. Only Roman citizens could serve in the legions; Narbonese Gaul, in the early days, was a useful source of man-power.

Each landed proprietor had to declare the value of his property, and was taxed accordingly. As we have seen, the fiscal archives had on record the areas of arable and grazing land and woodland; they also noted the number of fruit-trees, olive-trees, vines, etc., any given holding possessed. Persons owning property other than land were also taxed, so that tenant farmers, traders, artisans and the like shared the burden. Besides these direct taxes there were various indirect ones, including a purchase tax (1 per cent., later 2½ per cent.) and customs duties. These customs, called the *quadragesima Galliarum* (a charge of 2½ per cent.) were levied at the frontiers, Gaul being taken as a unit for the purpose. Inscriptions set up by

customs officers and their families have been found in the
Alps and the Pyrenees, at the ports and at certain large
towns. There were special taxes, such as those on in-
heritances of Roman citizens where the testator was un-
married. The provincials were liable for the maintenance
of the governor and his suite when on circuit and for
other public services. The mines constituted another
source of imperial revenue, for all the most important
ones, and also quarries, came to be held as imperial
domains.

Augustus returned to Gaul for a long sojourn from 16
to 13 B.C., handing over the vice-royalty of the new provinces to his stepson Drusus on his departure. The com-
pletion of the organization of Gaul was aptly celebrated
by the dedication of the altar of Rome and Augustus outside Lugudunum in 12 B.C., by Drusus, and henceforth an
annual festival of Augustus was celebrated there. At
this festival meetings were held of an assembly, the Concilium Galliarum, formed of representatives sent by each
of the tribes. The president of the Council was the high
priest, or *sacerdos*, of Augustus, chosen from among the
representatives. Besides participation in the festival, the
Council had a still more important function: the right of
making the views of the provincials known to the emperor.
Not only could it decree statues to be set up in honour of
worthy governors, but it could send deputations to Rome
with complaints to the emperor about bad governors or
other officials. The Council had some revenues of its
own and a staff to administer them. It marked at once
the new political regime and the continuation of Caesar's
custom of consulting gatherings of Gallic notables; it may
also be regarded as the successor as well as the supplanter
of the ancient assembly of all the Gauls held under the
auspices of the Druids somewhere in the region of Chartres.
Narbonensis and the Rhineland had their own provincial
altars and councils.

An inscription of 238 found at Vieux (Calvados) shows
the Council in action. It belonged to a statue set up in

honour of Titus Sennius Sollemnus by decree of the Council of the Three Provinces, on a site voted by his tribe, the Viducasses. He had represented this tribe on the Council, and had carried the day there in favour of the propraetor Tiberius Claudius Paulinus who had been unjustly accused. A letter from the grateful Paulinus is quoted on one face of the pedestal.

Another safeguard for the provincials was the survival of the old Republican custom of choosing a *patronus*— some man of eminence who was willing to watch over the interests of a particular community.

Cases of misgovernment did, of course, occur. There was a certain C. Julius Licinus, a freedman of Julius Caesar, who was made procurator of Gaul by Augustus. For several years he reigned like a king at Lugudunum, hated by all for his extortions. Of Gallic origin himself, he clearly knew where it was most effective to apply pressure. His exploits became legendary, and his rise was said to have been portended by a strange monster being cast up on the seashore. He presumably had his chance of spoliation at the time while the province was as yet only half organized, but, perhaps on the arrival of Agrippa in 19, he was bitterly accused by the Gauls, and soon disappeared from the scene. The Council of the Gauls was designed to remove the danger of similar cases arising.

Augustus next turned his attention to the problems of the German frontier. The campaigns across the Rhine which followed were part of the imperial plan for rounding off the Northern frontiers, of which the master move was the conquest of Illyricum up to the Danube. A permanent boundary on the Elbe would have greatly shortened the distance between the armies of Germany and those of the new Danube provinces. Gaul furnished its quota of auxiliary forces in the campaigns which opened in 12 B.C. It also provided the bulk of the supplies of the armies. Gallic ships carried the forces of Drusus, Tiberius and Germanicus in their adventurous voyages round the coast

to the Weser, Ems and Elbe in 12 B.C., A.D. 4 and A.D. 16
respectively. Gallic ties with the imperial house were
made closer by the constant presence of its leading princes
or their families. The future emperor Claudius was born
in Lugudunum in 12 B.C. General mourning followed the
untimely death of Drusus three years later, and the cities
of Gaul each year observed the day of his death with
prayers and sacrifices. For a time it seemed as if the
Roman Empire had been carried forward to the Elbe, and
a new province of Greater Germany was in process of
construction, but the destruction of Quinctilius Varus
and his army in the German forests in A.D. 9 showed that
it was not to be, and determined the historic role of Roman
Gaul.

ROADS

The chief administrative problem of Augustan Gaul had
been to survey the country and take a census for taxation
purposes. There was also the strategic necessity of
creating a network of Roman roads. Both these under-
takings could proceed together, for the road, in Gaul as
elsewhere, provided the base-line for the survey. Roman
roads already existed in the Province. The trunk road of
the south, the Via Domitia, bore the name of the conqueror Gnaeus Domitius Ahenobarbus, but the Roman
engineers simply straightened and improved this very
ancient track. According to Polybius, who died before
120 B.C., they had measured it and set up milestones along
it even before the conquest, which is not unlikely in view
of its importance, though no inscribed stones of earlier
date than 3 B.C. have been found. Strabo mentions that
in his day some of its bridges were of stone, others of wood;
the latter must be pre-Augustan.

Roman official traffic between Italy and Spain in the
second century B.C. seems to have gone mainly by sea,
ships coasting to Tarragona, calling at Nice, Marseilles and
Agde en route. Long voyages in bad weather in the small
ships of antiquity must have been singularly unpleasant,

and many travellers must have been glad to disembark at Marseilles and continue by land. The road enters Gaul from Spain by the Col de Pertus, and has been followed through Narbonne, Béziers and Nîmes to the Rhone-crossing at Beaucaire. It is often overlaid by the modern Route Nationale 9, but in places runs some little distance from it. It bears many interesting names, Chemin de la reine Juliette, Camin Roumiou, Chemin de la Monnaie among them. It must have been used in the centuriation of lands allotted to the colonists of Narbonne and Béziers.

From the Roman point of view it was obviously very desirable to be able to make the journey to Spain by land, but this was only intermittently possible in Republican times. The coastal tracks from Italy to Nice were dangerous and sometimes impassable, owing to the predatory habits of the Ligurian mountaineers. We hear of a Roman praetor travelling this way to his Spanish province in 189 and being attacked and fatally wounded by hostile tribesmen; this state of things was always liable to recur.

The armies of Pompey and Caesar used the Mont Genèvre route, keeping well inland from the coastwise Ligurians; but Caesar had even so to fight his way through in 58, and failed to subdue the mountaineers of the Vallis Poenina (Great Saint Bernard). After his death the various rival generals seem to have crossed the Alps freely, using a variety of passes, but Strabo mentions that Decimus Brutus, after Mutina, had to pay toll for his men. Only after the pacification of the Alpine tribes, celebrated by the erection of the monument of La Turbie in 7 B.C. (fig. 45b), was it possible to complete the coast road, the Via Julia Augusta, or Via Aurelia, which now ran right round the coast to Genoa and Pisa to join the original Aurelian Way coming up from Rome. Milestones of 3 B.C. are known along it, east of Fréjus. It had already been constructed west of this port, on which stretch occur milestones of 13–12 B.C. It is still called Camin Aurelian or Camin d'Aurian in Provence.

The third key road, now Route Nationale 7, which must

go back to Republican times, is the Rhone valley road.
The main road, then as now, ran along the east bank of
the great river. In Augustan times it linked Arles,
Orange, Valence and Vienne with the capital of the Three
Gauls, Lyons. At Lyons it forked, one branch continuing
up the Rhone valley to Geneva and the territory of the
Helvetii, and the other running north along the right bank
of the Saône.

The older, eastern branch was joined north of the Lake
of Geneva by one of the most important of the imperial
roads, that coming from Italy over the Great St. Bernard
Pass. The joint road then passed on through Augst
northwards to the Rhineland. The Great St. Bernard
route was thus the most direct line of communication
between Rome and the armies of the Rhine and, as such,
plays a big part in history. The pass lies in the territory
of the Vallis Poenina, thus outside Gaul proper, but its
history is intimately bound up with Gaul.

Returning to the heart of Gaul we follow the Saône
road from Lyons to its next fork at Châlon-sur-Saône.
From here it strikes across the Langres plateau and then
to Metz and Trier. Its more easterly branch heads for
Besançon and the Belfort Gap. It was the best route for
the armies of Germany to take when bound for the south
of Gaul, and was followed by the legions of Vitellius and
Valens in their fatal march of 69. A north-western
branch from Langres led to Reims–Soissons–Amiens and
the Channel. This was the original great north road to
Britain, but another, Châlon–Autun–Auxerre–Sens–Paris–
Beauvais, became scarcely less important.

Two main east–west roads ran to the coast from Lyons,
at least from the time of Claudius, whose milestones have
been found along them: one by Roanne, Vichy, Aigue-
perse, Néris. Here it passed round the north side of the
Massif Central on its way to Poitiers, from which branches
went to Bordeaux and Nantes. The second ran west
from Lyons to Feurs on the Loire, then via Clermont to
Limoges, and thence to Saintes or Bordeaux.

Lyons, as Strabo says, 'is an acropolis of Gaul, not only because the rivers meet there, but also because it is near all parts of the country. And it is on this account, also, that Agrippa began at Lugudunum when he cut his roads, that which passes to the Cemmenus Mountains as far as the Santoni and Aquitania, and that which leads to the Rhenus, and that which leads to the Ocean by the Bellovaci and the Ambiani and, a fourth, that which leads to Narbonitis'. No milestones earlier than those of Claudius, however, have yet been found in the Three Gauls.

The chief route into Aquitania was the road from Narbonne, of which the sector Narbonne–Carcassonne–Toulouse cannot be much later than the Via Domitia itself. After Toulouse this road followed the Garonne closely to Bordeaux, but in the later empire it seems to have been less favoured by through traffic, which took a road swinging slightly southwards along the higher ground in order to avoid those districts liable to flooding. It is this second road which is given in the late Roman itinerary for the pilgrims bound from Bordeaux to Jerusalem.

Aquitaine also had its north–south trunk roads, and northern Gaul was amply provided with roads crossing those coming up from Lyons—for example, the road to Trier from Reims and, farther to the north, the important Cologne–Tongres–Bavai–Boulogne highway, which must probably date from the time of Claudius because of its great strategic value as the main line of communication between the legions of Germany and of Britain. It is one of the roads ascribed by the Middle Ages to Queen Brunehaut or Brunhilda.

This network remained the main system of France until the eighteenth century. France is a land of long straight highways, and more than half of them follow the line laid down by the Roman engineers. The modern system is, however, orientated differently from the ancient one, for it radiates from Paris, whereas the Roman one is primarily a network linking the provincial capitals.

The lion's share of building the roads was borne by the Roman army. To the military engineers fell the surveying of the territory and the laying out of the lines which can still be followed across the French countryside. Much of the labour would, however, be carried out by gangs recruited locally, and the materials for the causeways were quarried from the land through which the roads passed. The standard road is a causeway of macadam type; first a closely packed foundation of large stones was built, and on that was rammed a thick layer of gravel. The causeway was further held in place by kerbstones, and ditches ran along both sides of the road. In and near towns an additional layer of paving-stones was often added, and a good stretch of such paving has been preserved at Vienne. A main road averages 5 metres in width.

This basic construction is varied where necessary. In mountainous districts the roads were frequently rock cut, and on such stretches, especially where they were very steep or where one side was on the edge of a ravine, ruts were deliberately hewn to render them safer for vehicles. Such ruts are known in the Alps, the Jura and Alsace, and are sometimes found in city gateways, as at Reims. Their distance apart varies, with averages 1·10, 1·40 and 1·55 metres. Axle-widths must have differed, but the narrow axle seems to have predominated in the higher mountain districts.

In some mountain passages (e.g. Pierre Pertuis near Basle) the roads passed through short tunnels. Elsewhere roads were carried across swamps on log corduroy rafts which were used as the base on which to build the causeway. In a swampy tract of the road from Trier to Maestricht (the *Via Mansuerisca*), a striking example of this was followed for a distance of seven kilometres and a model of it is shown in the Brussels Museum.

We know that bridges were built across the chief rivers, but few traces of them remain. Arles had a bridge of boats, of which a mosaic in the Piazza delle Corporazione at Ostia seems to preserve a picture, and part of its abutments remains. The Saône was bridged at Lyons, but there is as yet no evidence that there was a Rhone bridge there. The positions of both the Gallic and Roman bridges over the Rhone at Geneva have been ascertained. The iron-shod piles of the bridge at Mainz have been dredged out of the Rhine. They were driven into the river-bed in a compact mass with cut-waters against the current, and the stone piers of the bridge were erected on them. The superstructure of the bridge seems to have been timber, and a lead medallion of Diocletian and Maximian found at Lyons gives some idea of its appearance, with the fourth-century fortified town of Mainz, and its bridgehead at Castel, on either side. Portions of the Roman piers support the present bridge at Trier; and its ancient superstructure was probably timber. Similar Rhine bridges existed at Cologne and at the fortified stations of Augst, Zurzach and Stein in Switzerland.

Caesar frequently mentions bridges in his *Commentaries*, such as those across the Allier which Vercingetorix broke down. Many bridges of Roman period crossed beside earlier fords, and in some cases fords were maintained and paved. Among known fords is that of Saint-Léonard, where the road from Jublains crosses the Mayenne, in which about 17,000 Gallic and Roman coins have been found—offerings to the divinity of the ford. This ford seems to have been marked by a wooden passage-way. Paved fords have been found in Provence at Saint-Rémy and at Saint-Maximian-du-Var.

A considerable number of Roman bridges are known along the Via Domitia, in various degrees of ruin. Among notable examples is the Pont Ambroix over the Vidourle on the borders of the Departments of Gard and Hérault. Another famous bridge is that at Saint-Chamas, with its two monumental arches, erected in the first century by a local dignitary in the vicinity of the now vanished town of Mastrabala. The arch of the bridge at Vaison is believed to be Roman. Examples in the Three Gauls are much rarer. The handsome bridge at Montignies

Saint-Christophe in Belgium has now been shown to belong to the eighteenth century. A few fragments of bridges have been identified in Switzerland.

The main roads were used by the Imperial Post, or *Cursus Publicus*, the system carefully organized by Augustus whereby the Roman emperors, like the Persian kings of old, could keep in touch with the remotest corners of their empire. At regular intervals along the roads relays of horses were maintained for official use, and by this means messages were rapidly transmitted. Besides couriers on horseback, post-chaises were provided, and officials and important persons travelling on public business were able to use them. Startling evidence of the changed relations of the Roman state to the Christian Church was provided when Constantine invited the bishops attending the Council of Arles (314) to use the Imperial Post. In the fifth century Sidonius Apollinaris could still use it without any difficulty between Lyons and Rome.

The upkeep of the Imperial Post was at first a charge on the local *civitas*, but Hadrian remitted this and put it directly under the *fiscus*, the imperial exchequer. In the late empire it had once again become an almost intolerable charge on the local man. The relay stations became important points along the roads. They had to be large enough to provide stabling for a number of horses, and coach-houses for the vehicles, also to house the postboys, ostlers, etc. The system is neatly shown by the Jerusalem Itinerary of A.D. 333, with *mutationes* at intervals of ten or twelve Roman miles, and generally a pair of *mutationes* between each two *mansiones*—the larger stations where travellers could put up for the night. Private travellers had to make their own arrangements, and inns grew up to meet the demand. The names Saverne and Rheinzabern come from the Latin *tabernae*.

The road stations tended to attract further settlement, and villages or small towns often grew up around them. In the late empire State granaries, to which the farmers brought their taxation in kind, were set up in the small fortified *castella* which were built at these points to protect communications. There must have been some provision for road policing from the first, but it is in the middle and late empire that it becomes clearest. *Beneficiarii*, or senior non-commissioned officers, were specially detailed as road police. Their inscriptions are found at many posts along the roads from the second century onward, and they increased in importance as highway robbery and brigandage became serious problems.

Among road stations may be cited the *castellum* of Jublains (Mayenne), a stoutly built structure within a fortified enclosure; the small fortified village of Tournus (Saône-et-Loire) on the Saône Road, and the station of Petinesca, Switzerland, where the entrance of the Roman road through a fortified gateway has been traced, and its passage to a large building with various rooms round a court, which was probably the hostel. A *mansio* stood at the top of the Great St. Bernard Pass, and among the inscriptions there is one to the *genius stationis* set up by a military policeman in the time of Severus Alexander. A very large ruin at Thésée (Loir-et-Cher) probably represents the Tasciaca road-station, on the road from Tours to Bourges. The building still visible is the large basilical hall ($44 \times 13 \cdot 50$ m.); the rest of the rectangular enclosure (80×60 m.) in which it stood is not now to be seen. The building is not fortified, and may be dated to the second century; it has been suggested that the great hall could be used for the local assizes by judges on circuit, or as a place for displaying merchandise.

The standard milestone is cylindrical in form, set firmly into a square base. It bears the name, titles and year of the emperor in whose reign it was set up, and a figure to indicate the distance from the nearest important town. From the third century the milestones of the Three Gauls carry distances in Celtic leagues; those of Narbonensis adhere to the Roman mile.

At important towns special milestones, or, rather, itineraries, were set up, indicating the chief roads passing through the town and the stations along them. Gaul has the remains of two or three of these, the best preserved and most interesting being that of Tongres, an eight-sided pillar now in the Brussels Museum, which must once have embodied a great deal of useful information. The pride of place on the remaining fragment is enjoyed by the Cologne–Boulogne road on which a few stages are given; the other roads still represented are the Cologne–Worms section of the Rhine road, and the Reims–Soissons–Amiens road.

Road-maps must have been common in the Roman Empire, and we hear of official itineraries supplied to the army. Certain itineraries have come down to us in mutilated form, which are nevertheless valuable aids in studying the topography of the provinces. The Antonine itinerary is based on an original which probably dates from the time of Caracalla. It lists the chief roads of the empire and the mileage between the stations along them. There are some big gaps in the Gaul section, which must mean that part of the manuscript is lost—nothing is given in the whole Loire basin below Orleans, the roads of the Massif Central are missing, and a section of the main Rhone road between Tarascon and Valence has dropped out. More roads are given in the curious Peutinger Table, an ancient map of which the extant copy was made in 1265.

A group of unusual souvenirs—four silver cups—was found among a great mass of ancient offerings in the hot medicinal spring of Vicarello, once Aquae Apollinares, at the north end of Lake Bracciano, 26 km. north-west of Rome. These cups were evidently a speciality of some Gaditanian firm, and are ascribed to the first or second century. They are cylindrical, in imitation of milestones, and engraved on them are the names of the posts along the route from Cadiz (Gades) to Rome, via the Col de Pertus–Narbonne–Nîmes–Saint Rémy–Mont Genèvre and so to Turin. Another interesting document is the Itinerary from Bordeaux to Jerusalem, dating from A.D. 333, a time when Christian pilgrims were beginning to travel to visit the holy places of their faith. The travellers went to Narbonne, and then followed the Via Domitia to Arles.

We have a number of stories of journeys made at high speed along the Roman roads, one of them being Hadrian's race to Upper Germany to be the first to announce to Trajan that he had been adopted by Nerva. A record journey was made by Caligula in the autumn of 39 on his way to put down the revolt of Gaetulicus. His party, which included his sisters Agrippina and Julia Livilla, an escort of Praetorian Guards, and his special German bodyguard, covered the 966 Roman miles from Rome to Mainz in about forty days.

THE LEGIONS AND THE FRONTIER

One of the gaps in our knowledge of Roman Gaul is the location of its military forces after the departure of Caesar, and in the early years of Augustus, before the legions were moved to permanent homes on the Rhine. Where were the winter quarters of Agrippa's legions, where his marching camps? When the legions did move forward, were no detachments left inside Gaul, were there no auxiliary regiments at strategic points? Gaul was not without its security measures: there were the veteran colonies in the early years to lend stability to the scene; the legions could move quickly if necessary; there was the Urban Cohort at Lugudunum; and there was another military force of three legions just across the Pyrenees in Northern Spain. But many semi-permanent or temporary camps, especially those used during the Aquitanian campaigns, must await the fortunate chance of discovery.

One marching-camp of the Augustan or pre-Augustan period is known at Urmitz on the banks of the Rhine, near Andernach. It measures 410 × 370 metres, and lies within a much larger prehistoric fortification. Inside it is another, later, camp of the Augustan period, which is usually identified as one of the forty *castella* which Drusus built along the banks of the Rhine. So the larger camp, which would take a legion, may be Agrippa's, or even Caesar's. There is another smaller marching camp at Ermelo in Holland, but its date is obscure. The entrances are protected by traverses (*tutuli*), not *claviculae*.

There are various signs of the movement of Roman troops in Gaul during the first century A.D. Inscriptions at Aunay, between Saintes and Poitiers, mention men of the II and XIV Legions, which left the Rhineland for Britain in A.D. 43. They must therefore have been here either before the move to the Rhine, or detachments must have come to Aunay before 43, perhaps in connection with the revolt of Sacrovir (p. 43). The traces of two camps are said to have been found at Néris-les-Bains. From the larger one were collected tiles of Legion VIII Augusta marked LAPPIO LEGATO. This legion had its headquarters at Strasbourg from 70, and A. Lappius Norbanus Maximus was the officer who suppressed the revolt of Saturninus, legate of Upper Germany, in 88. The camp itself, however, is suspected of being older than this, in which case we may also be on the tracks of the events of 21 or 68–70.

The most interesting and convincing series of tiles comes from Mirebeau-sur-Bèze (Côte d'Or), in the territory of the Lingones. Three groups are marked with the stamps of more than one Legion, viz.: VIII, XI, XIV and XXI; I, VIII, XI and XXII; II and VIII. The only time that this great concourse of seven legions came together was under the command of Cerialis for the campaign of 70, so their significance is clear. In addition, there are tiles of VIII Augusta of the LAPPIO type, showing that Mirebeau was used again in 88, and there are a good many other tiles of this legion, so it appears likely that it maintained detachments here for a protracted period.

Another site is on record on the southern edge of Dijon which has yielded more than 500 tiles of VIII Augusta, again including LAPPIO and later types, so the Legion may have kept in permanent touch with this post as well as with Mirebeau.

There are some interesting records from Gallia Belgica. The most notable case emerges from excavations carried out in 1850, at Arlaines, near Vic-sur-Aisne. The complicated structures unearthed were thought to be a villa, but their plan appears rather to be that of a Roman auxiliary fort, resembling the Flavian fort of Wiesbaden. It may well be that after the unrest at the end of Nero's reign it was considered expedient to maintain garrisons for some time at strategic points in north-eastern Gaul.

The backbone of the defensive and policing system of Gaul was, of course, the legions. Three of their fortresses on the Rhine may be briefly noticed: first, that at Neuss (Novaesium), because of its classic regularity. Fig. 4 shows the plan of the fortress as it was rebuilt after the disaster of 70, with its ranges of barrack buildings, familiar to students of Roman Britain from their own legionary fortresses, its granaries and hospital, the legate's house, and finally the brigade headquarters building, with the chapel for the eagle and other standards.

Before the time of Claudius the Roman fort was an earth-and-timber structure, the earthern ramparts being revetted with timber and provided with wooden towers and gateways, while the internal buildings were also of wood. The Claudian period was one of great building activity on the frontier, and the legionary fortresses were made over with stone in place of the wooden revetting, while the buildings inside were replaced by stone ones, sometimes of great magnificence. Most splendid of all were the buildings of the ill-fated double fortress of Vetera (Xanten), which met with a horrible end in A.D. 70. This was occupied by the two Legions XV Primigenia and V Alaudae, and the exactness with which the labour of building was shared by the two is shown by finds of their tiles. Each was allotted one side of the fortress, and the dividing line ran straight through the centre. The finish of the monumental gateway to the headquarters building was, however, left to the XV, as the senior legion. The most astonishing features of this lavish ensemble are the

D

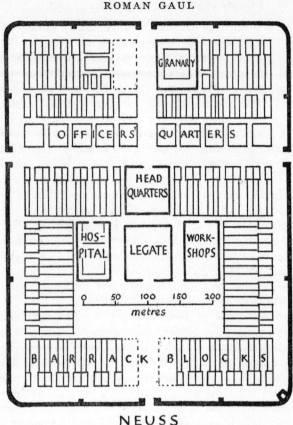

NEUSS

Fig. 4. Neuss Legionary Fortress

two palaces, one for each legate, with their ranges of peristyled courts and their beautiful porticoed gardens. The wonders of these great buildings in the six fortresses from Vindonissa to Vetera must have made a great impression on the simple northerners and set a keynote for the development of provincial architecture (fig. 5).

Some features of the legionary fortress of Vindonissa (Windisch), including its irregular outline, show that the rigidity of Roman military construction can be exag-

gerated.   There are also large baths within the perimeter,
and the west gateway is irregular, following a fashion of
the very early empire to be seen in towns like Fréjus and
Arles.   The conversion from earth-and-timber structures
to stone came in about A.D. 47, along with the other
building of the Claudian period.   The walls now had
stone facings with earth fillings.   A feature of special
interest is the *valetudinarium* or hospital (fig. 6), which
has been fully excavated.   This was a one-storey building,
70 × 62 metres.   It consisted of two ranges of rooms

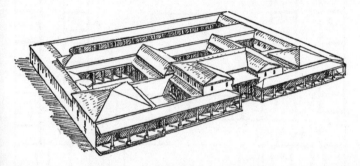

FIG. 5.   Legate's Palace at Vetera

round a corridor.   The rooms were in groups of three—
a pair of small wards, with a smaller room between them
which could serve as ante-room or store-room.   Each
ward could hold eight patients, so in all there was accommodation for 480 sick.   There is a large central court, in
the middle of which is a small building, perhaps for the
staff.   From the entrance portico arrivals entered a large
reception-room, where casualties could be brought before
being allotted to their wards, or where walking cases
could be treated.   This stone *valetudinarium* was preceded
by a similar building in wood.

From the early second century the military zone—that is,
the provinces of Upper and Lower Germany—was held by
four legions only, instead of the eight stationed there during
the first century.   In Upper Germany the VIII Augusta

remained at Strasbourg and the XXII Primigenia at Mainz; in Lower Germany the I Minervia was at Bonn and XXX Ulpia Victrix at Xanten. At intervals between the legions along the lower Rhine were the forts

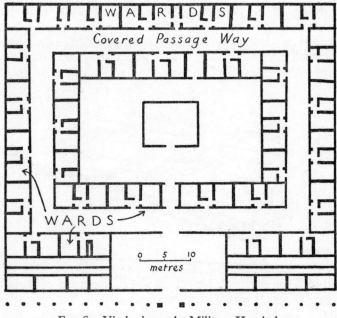

FIG. 6.   Vindonissa: the Military Hospital

of the auxiliary regiments. These were of the standard rectangular pattern, smaller editions of legionary fortresses. The auxiliaries of Upper Germany had, since Flavian times, been stationed in the newly conquered territory across the upper Rhine and the upper Danube. The consolidation of this land frontier or *limes* was undertaken by Domitian and completed by Hadrian, who marked it off by a continuous palisade running from the Rhine near Coblenz to the Main near Frankfort, and thence to the Danube above Regensburg. Like the British frontier, this line was protected by auxiliary forts and signal towers.

III

FROM TIBERIUS TO DIOCLETIAN

TIBERIUS, who succeeded Augustus in A.D. 14, was well known and respected in the Gallic provinces, and seems to have encouraged Gallic commerce. So we have the inscription of the shipowners of Paris stating that they presented him with a crown (see p. 106) and an altar to him set up by the *laniones* (butchers) of Périgueux. Money was not so abundant as in the days of Augustus, so there are no records of lavish building programmes on the Augustan scale. There is, however, one fine ornamental archway of his reign—that of Saintes.

The rising of Florus and Sacrovir in A.D. 21 was the first serious disturbance in Gaul for nearly half a century, and it was more of a potential than an actual danger. It is ascribed by Tacitus to discontent at the growing burden of taxation. Tiberius, it would seem, had withdrawn certain fiscal privileges enjoyed by a few Gallic communities, notably the Aedui and Treveri, and it is just among these peoples that the worst trouble came. There was also the occasional case of the oppressive procurator to create genuine grievances.

The unrest started, however, among the Andecavi and Turones of Anjou and Touraine. The Urban Cohort from Lugudunum speedily went into action and dealt with the former, while detachments from the Rhine army came up and disposed of the Turones. The Treveri and Aedui then decided to move, but, true to Gallic ineptitude in such matters, acted separately. Julius Florus, the Treveran leader, was soon cornered in the Ardennes. Julius Sacrovir, the Aeduan, was a more dangerous proposition. Like Florus, he had served with the Roman

43

army as a commander of Gallic auxiliaries, but he had given rather more thought to his preparations for revolt, having had a supply of arms forged secretly in Augusto-dunum (Autun). With some of the troops under his command he seized the city, gaining valuable hostages in the persons of the Gallic youths of high birth attending the schools there. The Sequani joined his venture, and he was able to muster a force of 40,000 men, about one-fifth of whom he armed as legionaries. There was also among them a stiffening of heavy armed gladiators. It was easy enough to march out from the city full of hopes, but as soon as the dreaded regular legions of the Rhine came in sight the heart went out of the adventure, and Sacrovir's motley army was rapidly dispersed. He escaped with some followers to his own country villa which he set alight; the members of the party then slew one another. The economical Tiberius had an inscription commemo-rating the defeat of Sacrovir added to the arch of Orange.

The doings of Caligula in Gaul are hidden in a spate of malicious tittle-tattle. His mild show of force across the Rhine in A.D. 39 was probably well-advised. It is less easy to know what to make of the muster on the sea-shore near Boulogne the following spring, but one substantial memorial of it remained: the eminently practical trophy in the form of a lighthouse which Suetonius tells us he set up. It is very possible that this was the Roman lighthouse known as the Tour d'Ordre which remained on the cliffs north of the port until the sixteenth century (fig. 1). As for the junketings at Lugudunum, they, too, are a curious mixture. It was manifestly good for the prestige of the ruling house that the son of Germanicus should once more show himself at Lugudunum and preside at its festivities. The introduction of contests in Greek and Latin oratory, however much cynical Romans might make fun of it, was very much in the Gallic tradition and furthered the spread of the Latin language, while the ingenious idea of auction-ing off the contents of the imperial lumber-rooms did no particular harm to anybody. His general extravagant behaviour perhaps did not alienate the lively Celts as much as the more sober Romans. We need not believe that even he would have been mad enough deliberately to have his uncle Claudius, son of the great Drusus, ducked in the Rhone, as malicious rumour asserted. There are a number of inscriptions in Gaul in honour of Caligula, and the people of Vienne owed to him their promotion to full Roman citizenship.

It fell to Claudius to carry out Caligula's intentions and to succeed in an undertaking which, whatever its wider implications, brought great advantages to the merchants and shippers of Gaul—the conquest of Britain. Once more the coast of the Pas de Calais was thronged with troops, and ships converged on Gesoriacum ready to convey the oncoming legions to the island. Old roads were repaired and new highways built. On his way to and from Britain, Claudius enjoyed a triumphal progress through Gaul and spent some time in his birthplace, Lugudunum.

The liking of Claudius for the Gauls was made a matter of numerous jokes in Rome, partly because of his notable speech to the Senate in 48 on the subject of admitting Gauls to that body. He asked that newly-enrolled citizens from the *civitates* of Gallia Comata should be regarded as eligible for membership of the Senate, on the same conditions as Italians, a privilege which had so far only been enjoyed by men from Narbonese Gaul. Tacitus has given a paraphrase of the speech, but we have part of the speech itself, commemorated on tablets of bronze which were set up at the Confluence and were found by exceptional good fortune in 1528. They are now in the Lyons Museum.

The rambling speech is an odd mixture of erudition and optimism, but it shows a feeling for the continuity of history and for Rome's imperial mission, and it is a fine statement of faith in the wisdom of political generosity. 'Do not be horrified at the idea of introducing this reform on the ground that it is new, but consider how many things in this City have been changed and renewed, and how many forms and stages our institutions have passed through, from the very foundation of the City.'

The interest of Claudius in Gaul and the frontier has another monument—the city of Cologne, the old town of the Ubii, which he raised to colonial status as Colonia Claudia Agrippinensis.

Nero, despite his ancestral connections with Gaul, never went near the province. After the great fire of Rome in 64, Lugudunum sent a donation of 40 million sesterces towards the rebuilding of the city. Lugudunum was fated itself to endure an equally terrible disaster a year later, when a great fire burnt much of it to the ground. The emperor returned the donation. Four years later the city had recovered much of its glory.

We have now arrived at the fateful years 68–70 when, as Tacitus so justly summed up, the discovery was made of the terrible secret that emperors could be made elsewhere than at Rome. And the seat of this discovery was Gaul. Nero's exactions from the provinces are a familiar, if not very precise story. They were sufficient to goad the Governor of Lugudunensis, Gaius Julius Vindex, a Gaul himself, of princely family, to revolt. His revolt follows the inevitable Gallic pattern. It starts with the usual assemblage of Gallic chiefs and the usual impassioned harangues. Nero had despoiled the whole Roman world: 'Therefore rise now at length against him; succour yourselves and succour the Romans; liberate the entire world.' Vindex speaks as a Roman, if also as a Gaul. He is not fighting for Gallic independence, but to get rid of an unworthy emperor. With a wit that delighted both Roman and Gaul and infuriated Nero, he dared to proclaim that not only was Nero a bad emperor, he was also a bad lyre-player.

He got into communication with the legate of Hispania Tarraconensis, the military province of Spain, which had one legion, and persuaded him to make a bid for the imperial power. This legate was Servius Sulpicius Galba, of ancient senatorial family, who had once been governor of Aquitania and who was *persona grata* with the Gauls. The great tribes of the centre, the Arverni and Aedui, and the Sequani farther north-east, were the chief supporters of Vindex, and thus of Galba, but Gallia Belgica held aloof. The rebellion succeeded, if only for a brief time, in imposing Galba as emperor on Rome, but Vindex himself, and his army, were annihilated in a clash with the Upper German army near Vesontio, a conflict of which the details are obscure. The campaign of Vindex, however, was a serious operation. It is called *Bellum Gallicum* in ancient sources, and Vindex obviously disposed of larger forces than had Sacrovir. The Augustan monument at Lugdunum Convenarum was destroyed at this time, and it is tempting to ascribe this to the supporters of Galba and Vindex.

The events of the next year belong to general Roman history and have been treated of time and again. They were, however, all too closely bound up with Gaul. The first point that strikes us is the way that the old local rivalries are ready to burst out with the smallest encouragement. They begin with the mutual jealousy of the Treveri and the tribes to their south-west who had supported Vindex. The Treveri were closely bound up with the Rhine legions, and disliked Lugudunensis and Galba. Galba could not leave well alone, but fanned the flames by confiscating territory belonging to the Treveri and Lingones and handing it over to the Sequani, so now the Treveri had a genuine cause for complaint. When the Rhine armies declared for the legate of the Lower German Army, Vitellius, on 1st January 69, the Treveri backed their choice.

With that began the march on Italy. Caecina led his troops through the land of the Helvetii and made a remarkable mid-winter's march over the Great St. Bernard. But before the legions disappeared up the pass they had left a trail of desolation, for the Helvetii elected to oppose their passage, and many of them were massacred.

Ugly incidents marked the march to the Rhone Valley of the second column under Valens. Some civilians, too, were not unready for trouble. The people of Lugudunum urged the Vitellians to attack Vienna, their rival and the friend of Vindex and Galba. Valens calmed them down, but took a heavy ransom from Vienna. It is therefore to be observed that Vienna and Aventicum, though threatened, were not in fact pillaged or burnt, so that it is easy to exaggerate the damage done by the armies. The Riviera coast suffered from a conflict between the Othonian fleet and Vitellian detachments, and the mother of Agricola was killed on her own estate near Ventimiglia by a band of Othonians.

Vitellius himself followed more slowly, sailing by barge down the Saône, while his men marched along Agrippa's road. On arrival at Lugudunum he held court and celebrated the defeat of Otho. At this point he was confronted by a curious incident—the uprising of a few thousand men of the small tribe of the Boii in the region of Nevers at the bidding of a Celtic messiah called Mariccus. Mariccus declared that he was sent by the gods to be the liberator of the Gauls. His movement caused no small stir in his own tribe and among neighbouring Aeduan villages, but cohorts sent by Vitellius and militia from Augustodunum made short work of his following. Mariccus was captured and exposed to the beasts in the amphitheatre but, so went the story, the beasts refused to touch him, and he had to be executed. This, says Tacitus, happened before the eyes of Vitellius himself, so it is to be assumed that it took place at Lugudunum.

Mariccus may be taken as a symbol of the unrest still simmering here and there among the Gauls. Vindex had undoubtedly created a strong impression in Lugudunensis, but more serious matters were soon afoot on the Rhine frontier, where a dangerous revolt was started by Julius Civilis, a Batavian officer in the Roman army. He posed at first as a supporter of Vespasian, but when news reached the Rhine of the collapse of the Vitellians at the end of the year, he threw off the mask and fought as the leader of a Germanic rising, backed by the power of a mysterious prophetess, Veleda, who lived in the Westphalian forest. The discontent among the Treveri and Lingones had meanwhile come to a head. Late in 69 Julius Classicus and Julius Tutor of the Treveri, and Julius Sabinus of the Lingones, jointly proclaimed an *Imperium Galliarum*. The proclamation was made in the legionary fortress of Novaesium, where the Roman commander was murdered. Classicus, who had just before deserted, at the head of his auxiliaries, now came before the soldiers in the purple cloak of a Roman general, and administered the oath of allegiance to the new empire. Civilis meanwhile took Vetera, which had undergone a long siege, and let his men butcher the surrendered garrison as it marched away. He then raided Gallia Belgica, and the Nervii and Tungri went over to him.

The enterprise of the Gallic Empire foundered on two obstacles. The first was the emperor Vespasian, the second the people of Gaul. The accession of Vespasian did not mean a continuation of anarchy, as Civilis and the others must have hoped, but a restoration of strong rule. The peoples of Gaul from the first held aloof from the rather shabby empire of Classicus and Sabinus, with its second-hand Roman trappings, its disgruntled soldiery and its German allies. The neighbours of the Treveri, the Mediomatrici and Sequani, had bitter memories of the passage of the armies of Vitellius, and the Sequani defeated Sabinus and his Lingones in a border skirmish. The Remi at last took the lead in summoning one of the most remarkable gatherings of Gallic history. They invited representatives from all the chief tribes of Gaul, including the Treveri, to meet at Reims, to study the situation and decide what action to take. Here was a *Concilium Galliarum* of the old traditional style, and Tacitus reports briefly its momentous deliberations. Should the Gauls choose peace or liberty? Tacitus concludes characteristically by saying that the assembly applauded the Treveran speech in favour of independence but voted for peace. A letter was accordingly sent to the Treveri 'in the name of the Gauls' bidding them to lay down their arms. Naturally enough, the Treveri paid no attention, but their doom was sealed.

Vespasian did not let the grass grow under his feet, and early in 70 the army of Petilius Cerialis crossed the Alps and made for Moguntiacum. Cerialis scornfully dismissed all the Gallic recruits he found in the forces there, saying that Rome could win back Gaul without their aid. He then proceeded to Augusta Treverorum, where he gave the rebels short shrift, despite some anxious moments. Civilis gave him more trouble, but the XIV Legion arrived from Britain, and as it approached, the Nervii and Tungri along its route prudently abandoned the revolt. Civilis, after long and bitter resistance, retired to the island of the Batavi—the Rhine delta between Waal and Lek. Here lay the oppidum of the Batavi—Ubbergen by Nijmegen —which the Romans stormed, and by the end of the year Civilis disappears from history.

Cerialis treated the vanquished with clemency. To the miserable remnants of the perjured legions he said that bygones should be bygones and that their leaders, rather than they, were to blame for what had happened. To the Gauls he made a famous speech, which embodies something of what the best Romans felt that imperial rule should be.

He began by recalling how the Romans had saved the Gauls from tribal warfare and German invasion, and went on: 'Do you consider yourselves more dear to Civilis, to the Batavi and the nations across the Rhine than your fathers and your grandfathers were to their ancestors? . . . We have not used our right of victory but to ask from you the means of assuring peace; for it is not possible to maintain the peace of nations without an army, there can be no army without pay, no pay without taxes: everything else we hold in common with you. You yourselves often command our legions, you govern these and other provinces; there is neither privilege nor exclusion. And if, which the gods forbid, the Romans are vanquished, what else can happen but universal war? Eight hundred years of happiness and wise policy have built up our edifice: it cannot be thrown down without dragging with it those who wished to destroy it. Think of peace and remember the City which secures for all of us the same rights.'

The restoration of peace by the energetic Cerialis, under the wise guidance of Vespasian, marks another epoch in the history of Gaul. One notable development in frontier policy is due to the Flavian emperors: under Vespasian the Romans advanced into the territory called the *Agri Decumates*, between the Upper Rhine and the Upper Danube, the land of the Black Forest and the Suabian Alb, and his son Domitian rounded this off by annexing land north of the Main. A land frontier therefore now extended from the neighbourhood of Coblenz to Eining above Regensburg. Domitian also finally recognized the special position of the Rhineland by cutting it off from Gaul and creating two new provinces, Germania Superior and Germania Inferior. The two German provinces remained closely bound up with Gaul, upon which they depended for their supplies, and in fiscal matters they continued to be administered by the Procurator of Gallia Belgica.

Gallic and German auxiliary regiments are still found in the Rhineland, but, after the events of 70, a higher proportion of them were sent to serve in other provinces. In the second century, when auxiliaries were settled permanently in their forts, recruitment became local, whatever the original tribal characters of the regiments.

The Flavian emperors continued the policy of favouring urban development. Vespasian advanced Aventicum, the chief town of the Helvetii, to colonial status. This would atone to the Helvetii for their sufferings at the hands of the Vitellians, and may also have marked the interest of the family of Vespasian in the tribe, for his father had carried on a banking business in the land of the Helvetii, and had died there.

Gaul now settled down to enjoy a century of almost unbroken peace. There was a moment of excitement when the legate of Moguntiacum revolted against Domitian and the emperor himself hurried north and summoned Trajan, at the head of the VII Legion, from Spain, but before either could arrive, Lappius Norbanus, the legate of Upper Germany, had quelled the revolt. After this the custom of having two legions sharing cantonments was abolished, and henceforward the Legion XXII Primigenia occupied the fortress at Moguntiacum alone. The military history of the second century belongs to the Danube, not to the Rhine, but the emperors kept in close touch with the western provinces.

Trajan himself was governor of Upper Germany at the time of his adoption by Nerva in 97, and he remained on the Rhine until Nerva's death. Hadrian made long journeys in Gaul in 121 and 122, and many new buildings arose after his visits. We are told that while at Nîmes he ordered a basilica to be built in honour of Plotina, Trajan's widow, news of whose death reached him there. The historian Dio writes that when Hadrian's favourite horse Borysthenes died in Gaul 'he prepared a tomb for him, set up a slab and placed an inscription upon it.' The site of this tomb may be Apt (Colonia Apta Iulia), where a metrical inscription came to light in 1604, stating that here lies Borysthenes, Caesar's charger, but perhaps this is too good to be true.

THE PROGRESS OF ROMANIZATION

With Antoninus Pius we have a son of a citizen of Nîmes attaining the purple. The Antonini were doubtless the descendants of Italian soldiers settled in the province, but their advancement marks the growing integration of the empire. This is perhaps a suitable point at which to assess what we know of individual Gallic citizens during the first two centuries of our era. It must be admitted that it does not amount to very much. Gaul was a province of manifold activity, which produced the most active traders and manufacturers of the west, and also the finest of the cavalry regiments in the Roman army, but surprisingly few eminent Gallo-Romans of the period have survived in our records.

Rome had gone to some pains to encourage the education of young Gauls of good birth. A school for sons of chieftains took root very early in Autun, which became an important centre of Romanization and later of higher education. This famous school, the *Maenianum*, lasted on into the third century and beyond, for one of the Panegyrics addressed to the emperor Constantius Chlorus contains an impassioned plea for its restoration after it had been destroyed in the siege of 272. Massilia was a celebrated centre of learning. Roman fathers sent their sons to study Greek letters there, feeling that in its sober provincial atmosphere they would be exposed to fewer temptations than at Athens. One of the youths of Narbonese Gaul educated there was Gnaeus Julius Agricola, who became governor of Aquitania in 74–76, shortly before he entered upon his governorship of Britain. Massilia was also a centre of medical studies. Pliny mentions two celebrated doctors of the town, describing their methods and the fortunes they amassed.

Schools, in which the rhetorical training, the ancient world's equivalent of a university course, was given, thus arose all over Gaul. Some of which we hear are those of Toulouse (referred to by Martial as Palladia Tolosa, city of Minerva), Vienne and Lyons. Fronto goes so far as to speak of Reims as an Athens, and Bordeaux, Arles and Trier did not lag far behind. We have, unfortunately, almost no literature of the early empire from Gaul, in striking contrast to the rich literary remains of fourth- and fifth-century Gaul, but some indication of the spread of at least a veneer of Latin culture is to be found in the popularity of mosaic pavements showing famous legends of classical literature and expressing devotion to the Muses. Rhetoric and oratory appealed strongly to the Gauls. A number of orators from Gallic towns are mentioned in our sources, including Gnaeus Domitius Afer of Nîmes, Consul in 39, who was an important figure in the Roman Senate from Tiberius to Nero; his contemporary, Julius Africanus of Saintes; Rufus of Vienne, famous under Trajan and Hadrian; Favorinus of Arles, acquaintance of Hadrian and teacher of Herodes Atticus. Many of these men must have had Gallic blood in their veins. A Narbonese Gaul of whom this is expressly stated is the historian Pompeius Trogus, a native of Vaison and a contemporary of Augustus. In one of the fragments of his writings he mentions that his grandfather, from Vasio, owed his Roman citizenship to Pompey the Great, for his services in the Sertorian war. It is at least possible that one of the most illustrious names in Roman letters comes from Narbonese Gaul, and that Publius Cornelius Tacitus himself, like Agricola his father-in-law, was descended from a Romanized Gallic family of the old Province.

Of politicians, we have already noted the attractive but unfortunate figure of Julius Vindex, governor of Lugudunensis in 68. Earlier, there was Marcus Valerius Asiaticus, native of Vienna, and one of the richest men in the empire in the time of Caligula and Claudius. He was twice consul, and was mixed up in the conspiracy to get rid of Caligula; later, he excited the cupidity of Messallina, who secured his condemnation on a trumped-up charge. He retired to the gardens of Lucullus, which he owned, and opened his veins.

Another leading figure is Marcus Antonius Primus of Toulouse, who was made legate of Legion VII Gemina and sent to Pannonia by Galba. He declared for Vespasian, and was one of those officers chiefly responsible for the success of the Flavian faction.

Towns continued to maintain links with powerful Romans who became their patrons. Sometimes these patrons were their own sons who had had distinguished careers. One such was M. Valerius Asiaticus, noted above; another was Sextus Afranius Burrus, the Praetorian Prefect of Claudius and Nero. He was a native of Vasio, and is mentioned in one of its inscriptions as patron of the city.

Rome's greatest and most enduring conquest was the spread of the Latin language over half Europe. Nowhere was that conquest more important than in Gaul. Throughout the Gallic provinces, save in the far north and west, Latin was to prevail. Only in Flanders, in the land of the Salian Franks, and along the Rhine, did a Germanic tongue emerge triumphant. How was it that Latin gained so complete a victory over the Celtic language that where it was supplanted it was by a new intruder and not a resurgent Gallic speech? The most notable evidence of the disappearance of Gallic is, paradoxically, from Brittany. There the language of the Middle Ages was not Gallic, but another Celtic tongue brought by settlers from Britain. Philologists say, however, that the distinctiveness of French may come from its Celtic background and that perhaps Gallic made its mark, after all. The language presents certain peculiarities which are not due to Germanic infiltration, nor are they normal modifications of a Romance tongue. This divergence of French from the Latin is very interesting to compare with the much more regular Romance tongues of Spanish and Italian. The Langue d'Oc, too, gave way before the Langue d'Oïl, and the latter, the ancestor of modern French, was developed precisely in those regions where the Celtic tribes were strongest.

The chief reason for the victory of Latin was that it was a written language, the language of education. The small beginnings of Celtic writing could not make headway against the Latin of the schools. Latin was also the language of commerce, of the law and of worldly advancement. It was the language of military service, and large numbers of Gauls passed through the Roman army. Celtic proved resistant in the country districts, but its

E

final submergence came with the disappearance of paganism, for Latin was the language of the new church and its priests, and their influence was in due course added to all those enumerated above.

Some Gallic words continued in common use. Here and there a town magistrate was still called *vergebret*, but the title had changed to *duumvir* by the time of Claudius. The *leuga*, or league, was able to displace the Roman mile from milestones in the third century, and inscriptions and *graffiti* show that Celtic numbers were commonly used for a long time. A few Gallic words, such as *bracae* for trousers and various names of carts, were taken over into Latin. An interesting case is the Gallic word for the lark, which was adopted by Latin and passed on to modern French, so that French Canadians singing their famous song 'la gentille alouette' are using the old Gallic word *alauda*.

A number of inscriptions in the Gallic language in Latin characters, and a few in Greek letters, exist, but they are mostly very brief and have not proved of great help to the ardent Celticists who still endeavour to reconstruct the ancient tongue. One only is very large, a calendar found at Coligny (Ain), probably belonging to a temple. It was inscribed in sixteen columns on a bronze tablet of which the fragments are preserved at Lyons. Unfortunately it gives very few Celtic words except proper names. Alongside the columns of days, which are divided into lunar months, are peg-holes for marking the date.

Celtic was quite common in the third century. Severus permitted its use for wills, and there is occasional mention of Celtic used by seers and sorceresses. Irenaeus refers to its widespread use in his diocese in the late second century.

It is difficult to estimate the amount of literacy in Roman Gaul outside the circles of the well-to-do. There was no such thing as universal compulsory education, and even in recent years the illiteracy figures in England before the Education Act—in a country where the printing-press had been known for 400 years—were very high. Therefore the occurrence of numerous *graffiti* in Roman Gaul does not compel us to believe that everybody could read or write. One may even learn the alphabet and be able to write one's own name and read the figures on a milestone, without aspiring to further literacy. House-hold slaves, no doubt, would be taught a minimum, shopkeepers had to know a little, and so of course did minor functionaries and artisans, but beyond that there is little to go on. There are, however, some interesting *graffiti* which do attest considerable penetration down-wards of Latin: on a tile found at Vichy: *ego achillis donavi figvlis amph vini* (I Achilles gave the potters an amphora of wine). Lead cursing-tablets were inscribed, in Latin, with ill-wishes destined for the suppliants' enemies, and then consigned to Pluto and the powers below by being buried in the ground; a few have been found in Gaul.

Another hint of widespread, if limited, literacy, is given by mottoes on drinking-vessels (fig. 25). The potters in the territory of the Gabali (Banassac, Lozère) produced cups with decorative legends, sometimes intended for particular tribes, like the cup with *Sequanis feliciter* found at Geneva. This recalls the 'present from Brighton' type of crockery. At the opposite end of Gaul the Treveri of a later period made wine-cups with convivial mottoes, from *gaudiamus* to *parce aquam adic merum* (spare the water and add more wine) or *vinum vires* (wine for strength).

Gallic society, like that of the Roman Empire in general, was aristocratic. Rome's policy throughout her history was almost invariably the conciliation of the aristocratic, conservative elements among the peoples whom she con-quered. By assuring stable government and security of property she obtained their co-operation. She could hardly have done otherwise. Nothing approaching an industrial proletariat was in existence, certainly not in the western countries, and the poor were illiterate and incapable of government. There had, it is true, been signs of unrest among certain impoverished elements in the generation of the conquest. These had been just the groups which supported leaders like Vercingetorix who were opponents of the ruling castes, but their defeat by Caesar was utter and complete. What became of them, and why is it that we do not get further unrest in any marked degree after the Roman conquest?

Many of them were, of course, dead, and there were the survivors of the siege of Uxellodunum with their severed hands, a horrid warning to all who would oppose Rome. Let it be said, in fairness to Caesar, that Vercingetorix himself had been capable of encouraging the laggards among his own following by not dissimilar methods. Some of the hardiest and most adventurous of the Gauls were promptly drawn off into the armies of Caesar and, later, of Augustus. One such group became Cleopatra's bodyguard and was handed over by Augustus to Herod the Great. Then, also, the coming of Rome meant work for the poor and prosperity for the nation as a whole. Even allowing for the work done by the Roman army, the building of the network of roads and the fine new cities must have kept large gangs of men occupied for long periods. As has been noticed in modern times, when the building industry flourishes, so do most other industries, for the requirements of the builder are countless. The rise of the towns necessitated a vast amount of quarrying, tile-making, wood-cutting, carpentry, mosaic-laying, drainage, and this kept people busy and free from want. So the first century of the Roman Empire in Gaul was a century of great economic prosperity. The restless enterprising spirit of the Celt was able to find plenty of outlets in commerce, and adventure did not cease with inter-tribal warfare.

The poor or busy man and woman had to rise early, and work long hours. Rich and poor alike generally retired to bed much earlier and arose much earlier than their counterparts to-day. The absence of good artificial lighting and of spectacles to aid the vision must have militated against late night reading after one had reached a certain age. We also have to picture a civilization without the printing press, where, therefore, despite the employment of thousands of slaves as copyists, reading-matter was not at all easily come by, and indeed the most ordinary book must have been a cherished possession. Hence the importance of the spoken word.

Time spent now in reading the newspapers and magazines would be spent in the forum or basilica gathering news for oneself or listening to the cases before the magistrates, or in that other popular gathering-place, the public baths. Here men could meet, bathe, talk, do gymnastic exercises in the *palaestra*, play games and gamble. Women too, had their baths.

The greatest sport of all was the chase, and, of course, Gaul was a famous hunting country. We get an interesting picture from the letters of Sidonius of his friends hunting the abundant game on their estates, and there is other evidence of this pastime. Sport and business could meet in field and forest, because there was the larger game to be trapped for the amphitheatre. In those days there were bears in Gaul, and wolves, besides the wild boars which have never disappeared from its remoter tracts.

From the pleasures of the field we move to the pleasures of the amphitheatre. The numerous amphitheatres of Gaul show that the Games took as great a hold here as in Rome itself. They provided occupation and amusement for large numbers of people. The Gauls also took passionately to the great sport of chariot-racing.

Dinner-parties were one of the chief social pleasures. The well-to-do Gauls, imitating Roman fashions in all things, adopted the Roman type of dining-room, the *triclinium* with its three couches, each with room for three diners, round a central space where there were tables and where slaves could easily move about. Meals could last a long time, and the host might arrange entertainments of music, conjuring, dancing, juggling, etc. Humbler folk had their societies, just as to-day. Very often these seem to have done little more than to have held club dinners at intervals or to have acted as burial societies to ensure decent funerals for their members. But they filled a need and made life more interesting for many simple people.

GAUL AND THE BARBARIAN WORLD

The first half of the second century passed auspiciously for Gaul. But great changes were going on in the barbarian world, migratory tribes displacing their neighbours and setting whole peoples on the move. A first tidal wave broke into the empire in 167, when a horde of Germanic tribes crossed the middle Danube and surged southward. The terrible Marcomannic War which ensued (167–180) had its repercussions in Gaul, as throughout the empire. Gaul could not fail to be affected by the drain on man-power and, still more, on finance. The plagues which swept Europe in 165–166, brought back by troops returning from a war on the eastern frontier, had their inevitably weakening effects. An ominous incident occurred in 174, when a piratical horde of Chauci swept down the coast and into Gallia Belgica, a presage of the later Saxon sea-raids. Against them levies of local militia were hastily assembled by the governor, Julianus, who drove them out.

There were other signs that things were not going too well. The aftermath of the Marcomannic War was apparent in the outbreak of bands of deserters, in particular of a large group under a certain Maternus, with whom the government of Commodus had to cope (186). Septimius Severus was then governor of Lugudunensis, and his future rival, Pescennius Niger, was sent against the deserters. Thus with the reigns of the heroic philosopher-emperor Marcus Aurelius and his unworthy son Commodus we enter a darker world. The twin curses of the empire, barbarian invaders and disputed successions, were now again to threaten its tranquillity. The assassination of Commodus (192) brought back to Gaul the troubles of the year of the four emperors.

When the legions of Britain declared for Clodius Albinus, they found many supporters in Gaul, and the army of Lower Germany joined them. Civil war followed, reaching its climax towards the end of A.D. 196 with the approach of Severus, the candidate of the powerful Danube army. The final clash between these two able Africans, the aristocratic Albinus from Hadrumetum and the Punic-speaking Severus, citizen of Lepcis Magna, took place outside Lugudunum (197). After a bitter contest, in which the tough legions from Britain acquitted themselves well, Severus gained an overwhelming victory. His record is disgraced by his permitting the brutal sack of Lugudunum by his soldiery. It may have been in part prompted by anger that a city where he had recently been governor and where his eldest son had been born should have gone over to the foe; or it may have been that he could not really be sure of restraining his troops. After taking condign vengeance of his defeated opponents, Severus let the provinces settle down, and in general they benefited considerably from the rule of the Severan house.

In our story of Gaul we still have many prosperous years to record. Lugudunum recovered much of its old preeminence, and the Council of the Gauls was still functioning peacefully in 238. Altars in honour of the imperial family sprang up on all sides, and there was a new period of building activity. Justice was administered efficiently, and the civil service was strictly supervised. A noteworthy feature of the epoch is the favour shown to native provincial life. Native languages, especially Punic and Celtic, were given some encouragement, for it was now permitted to use them in the law-courts. The Severans also encouraged the corporations of the lesser folk in the towns, and finally there is the famous *Constitutio Antoniniana* of 212, the Edict granting the Roman citizenship to all free citizens of the empire—the logical conclusion of a long development.

The German menace, banished for 200 years by Caesar and Augustus and held off by Marcus Aurelius, was returning to the Gallic scene. The old familiar neighbours —Hermunduri, Chatti, Chauci—disappeared, and big new confederations took their place—the Alemanni, Franks and Saxons, with Goths appearing farther east. A foretaste of what was in store came with the Alemanni breaking through the *limes* of Upper Germany in 215, with which Caracalla, despite his many faults, coped adequately. He drove them out and strengthened the old frontier line, Hadrian's wooden palisade, with a continuous bank and ditch in Upper Germany and a stone wall in Raetia.

The Alemanni were thus not to reach Gaul itself yet awhile. The young Severus Alexander went to Moguntiacum in 234 to meet their next threat. He was murdered by discontented soldiers early the following year, but his project was carried out by his successor, Maximinus Thrax, who took the war into German territory, and so staved off the threat to the Empire, before he in his turn was murdered. Army after army put forward its pretenders and left its post to back its choice. The weakness was clear to the barbarians, perhaps clearer than to the Romans, and attacks on the empire multiplied, but as yet Gaul was not seriously affected, and life remained untroubled by the rapid changes of ruler during the next ten years. Gallic industries continued, and large funerary monuments of the first half of the century attest the wealth and peace of the country. So time flowed on towards the year 247, when the emperor Philip, of Arab descent, celebrated the millennium of Rome, and Gaul emerged comparatively unharmed from the first half of the third century.

The signal for the crash came in 253, when the troops of the frontier again left their posts to participate in a new civil war, as a result of which Valerian emerged as emperor. The barbarians moved against the frontier as its garrisons had marched away. The exact dates of their incursions is not clear, but numerous coin hoards of the fifties all over Gaul show how the inhabitants were endeavouring to protect their wealth against the perils of the time. The Alemanni swept over the frontier and occupied the parts of Germania Superior east of the Rhine, while some of them advanced into Gaul itself, harrying the land as they went.

To this period belongs the half-legendary Alemannic king Chrocus described by Gregory of Tours, who tells us that he pillaged Auvergne, and destroyed the temple at Augustonemetum called Vasso Galate, before passing on to Arelate, where he was finally captured. At the same time the Franks passed across the lower Rhine on plundering forays. The trail of ruins can still be traced. Not since the days of the Cimbri and Teutoni had such a visitation overtaken Gaul, and the damage done by the Cimbri cannot be compared with that done to a rich, thickly settled land, with its numerous undefended urban centres and isolated farms by the Franks and Alemanni.

Valerian, as soon as his own position was assured, had despatched his son and co-Augustus, Gallienus, to take supreme command in Gaul, where the provinces were once more grouped together as in the days of Drusus, and Roman Germany ceased to have an independent existence. Gallienus, using Colonia Agrippinensis as his headquarters, acted with energy, and about 256 was able to carry the war across the Rhine with some success, so that the title *Restitutor Galliarum* appears, not unjustifiably, on his coins. The territory east of the Rhine was now, however, virtually Alemannic, and there is no sign of occupation of any of the old frontier forts after 259. Gallienus had to depart for the Danube about 258, and almost at once, two years later, lost Gaul to his general Postumus. Postumus, after being saluted as emperor, sent a manifesto to Gallienus to the effect that his intention was to stay in his province and protect and prosper Gaul.

The 'Roman Empire of the Gauls' is an interesting

episode of which some historians have tended to make too much. Recent work has shown it to have been a fairly unsubstantial thing, and its ruler simply a would-be emperor of the world whom the circumstances of the day prevented from asserting his power over the whole empire. Despite his interesting initial proclamation, after the repulse of Gallienus Postumus seems to have cherished the ambition of ultimately extending his rule all over the empire. He brought Britain and Spain into his sphere, while in 268 he even succeeded momentarily in penetrating into northern Italy.

Postumus endeavoured to carry out his basic duty of keeping the barbarians at bay, though bands of them continued from time to time to roam the interior, and the loss of the *Agri Decumates* was not retrieved. Under him, too, Augusta Treverorum moved towards its destiny as an imperial capital, and the re-fortification of Gaul was begun, but there is no indication of any kind of Gallic nationalism.

Having defeated a rival by taking Moguntiacum, he was murdered by his own troops, when he had refused to allow them to sack the city (c. 269). Emperors now followed one another rapidly. The last of the Gallic emperors was Tetricus. He had been made governor of Aquitania by Postumus, and was essentially a civilian— a worthy senator, of Celtic blood, judging by his name, Esuvius, which may denote connection with the tribe of the Esuvii.

The murder of Gallienus in the same year was followed by the elevation of one of the conspirators, Claudius Gothicus, to the purple. The Gallic empire, too, was breaking up, and Autun declared for Claudius. For seven months the city was besieged by lawless bands masquerading as the army of the unlucky Tetricus. They finally overcame resistance by cutting the aqueducts, and looting and destruction of the worst kind followed. This siege made a great impression on contemporaries and seemed to be the culmination of the woes of Gaul.

In due course Claudius was replaced by Aurelian, who had to deal with the east before turning his attention to Gaul. When he did come (in 274), Tetricus made no attempt to prevent the passage of the Alps, and was an unwilling follower of his own army, which was beaten at the Catalaunian Fields. Tetricus, who is said to have sent the Virgilian message *Eripe me his, Invicte, malis* to Aurelian, 'Deliver me from these woes, unconquered one', seized the first possible chance of surrender. Aurelian did not spare him the indignity of marching, with Queen Zenobia, in his triumph, clad in full Gallic costume, but his story has a happy ending which does great credit to both parties, for he was allowed to revert to his career in the higher civil service, and became Governor of Lucania. He was thus one of the few third-century emperors who died in their beds. The troubles of Gaul, however, were not yet over, for in the years 275–276 fresh barbarian hordes fell upon the land and swept into every corner.

The real *Restitutor Galliae* was the emperor Probus (276–282), who hastened to the scene in 276, drove the invaders out, recaptured much booty, and followed them into their own territory. Under him the weary business of rebuilding was begun again, and the land was once more cultivated. His edict encouraging the provincials to grow vines may well be an attempt to assuage the scouring of the provinces and to aid their recovery.

Probus went the way of other emperors of his age, good or bad. The empire's luck at last turned in 284 with the choice of the obscure but able Diocles by the army of the east. The new emperor, now calling himself Diocletianus, brought to his task something of the cool ability of Augustus. He also was a civilian rather than a soldier, but, like Augustus, he knew how to choose good soldiers and to keep their loyalty.

IV

TOWN PLANNING AND BUILDINGS

THE well-known generalization that the civilization of the ancient classical world was a city civilization is only partially true of Roman Gaul. It is true that under Roman rule many cities grew up, but city life in Gaul, except in the south, was never quite the same as that of Italy or Greece. In Gaul the city rarely succeeded in dwarfing the tribe; the 'sixty cities' of Gallia Comata are the sixty tribes. The inhabitant of Lutetia did not forget that he was a Parisian, and the inhabitant of Augustone-metum was an Arvernian. The importance of the tribe is attested by the final victory of tribal names over city names. So Durocortorum of the Remi becomes Reims, Samarobriva of the Ambiani, Amiens, Avaricum of the Bituriges, Bourges, Augustoritum of the Lemovices, Limoges. The exceptions are instructive, and occur where Roman influence was strongest: Augustodunum of the Aedui retains its Latin name in Autun; Colonia Agrippinensis, created by Rome, is still called Köln or Cologne. A few dominant cities, where there was no important tribe, retained their Celtic non-tribal name: Burdigala, Lugudunum, Moguntiacum.

Gaul was, in fact, too large, its tribes too backward and scattered, to be welded into the Italian type of a network of municipalities. A tribal territory was like a French department, or often larger. The link between the Gallic *civitas* and the Italian *municipium* proper is found in Narbonensis, where tribal territories were reduced by making grants of land to the colonies of Caesar.

A *civitas*—that is, a tribe and its territory—had to be divided up for administrative purposes, and its divisions

66

were known as *pagi*. Many of these were based on sub-
or client-tribes already in existence. Thus the Parisii
were a sub-tribe of the Senones, and the Verodunenses of
Verdun were a sub-tribe of the Mediomatrici. From the
Latin *pagus* comes the French word *pays*. The *pagus*, like
the parent *civitas*, had its centre—a *vicus*, or small settlement—and its presiding magistrate, the *praefectus*, *aedilis*
or *magister pagi*. The subsidiary market towns of the
civitas would tend to be the chief towns of the *pagi*. Some
of these towns, as the Celtic suffix -*magus* (market) suggests,
were already established before or very soon after the
Roman conquest, as Rotomagus (Rouen). Germanicoma-
gus (Saint-Cybardeaux in Charente), however, shows the
Celtic termination still being used for a new foundation
of about A.D. 15. Or we find the Latin *Forum* being
used, e.g. at Forum Domitii (Montbazon, Indre-et-Loire),
Forum Claudii Ceutronum or Axima (Aime-en-Taren-
taise).

As time wore on some *pagi* were promoted to the rank of
civitates, so that the fifth century gazeteer, the Notitia
Dignitatum, lists 104 Gallic cities as against the eighty
(including Narbonensis) of the time of Augustus. Among
the promotions are the Parisii and Rouen.

Small settlements, often little more than hamlets,
tended to grow up, as always, at cross-roads, around
sanctuaries, at fords or bridges, or where important roads
crossed tribal boundaries. The stations of the Imperial
Post also acted as nuclei (see p. 34).

TOWN WALLS OF THE EARLY EMPIRE

In the Republican period, while the land was still
occupied by warring tribes, towns had to have defences,
but of the early walls of Narbonne and of the *castellum* at
Aix no sure trace remains. Here and there fragments of
what is believed to be the venerable Greek wall of Massilia
have been found deep in the ground; some fine masonry
of the Greek fortress at Saint-Blaise (Bouches-du-
Rhône) has been recovered, and remains of the Greek

fortifications of Olbia (Hyères) and Antipolis (Antibes) have also been traced.

The Caesarian and Augustan towns rose in a land pacified, but only recently pacified, and fortifications were desirable. They were also a matter of imperial propaganda and of civic pride. Towns enjoying the distinction of colonial status were provided with walls. The colonies of Roman citizens, like Arelate and Forum Iulii, were not only settlements for retired soldiers, but had a military function to perform, so they were, as a matter of course, fortified; colonies with Latin rights, like Nemausus and Vienna, were given a girdle of walls as a mark of imperial favour and a sign of the might of the Roman civilization which was now embracing the country.

The standard walls of this period are some 2½ metres thick, with heavily mortared rubble cores faced with small dressed blocks of masonry, carefully laid. There are no bonding courses of tiles. The best examples are at Arles, Nîmes and Fréjus. Autun, Vienne and Lyons also had Augustan walls. They are constructed in the tradition of the walls of the Augustan colonies in Italy, and are massive structures, thick enough to have carried a rampart walk. All these walls were provided with circular towers, generally about 10 metres in diameter, set at intervals from 50 to 100 metres apart. Nothing is known of early walls of Colonia Iulia Equestris and Augusta Raurica, the colonies in the north. The walls at the latter, backed by an earth bank, of which two stretches have been investigated, appear to belong to the third century, and may never have been finished.

In the Flavian period we know of one nominee to colonial status, Aventicum, which received walls on a generous scale. They made a wide sweep round the openly spaced buildings of the colony. These walls are only 1·35 to 1·65 metres thick, although the foundations reach 2 metres across and are in places built on piles. All round the walls are curious semi-circular towers, projecting inwards, 5 metres across. The whole construction gives the impression that the wall must have been backed by an earth bank, like town walls in Britain, but of this apparently no trace has been discovered. The walls of the Trajanic colony, which grew out of the old civilian settlement outside the legionary fortress of Vetera, had an earth backing and a ditch.

The best example of an early second-century wall is that of Tongres, built of flints bedded in mortar and faced, above ground, with ashlar. The foundations are 2·10 metres wide, the wall 2·07 metres (= 7 Roman feet). There are the usual towers, 9 metres in diameter. In the marshy ground which part of the wall traverses, its foundations are laid on oaken piles about 5 metres long. In front of the walls are two ditches, the outer one being the deeper and broader of the two.

Some of the earliest gateways, belonging to the end of the Second Triumvirate, have the entrance set back in a half-moon recess in the walls, with towers at the ends of the horns from which an enemy trying to enter could be attacked. Examples of this development are found at Arles, Fréjus and, in its latest modification, at Vindonissa. Fig. 7, of the Porte des Gaules of Fréjus, illustrates the point clearly. It has been plausibly conjectured that such a half-moon gateway lay round the Arch of Triumph at Orange. This seems to have been an experimental form, however, and was not generally adopted. Two good examples of the more orthodox type of Augustan gate are those of the Porte d'Auguste of Nîmes and the gates of Autun. The early gate through the half-moon wall at Arles was replaced, under Augustus, by a more elaborate structure of the Nîmes type (fig. 7).

At the Porte d'Auguste the wall ended in two towers, rounded in front, rectangular in the rear; between them was the gateway, of monumental proportions, with four passages, two for foot-passengers, two for vehicles, leading into an inner court, 10·60 by 7·60 metres. There was a portcullis in the front, and the towers held guardrooms.

In Autun's gates the courtyard has disappeared, but

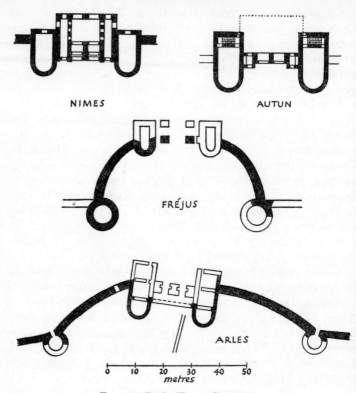

NIMES

AUTUN

FRÉJUS

ARLES

Fig. 7. Early Town Gateways

there are towers with guardrooms. The Porte d'Arroux
had a portcullis, but this was not provided for in the Porte
Saint-André. In time gates tended to be built for the
adornment of a town rather than for its defence. It has
been observed that the upper storey of the Porte Saint-
André is far more lightly built than the stout lower part,
and it is taken to be a post-Augustan alteration.

Gaul also possesses a number of gateways which are
normally classified as arches of triumph, but which are
often, though not necessarily, connected with town gates.
The arch of triumph at Orange (see p. 163) stands at the

entry of the town.   Like the arch at Reims, it has three
passage-ways.   The arch at Reims, it has now been
argued, is probably one of these first-century arches of
triumph put up in association with a gateway.   This is
a hypothesis with much to be said for it, for no Gallic
tribe deserved more consideration by the victors than the
Remi.   A much later example is that of Langres, set up
by the Lingones in honour of Marcus Aurelius; that at
Vesontio is also regarded as belonging to the second
century.

Bridges were also favourite positions for erecting
ornamental archways; and the chief example is that at
Saintes, which once stood on a bridge.   Other, smaller
ones belong to the bridge at Saint-Chamas (Bouches-du-
Rhône).

PUBLIC BUILDINGS

Roman Gaul had no large cities by modern standards.
It had few even by eighteenth-century standards, which
it is more appropriate to use when considering Roman
times.   Augusta Treverorum, which became an imperial
capital, covered only 285 hectares (704 acres), and the
walls of Augustodunum only enclosed about 200 hectares
(494 acres).

A full account of the towns is obviously impossible in
this little book.   A few of the standard buildings of Roman
towns, with some of the best existing examples, will first
be mentioned.   After that a limited number of the most
interesting towns, both large and small, will be discussed,
and any outstanding points in their history or archaeology
which may help to fill in our picture of the life of Gaul.

Regularity of plan was a feature of all towns constructed
under Roman auspices; and in this the Romans and the
modern Americans have a good deal in common.   The
foundation of large numbers of new towns had to be
carried out by both within a comparatively short time, and
it is natural that a standard type should be used.   This is
the chessboard pattern early adopted for the lay-out of

F

Roman colonies and also familiar in the Greek world, where it went back to the building of Piraeus, the port of Athens, in the fifth century B.C. Augst in Switzerland is a good example of a standard Roman colony (fig. 8).

Each town of any pretensions had to have its civic

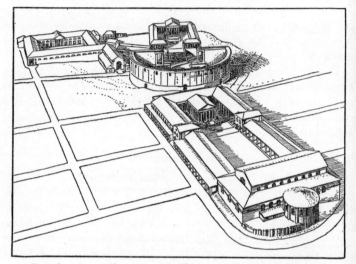

FIG. 8. Augst Forum, with Theatre and Temple beyond

centre—that is, its market-place or forum—with associated temple, town hall (basilica), and meeting place for the town council (curia). The planning of such a group of buildings in Augst is very striking (fig. 8). The forum consists of a rectangular open space, surrounded by porticoes, with the basilica at one end and a temple in the central part of the opposite end. The discovery of an altar dedicated to Jupiter in the court of this temple points to it as the capitolium of the town—the centre here, as in Rome, of the official cult of Jupiter, Juno and Minerva. Off the porticoes were rows of small shops.

The basilica was of standard type, with a nave supported by columns and aisles, somewhat austere externally, but richly decorated within. Abutting on its outer side was a circular building, the curia, in which the excavators found the steps on which the seats were set. Off it was a small waiting- or service-room.

The group of buildings as here described belongs to the second century. As most towns of Gaul have been inhabited continuously since Roman times, opportunities of excavating their fora have been rare, but in addition to Augst, large-scale investigation has been possible at Avenches and Alesia.

In a few cases basement or underground passages have been found running under the ranges of porticoes round a forum. Such a structure, called a *cryptoporticus*, was a good storehouse for perishable goods, and a pleasant place for cooling off in the hot climate of the south. The one at Arles can be reached from the Musée d'Art Chrétien; there is another at Narbonne; Reims, however, far in the north, had one, and what is probably yet another has recently been found at Bavai. This has narrow openings for cellar-type windows like those at Arles, and its double walls suggest that its builders were interested in keeping the damp out, and that therefore grain may have been stored here.

Many towns have secondary market-places, for the forum proper tended to be more and more the civic rather than the commercial centre, and Augst again provides us with a good example.

The public baths, after the fora the chief centres of social life, are one of the most prominent features of any Roman town, whether in the north of Britain or on the borders of the Sahara. The best-preserved baths of Gaul are, paradoxically, baths which were never quite finished, and so never used, the Imperial Baths (Kaiserthermen) of Trier. These are Constantinian in date, but their plan does not differ in any important respect from those of the earlier period. They virtually duplicated another vast, earlier, public bathing establishment, the

Barbarathermen, which was still maintained. They contained dressing-rooms (*apodyteria*), cold baths and swimming-baths (*frigidaria* and *piscinae*), warm rooms (*tepidaria*), hot baths (*caldaria* and *sudatoria*), promenade halls and a great court used as a gymnasium (*palaestra*). The Kaiserthermen at Trier have the particular advantage for the visitor that one can climb a narrow Roman staircase to a point high up among the ruins, from where one can look down on the ground plan of the enormous structure.

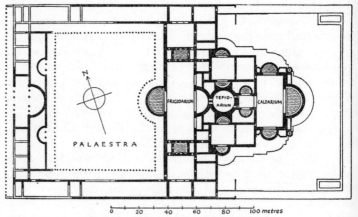

FIG. 9.　Trier: the Imperial Baths

Large portions of the system of underground passages are also preserved, which give some idea of the complex service needed for the upkeep of the baths (figs. 9 and 38).

Women bathed as well as men, and the smaller of the two sets of baths excavated at Augst would seem to have been women's baths, or at least to have been largely used by women, as large numbers of hairpins and beads from necklaces were found in the main drain of the building.

TOWN HOUSES

The well-to-do inhabitants of the cities of Gaul lived in houses which might equally well be found in Italy, and

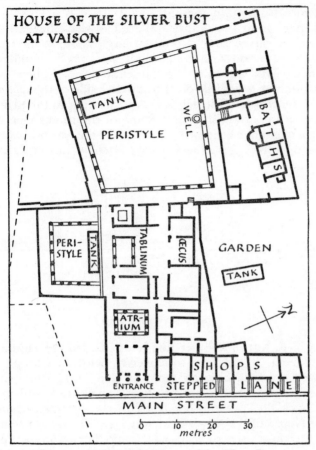

FIG. 10. Vaison: the House of the Silver Bust

of a type which is not unrepresented in Britain. A good specimen is the fine town mansion called by the excavator the House of the Silver Bust, at Vaison. Its entrance (fig. 10) leads from a narrow paved and stepped street with colonnade and shops. The mansion thus lay on the inside of an *insula* or block, fringed by shops and houses, whose rents doubtless formed part of the income of the proprietor. Within the entrance portico is a large hall, opening on to the square, pillared *atrium*. Beyond the *atrium* are the reception-rooms, a large salon on the right, with a vista through to a small *peristylium* or pillared garden, with an oblong ornamental tank. There is a much larger *peristylium* on the opposite side of the *tablinum* from the *atrium*, off which is a court leading to the private baths of the establishment. Some of the rooms near the *atrium* may have been bedrooms, and there was probably a second storey for others. The kitchen has not been

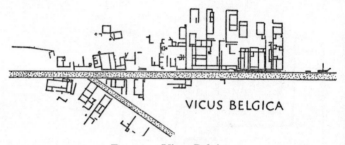

VICUS BELGICA

FIG. 11. Vicus Belgica

identified, but in another fine house, called the House of the Messii, it has been discovered, with two fireplaces arranged for burning charcoal or wood, and also a sink. One of its two doors leads to the kitchen yard, and so to the back door; the other leads to the reception-rooms. The House of the Silver Bust was given its name because a silver bust (see p. 178) was found buried under lead debris from its roof, due to a catastrophe during the third century. When the house was rebuilt it was not cleared completely, so the bust was not noticed. It perhaps represents one of the owners, of the end of the first century (see fig. 41*a*).

Unfortunately the houses of the less well-to-do are more difficult to describe, because, being smaller and closer together, they present a less clear picture to the excavator. When he is uncovering walls of which only the lowest courses remain, he rarely finds doorways, so that it is hard to know where one house ends and another begins. Two long, narrow *insulae* at Vaison are believed to have contained blocks of flats. If the doorways have been correctly identified, the ground-floor units appear to have been fairly commodious.

Elsewhere the smaller town houses are often long and narrow, so that as many tenants as possible could share the advantage of a street frontage. Fig. 11 shows examples of this occurring at the small road station Vicus Belgica on the Tongres–Cologne road. A good many houses, or fragments of houses, have been excavated in the last hundred years at Avenches. They seem to have been carefully aligned to the road grid, but they vary greatly in size and plan, and cannot at present be reduced to a standard. As in so many towns, they are often fronted by colonnaded streets. Other houses have been found at Alesia, where an outstanding feature is the popularity of cellars.

THEATRES, AMPHITHEATRES AND CIRCUSES

Theatres, rare among Romano-British discoveries, are frequent in Gaul, and very imposing remains of many of them are still visible. The Augustan theatre of Orange is the only Roman theatre in the western provinces whose façade (*scenae frons*) has survived. This great wall, 103 metres long and 38 metres high, looks gaunt as one approaches it to-day, but it once had a portico along its outside and was decorated with arcaded pilasters. Between it and the back stage wall (*proscenium*) were various chambers used by the actors. The *proscenium* was sumptuously embellished. Three portals led through it on to the stage. Above the central one is a niche which once contained the statue of the emperor Augustus. On either side of this were three tiers of columns with niches for more statues. There were other entrances from spacious green-rooms on either side of the stage. The wall along the front of the *pulpitum*, now vanished, was also decorated lavishly. Behind it was the long groove into which the curtain was lowered when performances began. Opposite the stage the auditorium (*cavea*) rested on the slope of the hill of Saint-Eutrope, crowned in a later age by the castle of the Princes of Orange. It was the incorporation of the theatre into this castle which assured its survival.

The semi-circle of the *cavea* (fig. 12), which could seat 9000 spectators, rose from the small, ground-level semi-

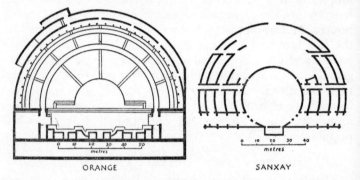

ORANGE   SANXAY

FIG. 12.   Classical Roman Theatre at Orange and Romano-
Celtic Theatre at Sanxay

circle of the *orchestra*.   This *orchestra* had originally played an important part in the Greek theatre as the place where the chorus danced and sang, but in Roman times the performers kept to the stage, so the outer part of the orchestra might be used for special seats brought in for city counsellors or visiting dignitaries.   The height of the now-vanished stage, however, precluded the use of the whole orchestra by spectators.   The stone seats of the *cavea* have been restored, for the theatre is now once more used for public performances, and probably more Greek tragedies are played to modern citizens of Orange than were ever played to their Gallo-Roman ancestors, who preferred, we suspect, coarser and more amusing fare. The seats were arranged in three tiers (*moeniana*), and at the top of the *cavea* was a portico, serving as a promenade and an entrance. Other entrances to the auditorium ran through vaulted passages at the side of the stage. Over these were boxes, in one of which sat the magistrate giving the show. During performances an awning (*velum*) was drawn across the theatre, and the sockets for the masts which held it still exist along the façade. Alongside this theatre was another public building which is thought to have been a gymnasium. This was afterwards converted into a colonnaded court round a temple.

Only small fragments of the sculptures and marble columns which adorned the theatre of Orange have survived, but some of the best works of art which have been found in Gaul come from the theatres of Arles and Vaison (see p. 167). Vienne and Autun had still larger theatres, each estimated as capable of holding 10,000 or 11,000 spectators.

While commenting on the theatres in the large towns, we must not forget the numerous small ones found in quite remote country places, near sanctuaries, as, for instance, at Champlieu on the borders of the Forest of Compiègne, at Sanxay in the department of Vienne (fig. 12) or at Vieux not far from Caen. Many of the theatres in the Three Gauls, like that at Verulamium in Britain, are of a special type, peculiar to the Celtic provinces of the empire.

These so-called cockpit theatres have a large, nearly circular orchestra and a narrow stage erected much farther back than in the standard Vitruvian theatre of the Orange type. This is not, however, the sign of a return of the Greek chorus, but the desire of small communities to make their theatre serve the double purpose of a small amphitheatre where cock-fighting or bear-baiting could go on, and an ordinary theatre. The *cavea* is separated from the *orchestra* by a deep wall, so that spectators should not be in danger from wild beasts, and it often extends round more than a semi-circle. As an easily accessible, but rather extreme, example, we may cite the Arènes of

Paris. Here the *orchestra* was elliptical, but there was also a stage. The theatre at Drevant has, in addition, small chambers which are evidently dens for animals.

The theatre of Lyons was recently cleared and close by it, another, much smaller one, was found and excavated (fig. 37*b*). This is with reason regarded as an *odeum*, or concert hall. These halls were roofed, wholly, or partially, and the thickness of the wall of the Lyons building gives the impression that it was designed to carry the weight of a roof. Another *odeum* has since been discovered at Vienne.

No province loved gladiatorial shows and the other sports of the amphitheatre more than Gaul. Two amphitheatres of the south—those of Nîmes and Arles —are still in almost perfect preservation, and are now used for bull-fights and for other amusements, like open-air cinemas, less directly derived from the Roman empire. The largest amphitheatre known in Gaul is that of Autun.

The amphitheatres of Arles and Nîmes, free-standing, with two tiers of arcades, resemble one another very closely. The Arles amphitheatre measures 136 × 107 metres and must have had seating for 26,000 spectators. On a number of seats inscriptions indicating the city corporations to which they were allotted were found: the shippers and oil merchants in the front row; farther back the *scholastici*, the students. In the Middle Ages the amphitheatre served as a fortress, and a whole quarter of the town grew up within it with a population of 1,500 and a church of its own. This was all cleared away between 1825 and 1837. The date of the monument is uncertain. It cannot belong to the earliest period of the colony, because a tower of the town wall has been found embedded in its substructures. On its podium, however, is a large inscription of the early second century in honour of a *duumvir* who had given games here.

The amphitheatre of Nîmes is only slightly smaller than that of Arles, and is even more completely preserved.

Its date is also not definitely established, but it overlies earlier Roman houses. It, too, became a medieval fortress. The outer wall remains to its full height, so that the sockets for the masts holding the *velum* are still to be seen. We may even have the name of the architect, if an inscription *T. Crispius Reburrus fecit* refers to him and not to some humbler participator in the work.

Sometimes these amphitheatres were built on earth banks, as at Trier. A legionary fortress like Vindonissa had its amphitheatre as a matter of course (110 × 98·5 metres, seating 10,000 men); this was hollowed out within earth banks.

Chariot-racing appealed strongly to the Gauls. A race-course could be cleared and maintained without elaborate buildings, but the larger cities had their properly laid-out circuses, modelled on those of Rome, with the long central island or *spina*, marked with obelisks and other monuments, round which the competitors galloped, and the long ellipse with ranges of seats. A tall obelisk in Egyptian granite was found south of the old walls of Arles, and now stands in the Place de la République. From time to time traces of a large structure were noticed in the region whence the obelisk had come.

Excavations in 1911 and 1912 revealed a small part of the circus ellipse with the walls intended to carry seating. The structure was built on oak piles. Nothing of this can now be seen, but at Vienne a monument belonging to the *spina* is still in position, and the dimensions of the circus (455 × 118 metres) have been worked out.

AQUEDUCTS

The most beautiful of all the monuments of Roman Gaul, the Pont du Gard, was, appropriately enough, built for utility, forming part of the aqueduct carrying water from springs near Uzès to the city of Nîmes. A Roman aqueduct was normally a cemented channel (*specus*), rectangular in section, with a vaulted roof. It ran as far as possible at ground level, carrying the water down a very gentle slope towards its objective. The maintenance of this slight slope was no easy matter, and often necessitated tunnels through hills, or the building of arches to carry the channel across valleys. The Pont du Gard on its triple arches is the most majestic of these bridges, but the tall arches of the Metz aqueduct are scarcely less impressive (fig. 40).

The aqueduct of Nîmes follows a winding course and covers a total distance of 50 kilometres. The drop in level is 17 metres. A group of springs, the *Fontaines d'Eure et d'Airan*, was tapped on the hills east of Uzès, and the water was led to the aqueduct. For most of its course to the Gardon river it is carried on low arches or on a wall; a three-arched bridge conveys it across the ravine of Bornègre. The Pont du Gard itself is 269 metres long and 48 metres high: the bottom tier has six arches measuring 18 to 22 metres across, the second tier has eleven arches of about the same dimensions, the third consists of thirty-five arches 4·8 m. wide and 8·50 m. high. The two lower tiers are wider than the top one, and provide a passage way of 1·07 m. which has always been used as a foot-bridge, but the road along the east side above the first tier, and the arcading built to support it (see fig. 13), date from 1747. After crossing the Gardon the course of the aqueduct becomes extremely sinuous, as it accommodates itself to the sides of the hills round which it has to pass. It had no fewer than six other bridges over small streams or gullies, one of which must have required two tiers of arches. At Lafoux it turns to run in a generally south-westerly direction towards Nîmes, most of its course now being subterranean. Where possible it was built in a rock-cut trench 3 to 5 metres deep, but in places it passes through tunnels, one being as much as 400 metres long and not running straight, as the engineers apparently sought out the softer veins of rock.

It enters Nîmes near the Citadel, close to which the *castellum divisorium* was found in 1844. This device is a circular basin 5·90 m. in diameter, 1·40 m. in depth, which the aqueduct enters by an opening 1·80 m. wide by 1·20 m. high.   On the opposite side of the basin, 56 centimetres above its bottom, is a row of ten circular openings, 40 cm. in diameter, into which were let the pipes to carry the waters off in double conduits in five different directions.   There were also three openings through which silt could be washed away into a drain below when the basin was cleaned out, and the inflow could be controlled by a gate.   The building containing the basin seems to have been adorned with columns.

The dimensions of the channel were 1·80 m. in depth by 1·22 m. in width.   It was cemented as far as the spring of the vault with an extremely thick cement.   Manholes for admitting persons into the aqueduct to clean it were 80–100 metres apart as a rule, but much closer on bends. The water was very hard, and a calcareous deposit 30 centimetres thick formed in the aqueduct in the course of years.

Many other Gallo-Roman aqueducts are known, and substantial remains are to be seen in many places.   Arles had more than one.   The best preserved is the one coming from the Alpilles to the north-east of the city; a stretch of several arches can be followed near Barbegal.   The remains of the forty-kilometre aqueduct of Fréjus are among the finest surviving, great piers still standing near the town.   It branched into two shortly before entering the town, one branch going to the port and one to the colony.   For part of the way it had a double channel. A good many fragments of the aqueduct survive along its course, including the initial collecting basin.

The principle that water finds its own level was known to the Romans, so that they were able if necessary to carry an aqueduct down a steep slope and up the one opposite. This course was, however, avoided whenever possible, as it involved costly outlay in lead or earthenware pipes and it was not possible to convey a great volume of water this way.   One of the Lyons aqueducts, which is 75 kilometres long, was carried to the city thus from Mont Pilate over the valleys of the Garon, the Baran and Saint-Irenée. It has been calculated that the four aqueducts of Lyons could bring into the city a total of 80,000 cubic metres of water daily.

The aqueduct of Rodez followed the contours of the hills with even more than the usual care, so that though its source is only 12 kilometres south-west of the town, the channel is 27 kilometres long. From time to time it is fed by tributary conduits. It had also to pass through two tunnels respectively 106 and 271 metres long. As it neared the town it went forward on arches which must have been 20 metres high; foundations of 133 of their piers have been found. For the last lap, the water must have been carried across the deep intervening valley in thick lead pipes under pressure.

The aqueduct of Metz moved an eleventh-century monk to describe it in a poem. It was 22 kilometres in length, partly underground, partly above ground. It was carried across the Moselle south of the city on a bridge 1,100 metres long, which must have been composed of about sixty arches. Two groups, one of two and the other of five arches, survive on the left bank of the river, and on the opposite side there is still a series of sixteen. A special feature is the double channel of the bridge section, probably constructed in order that while one was being cleaned the other could continue in use. These channels have now disappeared, but their ends were traced in the settling-basins found on either side of the river, of which that on the right bank is still visible. The aqueduct of Paris came 16 km. from Arcueil, where fragments of its piers remain beside aqueducts of the seventeenth and nineteenth centuries. The Cologne aqueduct brought water from springs in the Eifel Mountains 77 km. from the city.

Proprietors of land were compelled to attend to the cleaning of the part of an aqueduct that passed across their ground. An inscription of the time of Hadrian has been found at Chagnon, near a point where a tributary conduit enters one of the main Lyons aqueducts, stating that no man must plough, sow or plant on the ground reserved to the aqueduct.

The Romans also made large use of wells and cisterns as well as of the expensive aqueducts.

Fig. 13.   The Pont du Gard

V

SOME GALLO-ROMAN TOWNS

HAVING looked at some of the principal structures of Gallo-Roman towns, we will now make a rapid survey of some of the leading towns themselves, their lay-out and their chief features.

MARSEILLES, *Massilia*, has long been one of the world's greatest ports, and its antiquities have consequently been buried under the accumulation of centuries. The old Phocaean harbour, the Lacydon, still delights the eye as the Vieux Port, but knowledge of the Greco-Roman City which lay on its north side has had to be gathered piecemeal. Considerable advances have been made by recent excavations in demolished areas, and it has been possible to locate the forum, the Greek theatre, a number of house walls and mosaics, numerous wells and a large Roman warehouse of the first century (see fig. 14). Ranged in the ground floor of this last were fifty great storage-jars, each two metres deep. It is not known whether Caesar had the walls of Marseilles demolished after the siege of 49 B.C. We are told by Pliny that a rich Massiliote doctor gave a large sum of money to his city in the time of Nero for the building of city walls: but whether this involves rebuilding or extensive repairing, we do not know. A stretch of city wall was located and partially excavated in the area behind the Bourse in 1913 and 1928. It is built of large blocks in the Greek technique with tenons, but it might be the Neronic wall built in a still-remembered Greek manner.

It is generally stated that the commerce of Marseilles practically disappeared under the Romans, owing to the

rapid growth of Arles. This, combined with the tribulations of the siege and the silting-up of the *Fossa Mariana*
(see p. 8), did greatly reduce the wealth of the city, but
Marseilles was still the most convenient outlet for a large

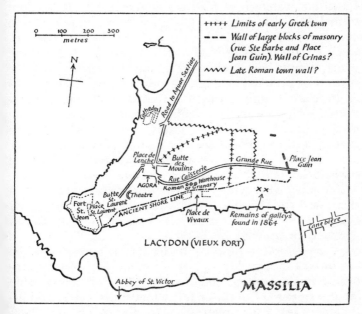

FIG. 14. Marseilles

hinterland. It also attained eminence as a centre of
learning and medical studies, and one of its most distinguished alumni was Agricola.

Traces of its early Christian community remain in a
cemetery lying above a pagan Greco-Roman one on the
south side of the Lacydon, excavated in 1947. Here
tradition held that Saint Victor had been buried in the
rocky hillside in the third century. One of the earliest
monasteries of Gaul was founded in his honour on this
spot by Cassianus in the early fifth century.

G

NARBONNE, *Colonia Iulia Paterna Claudia Narbo Martius Decumanorum*, dates from 118 B.C., but we know next to nothing of the early city, save that it was the outcome of the Gracchan schemes for colonization outside Italy, and that L. Licinius Crassus was concerned with the scheme. In 46 B.C. veterans of Caesar's favourite Legion X were settled here by Tiberius Claudius Nero, father of the emperor Tiberius. Neither the walls of the early period, when Cicero refers to Narbo as a strong point, nor those which it must have had under the early empire, if only for reasons of prestige, remain. More is known of the walls of the late Empire, which included numerous re-used stones. They were particularly massive structures 6 metres thick in their foundations, 3 metres thick above ground, but they enclosed only a small part of the earlier city. At one point, however, the foundations of a square tower belonging to an earlier wall have been observed.

The line where the Via Domitia crosses the city is clear, and the foundations of a temple, with colonnaded *temenos*, have been identified as those of the capitolium, which is mentioned by both Ausonius and Sidonius; a large *cryptoporticus* running under the colonnade of the forum was found close by; on its inner side were a number of small vaulted chambers which would be suitable for the storage of grain or other foodstuffs. The amphitheatre (121 × 95 metres) was discovered in 1838. Among the many inscriptions of Narbonne are records of the rebuilding of baths and a basilica after the disastrous fire which occurred in the reign of Antoninus Pius, and of the restoration of the bridge, the gates and the aqueduct in the fourth century.

Some light was shed on early Christian Narbonne by the discovery, in 1927, of the ruins of the basilica of St. Felix, mentioned by Gregory of Tours. On a marble lintel was the dedicatory inscription set up by bishop Rusticus, in 455. More recently a late fourth-century cemetery has been uncovered beside the old church of St. Paul.

The commercial importance of Narbonne is borne out

by its many inscriptions set up by all sorts of merchants, in particular by those of the *navicularii*, or ship-owners. An illustrous but commercially minded colony, it had something which appealed to the imagination of poets and Martial could write of it as *pulcherrima*—most beautiful—*Narbo*. Ausonius writes of the ships of the east, of Africa, Sicily and Spain, which made their way thither:

What shall I say of thy harbours, mountains, lakes?
What of thy peoples, with their varied differences of garb and speech?
.   .   .   .   .   .
The whole world over, no argosy is afloat but for thy sake.

Yet Narbonne lay 18 kilometres up the Aude, and the remains of its port are as elusive as those of the town itself. There are no great works resembling the ports of Ostia, Alexandria or Lepcis. The port is to be found in the group of lagoons which provided safe anchorage at the mouth of the Aude. The large sea-going ships could unload here into lighters which transported their merchandise upstream to the town. Finds at three different points strengthen this view. On the Ile Sainte-Lucie large quantities of amphoras and fragments of black and red Campanian bowls point to trade during the first century B.C. with Italy; near the Porte de La Capelle on the Étang de Bages there are remains of foundations, and numbers of sherds of the pottery of La Graufesenque and pieces of a very large storage jar were found; the Port de Couilhac in another lagoon farther east also shows traces of intense activity. From this point a Roman road has been followed to the south-east end of Narbonne.

It must, however, be admitted that of both port and town we know more from literature and inscriptions than from archaeology.

ARLES, *Colonia Iulia Paterna Sextanorum Arelatensium*, or *Arelate*—the 'Little Rome of Gaul', as Ausonius calls it—is the most famous of all the towns of Roman Gaul, both for its history and for the splendour of its monuments. It lay originally in the territory of the Saluvii, but it is widely believed that the Massiliote trading-station of Theline was here. Arles was occupied in the Republican period, for it is mentioned by Caesar, who had galleys built here for his operations against Marseilles in 49. Strabo mentions

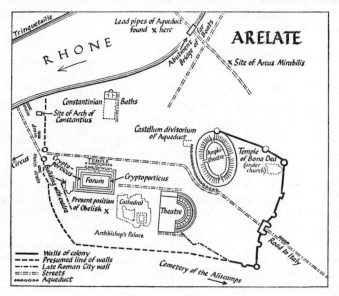

FIG. 15. Arles

Arles as an important emporium even in his days, over-shadowed only by Narbonne. It owed its commercial success to its position at a convenient point for tran-shipping goods from river craft into sea-going vessels (see fig. 36).

The Roman Arles which one sees so vividly to-day is the main city on the left bank of the river, the original *Colonia* of the veterans of Caesar's Legion VI, who were settled here in 46 B.C. The line of the town walls is still not fully known, but it is clear that they enclosed an area only about a quarter of that of Roman Nîmes. The best-preserved stretch of the walls is that on the south-east and east of the city, where much of the masonry of the early period is still to be seen (see p. 68). A tower of this early wall is embedded within the northern edge of the foundations of the later amphitheatre. Besides the walls and the eastern gate (the Porte de la Redoute), the outstanding early monument is the theatre (see pp. 79, 167). Outside the original walls, to the north, stood a triumphal arch, now destroyed, which remained in place during the Middle Ages and was then known as the *Arcus Mirabilis*. A second arch stood at the south-west side of the town until the nineteenth century, when it was removed, as it was becoming unsafe. Sketches which remain show that it was decorated with triglyphs and metopes containing bulls' heads similar to those upon the theatre, with which it must have been contemporary. It was given a new inscription by Constantius in the fourth century A.D. The civic centre of Arles lay in the western part of the town, where the ground was more level than on the slight hill later occupied by the amphitheatre. The remarkable *cryptoporticus* which lay below the forum has been noted above (p. 73). Whether this represents the whole of the forum, or whether there was an associated space on the site of the present Place du Forum, is not yet quite clear. The mainstreet of the town, the *decumanus*, ran through the latter parallel with the northern side of the *cryptoporticus*, which is here interrupted by the foundations of a temple of which two Corinthian columns and the half of a pediment are walled into the present Hotel du Nord. This temple was probably the Capitolium of Arles. The basilical building on the west side of the *cryptoporticus* may have been a temple. At one end of it was an open semi-circular court (*exedra*) with niches for statues and with stone seats, which is now preserved in the court of the Museon Arlaten. The official basilica is to be sought under the archbishop's palace and the post office. A temple to the Bona Dea stood near the eastern gate on the site of the church of Notre Dame de la Major.

By the second century the amphitheatre was built and,

about the same time, the bridge of boats. Portions of the abutments of the bridge still remain, for it was maintained until the fourteenth century. Across the river in Trinquetaille there was a suburb where private houses with some good mosaics, warehouses, and pottery kilns have been found, and also part of a large building of the first century B.C. The mercantile and fishing population lived along both banks of the river.

Along the Via Aurelia to the south-east was a cemetery, which was to continue in uninterrupted use through pagan and early Christian times into the Middle Ages. The Aliscamps (Elysian Fields), as it came to be called, became one of the most famous cemeteries of western Europe. From it come most of the fine sarcophagi which are now in the Arles museums. The early Christian tombs tended to cluster round the one ascribed to St. Genès (Genesius), above which a chapel was in due course built and then succeeded by the church of St. Honorat, who ousted the earlier saint.

The perimeter of Arles was slightly contracted in the late empire, but the town now attained its maximum political importance, for a number of emperors from Constantine onwards dwelt there for considerable periods. The Constantinian house did much for Arles, and provided it with large new baths, of which a considerable portion remains, recalling those of Trier. Constantius celebrated the 30th anniversary of his reign (354) at Arles with great magnificence, with theatrical displays and races in the circus. In the last days of the empire, when Trier had fallen into barbarian hands, Arles became the capital of the shrunken western provinces. During this period it was frequently visited by Sidonius Apollinaris, who mentions its forum with its colonnades and statues.

Nîmes, *Colonia Augusta Nemausus*, always maintained a special character of its own, as the chief town of the Volcae Arecomici with its important sanctuary of the healing god Nemausus. It was not a military colony, but enjoyed Latin rights. It is assumed that Augustus settled a number of Greek soldiers from Egypt here after the civil war, for this seems to be the explanation of the crocodile and palm-tree on coins of Nîmes dating between 27 and 12 B.C., and of the large number of Greek inscriptions and Greek names found here. An inscription of 16 or 15 B.C. records that Augustus gave the colony gates and walls. These walls run for 6 km. round an area of 220 hectares, so that Nîmes was for long the largest town in Gaul. Encased in the ramparts, on the summit of Mont Cavalier, the highest point in Nîmes, is the Tour Magne, which is presumably of Republican date. The walls form a re-entrant angle especially to enclose the monument, and their masonry is carried round it to form a sheath round its lower storey. The sheath is hexagonal, whereas the tower within it is octagonal. Its base is 19·40 metres across, and it must have stood at least 25 metres high. From its top, reached by a stairway, there is a wide view of the landscape from the Cévennes to the sea. The Tour Magne was therefore invaluable as a watch-tower, and traces of an inner core may represent a pre-Roman look-out post. The Roman structure had a certain amount of ornament. The four pilasters on the faces of the upper storey, deprived long since of their marble or other facing, give some idea of the decoration of the tower, and the bases of columns belonging to the next storey can also be seen. It recalls the Augustan monument at La Turbie (p. 165), and some authorities have gone so far as to claim it as a trophy erected by some Republican general. For the present this remains pure hypothesis, and we must remain content to enjoy the Tour Magne simply as one of the oldest Roman monuments in Gaul.

Of even greater interest is the sacred enclosure round the spring at the foot of Mont Cavalier, where the god Nemausus had his shrine. Much of the *temenos* was excavated in 1738 and incorporated into the handsome eighteenth-century ornamental park—the Jardin de la

Fontaine; there has also been some investigation in recent years. The waters from the spring flowed into a small lake, the outflow from which was controlled by a weir. The Roman structures immediately beside the lake are probably direct descendants of pre-existing Celtic shrines; south of this was a rectangular space surrounded by a portico. In the centre of the space was an altar set up on an artificial island round which the water from the spring was led. The altar complex is probably to be dated to the middle of the first century A.D. Another temple (third century) lay in the south side of the portico, and there was a theatre just beyond the portico to the north-east. The most interesting building in the complex is the rectangular hall called the temple of Diana, which still survives almost intact through having been taken over as a convent chapel in 991. It has an elaborate coffered barrel vault, and dates from the first half of the second century. It is not a temple and its purpose has been much discussed. One view is that it may have been the place in which pilgrims coming to seek a cure for their ailments passed the night within the sanctuary; but the existence of a series of niches round the walls lends much support to a recent suggestion that it was a library.

Agrippa's Maison Carrée (25·13 × 12·29 m.), surrounded by porticoes, faced the forum and was probably the capitolium. It now contains the local museum of antiquities. The rampart, gates, amphitheatre and aqueduct have been described above.

FRÉJUS, *Forum Iulii Octavanorum Colonia Pacensis Classica, Navale Caesaris Augusta.* Fréjus, the Toulon of Roman Gaul, is a site of particular interest which began as a market centre. Its entrance into history was in May, 43 B.C., when Antony arrived after his retreat across the Alps from Mutina and here, or close by, joined forces with Lepidus, a first step towards the formation of the Second Triumvirate. Very early in his consolidation of the west, probably in the course of his campaigns against Sextus

Pompey (39 B.C.), Octavian established a naval station at Forum Iulii. Hither were sent the galleys captured from Cleopatra at Actium in 31, and here a veteran colony of Legion VIII was settled. It was without doubt a valuable base for the pacification of the Ligurian coast-line.

Although we do not hear of Fréjus after Plutarch, who tells us that its fleet contained three hundred vessels, it is listed in the itineraries, and the amount of reconstruction carried out during the Constantinian period shows the importance which was still attached to the town. The excavations of the naval arsenal, however, indicate that little in the way of reconstruction or modification was ever carried out there, so Fréjus was probably not kept up as a naval base of first magnitude, though a police flotilla was doubtless maintained to keep an eye on the Ligurian coast.

The harbour, which still functioned in the Middle Ages, was an artificial basin (22 hectares) probably enlarging an existing lagoon and fed by a narrow channel diverted from the River Argens. It communicated with the sea by an entrance channel 83 metres wide and 460 metres long, along which the railway from Marseilles to Ventimiglia now runs. With the earth excavated during its construction two platforms were formed at the north and west ends of the harbour, and were fortified as citadels for its defence. All round the harbour were quays which broadened out along the north and west sides to hold buildings for naval stores. The northern part of the harbour and its quays are now under vineyards. There were towers at intervals on the walls; two of them, between which a chain boom was laid when necessary, guarded the entry to the port. A larger tower at the point where the dockyard rampart joins the east wall of the Citadelle Saint-Antoine was a lighthouse: it had at least three storeys, of orthodox build, each narrower than the one below. In the centre of the basin was an island on which probably stood some of the offices of the harbour-master. The harbour was not very deep, but the draught of ancient vessels was not great.

The ramparts of the citadels are continuous with those of the harbour. That on the west, the Citadelle Saint-Antoine, measures 170 × 104 metres. To support the thrust of the piled-up earth its west side has double walls, the outer one strengthened with buttresses. A postern gate is another feature of interest. On the northern side the citadel was bordered by the canalized arm of the river. Two small openings connected this canal with the barracks laundry or *fullonica*. The second citadel, known as the *Platforme*, does not conform to the plan of the familiar military forts of the first century A.D., but has its head-quarters complex in its south-eastern section. This had its own special gateway and appears to have contained the house of the Prefect in charge of the fleet with its private baths and a series of offices. There are also granaries and a large underground cistern. The most curious feature is an open court which has been identified by the exca-vators as an *auguratorium*. It has a central square block of masonry, believed to have supported the pyramid from which the augur determined the position of the signs he was observing.

The colony of Legion VIII lay to the north-west of the port. Its walls, gates and aqueduct have already been discussed (pp. 69, 83).

Fréjus also possesses in a remarkably complete state one of the earliest surviving monuments of Christian Gaul. This is its octagonal baptistery, which dates from the beginning of the fifth century at least. It is surmounted by a lantern in which eight small windows alternate with eight small niches. The original structure remains as far as these windows, but the roof has been restored. In the centre of the floor is the sunken, octagonal basin, to which steps descended. It was surrounded by a balustrade and eight small columns which carried the *ciborium*. A large jar sunk in the ground alongside is thought to have con-tained oil with which the newly-baptized persons were anointed. Some of the columns of the baptistery are taken from an earlier building, and the interior was once covered with painted plaster.

SAINT BERTRAND-DE-COMMINGES, *Lugdunum Convenarum*. Another very early example of a Roman town can be taken from the opposite end of Narbonensis—Lugdunum Convenarum, lying at the foot of a Celtic oppidum. It was a foundation of Pompey himself, who pacified this region in 77 B.C. Well placed on the banks of the Garonne, which is navigable up to this point, and on roads leading to the plains from the Pyrenees, it enjoyed considerable wealth. Its prosperity in the second century was largely due to the exploitation of the marble quarries of Saint-Béat. It was surrounded by a wall of which fragments remained above ground in the last century. They have not been securely dated, but in view of the exposed position of this outpost of the Roman world, it is tempting to postulate a Republican date. Remains of the ramparts along the Garonne consist of a retaining wall with buttresses recalling the wall of the Citadelle Saint-Antoine at Fréjus. The Roman walls abutted on to the old oppidum. This upper town contained public buildings in Roman times, of which remains have been discovered, though much space is occupied by the Cathedral and associated buildings. Saint-Bertrand escaped the barbarian inroads of the third century, but in the later empire the upper town was refortified and here the town lingered on rather miserably after its sack by the Vandals in 408 or 409.

The most interesting discovery at Saint Bertrand has been a handsome series of public buildings, the forum and adjacent structures, one of which was a trophy in honour of Augustus, under whom the Pyrenaean region had been pacified. This was destroyed in the time of Nero. The shrine was restored under Trajan and adorned with statues of him and of the empress Plotina.

GLANUM, near *St. Rémy de Provence,* is a site that rivals in interest even the famous places already described. This little Greek town of Glanon, later latinized to Glanum, lies on the northern edge of the chain of ruggedly chiselled Alpilles, 86 kilometres north of Marseilles and 24 kilometres north-east of Arles. The great interest of Glanum is, first, its Hellenistic character and, secondly, its well-attested remains of the earliest Roman occupation, which are so rarely found elsewhere in Narbonensis.

The excavators have distinguished three main early periods. Glanum I flourished in the second century B.C., and was preceded by a native settlement which had traded with the Greeks of the coast. The *raison d'être* for this little town, precariously placed in barbarian territory, must have been trade. Glanum lay close to the ancient track from Beaucaire to Cavaillon (a continuation of the Via Domitia towards the Alps), which is crossed here by a track coming from the south through the Alpilles and running north to the Durance. No walls of Glanum have yet been found, but only a small part of the town has been excavated. One of the streets of this early period has been explored, with handsome houses of Hellenistic type on either side and a main drain underneath, which shows that the Romans were not the first to bring sanitation to Gaul.

In the troubles of the second half of the century, when the Saluvii were pressing forward, much of the little town was destroyed. Glanum II belongs to the Roman republican period after the end of the Cimbric wars.

After the end of the Civil Wars money was spent on the town, and the new period, extending into our era, is called Glanum III. At the southernmost point yet reached by the excavators a large building with porticoed court and a basilica at one end has been found, but its purpose is not yet clear. It overlay a Hellenistic building with pediments and with a fine wall in the Greek tradition. It shows the high quality of Massiliote building and the fine heritage into which the Romans stepped in Provence.

The triumphal arch set up a little later than 45 B.C.

belongs to the early years of Glanum III. Beside it stands a very beautiful early mausoleum.

VAISON, *Vasio Vocontiorum*, has been one of the most fruitful sites excavated in recent years. The castle of the Counts of Toulouse towering above the left bank of the river Ouvèze marks the position of the old Gallic oppidum. The Roman town lies on the opposite side of the stream.

Vasio was one of the two chief towns of the Vocontii, and was an Augustan foundation on a monumental scale. Its plan shows the usual rectangular grid; there are baths, a theatre, a public hall (perhaps a basilica), colonnaded streets with shops and, at the heart of some of the *insulae,* great mansions. One very attractive feature is a large porticoed structure which seems to have been a public promenade and pleasure-garden. This sheltered garden (51 × 51 metres) is surrounded by a wall in which there were niches at intervals containing statues. In the centre of the garden was an elaborate pool and a pavilion which perhaps contained the statue of the donor and a small shrine. Porticoes of this type were usually given to a city by some wealthy citizen, and all manner of treasures were displayed in them, so that they were museums as well as places of recreation. The well-known statue of a Diadumenos now in the British Museum was found on the slope where the portico was subsequently excavated, so may well come from it. Many other works of art were found at Vaison, some of them in the theatre.

The lower part of the bridge over the Ouvèze is Roman. On the left bank, slightly below the bridge, a landing-stage of flagstones resting on piles was found in 1946. Portions of the aqueduct are also visible, and various underground conduits have been found, some running from a fountain near the theatre.

ORANGE, *Colonia Firma Iulia Secundanorum Arausio*, was a colony of Legion II. Its arch (p. 163) and theatre (p. 78) are dealt with elsewhere; its capitolium appears to have stood upon the hill behind the theatre. Over a hundred fragments have been discovered (most of them as recently as 1949–50) of tablets recording one or more Roman land surveys of the territory round the colony. The plans are divided into rectangles of 200 *iugera*, and the names of the holders are given. On one piece found in 1904 a *ludus*, or training arena for gladiators, is mentioned. This monument still existed in 1629 and looked like an amphi-theatre without the usual tiers of seating.

VIENNE, *Colonia Iulia Vienna*, was one of the most illustrious and wealthy cities of Gaul. It was laid out in terraces on the hillside and in the narrow space between hills and river. Parts of a monumental stairway mounting the hill have been laid bare, and there are a theatre and an odeum, as in its neighbour and rival Lyons. The summit of the town, the Mont Pipet, was surmounted by a temple, and, like Nîmes, Vienne had its Augustan girdle of walls. It is perhaps not too fanciful to call Vienne the Pergamon of Gaul, and there is indeed a certain extravagance about its history which has a Hellen-istic flavour. The fabulously rich Valerius Asiaticus was a citizen of Vienne and kept a private troupe of actors and buffoons to entertain his fellow-citizens. Here Archelaus, son of Herod of Judaea, was exiled and many less exalted easterners settled. Martial and other Romans of the early empire have much to say of the high quality of its wines. Martial's opinion of the city was all the greater because his poems were much appreciated there. Many fine works of art have been found at Vienne, and its beautiful temple is only surpassed by the Maison Carrée. A number of statues found in the remains of a large house in the suburb of Saint-Colomb are thought to have been taken there for concealment by pagans when the Chris-tians were threatening to destroy them. The 'Aiguille' of Vienne is one of the monuments of the Circus, an obelisk 15·50 metres high on a portico-base 7 metres high, still standing in its ancient position and to be seen on the right

of the railway-line shortly after passing through the station
en route for the south.

LYONS, *Colonia Copia Claudia Augusta Lugudunum*, or
Lugdunum.   Roman Lyons, founded in 43 B.C. by Lucius
Munatius Plancus, took over an oppidum of the Segusiavi, a client-tribe of the Aedui, and it is to be presumed
that the lands assigned to the colonists were taken from
the tribe.   The name Lugudunum means stronghold of
Lug, a Celtic deity known also from Irish sources, but
whether he was a god of light, or a raven- or crow-god, we
do not know.   The colonists do not seem to have been a
compact group of veterans from a single legion, but it is
clear that they were military and that the site was from the
first recognized as an important strategic point.   The
people of Lugudunum were proud, says Tacitus, of being a
Roman colony and a part of the army.   The colony
occupied Fourvière, the heights along the right bank of the
Saône close to the Confluence (fig. 16).

The line of the walls is fairly well defined by Roman
cemeteries, and the colony was about 140 hectares in
extent—i.e. considerably smaller than either Autun or
Nîmes—but its suburbs soon spread widely.   Between the
rivers were the sacred places of the Confluence, of which
Strabo has left such a vivid description: 'the temple that
was dedicated to Caesar Augustus by all the Gauls in
common is situated in front of this city at the junction
of the rivers.   And in it is a noteworthy altar, bearing an
inscription of the names of the tribes, sixty in number:
and also images from these tribes, one from each tribe,
and also another large altar.'   The altar is shown on
copper coins issued at Lyons in commemoration of the
dedication (see title page).   The temple seems to have
stood in the neighbourhood of the church of St. Polycarp
and the Jardin des Plantes, at the foot of the hills which
cut across the peninsula.   The letters RO from a very
large inscription, almost certainly *Romae et Augusto*, were
found here, and also the famous bronze tablets with the

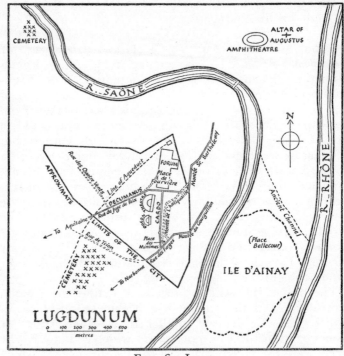

FIG. 16.   Lyons

speech of Claudius.   A group of inscriptions mentioning
the imperial cult and also numerous pieces of statues and
other sculptural fragments come from this neighbourhood.
Furthermore, the amphitheatre occupied the site of the
Jardin des Plantes, and inscriptions from it showing
places reserved for delegates from cities of Gaul (the
Arverni, Bituriges Cubi and Tricasses) still exist.   Their
allotted seating space was 39 centimetres broad.

Recent investigations, painfully conducted on Fourvière, in cellars and through Roman drains, have enabled
archaeologists to establish the lines of the principa
streets, the *Cardo* and the *Decumanus*.   The latter was 12
metres wide.   The sites of the forum and of various other

buildings are known. Behind the theatre (see p. 80), across a street, was a building with shops, afterwards modified into a large edifice, which was perhaps associated with the worship of Cybele.

Lyons had many government offices, for besides being the seat of the governor of Lugudunensis it was also the headquarters of the Procurator of Lugudunensis and Aquitania, and was the station of an Urban cohort, 1,000 strong, for long the only military force in Gaul proper. Strabo says: 'It is the most populous of all the cities of Celtica, except Narbo; for not only do people use it as an emporium, but the Roman governors coin their money there, both the silver and the gold.'

The mint was installed in 16–15 B.C., and here all the gold and silver coinage of the Augustan period was struck. No more telling evidence could be produced of the importance which Augustus attached to Gaul. The primary duty of the Urban cohort was the protection of this mint. Under Caligula the mint was removed to Rome, but the emperors from time to time struck coins at Lyons, notably Diocletian and Maximian. The bronze coinage of Lyons, too, is important.

We know something of the people who lived at Lyons both from ancient writers and from the rich series of inscriptions. The corporation of shippers was of very great importance. There was also an active gold- and silver-smiths' industry, and Lyons was one of the chief emporia for the oil trade. The younger Pliny refers to its bookshops, where his own works were on sale. There were numerous foreign traders, and also large numbers of functionaries of all sorts.

Quays stretched along both sides of the Saône. One series lay on the bend of the river north-east of the colony, near the bridge leading to the buildings of the Confluence; another series stretched south from the present church of Saint Georges. At both points a considerable number of inscriptions set up by the shipping corporations have been found. Near the latter group there may have been a

H

second bridge across the Saône, though both bridges are still somewhat conjectural. It is generally thought that the swift-moving Rhone was crossed by a ferry. On the east side of the Saône, opposite Saint Georges, where now the Place Bellecour stands, there was an island in Roman times, the Isle d'Ainay. Dotted about it were many fine private houses, and its western side was occupied by more quays, probably those of the wine dealers. About 4,000 lead seals have been found in the river at this point. During the late empire, Lyons was supplanted in political dignity by Trier, Vienne and Arles, but it remained no mean city, as is clear from the descriptions of Sidonius Apollinaris (see p. 180).

AUTUN, *Augustodunum*. Considerable parts of the walls and gates are preserved, as well as of the amphitheatre, theatre and a temple. Autun is the classic example of the transfer of a native population from a hill *oppidum* to a valley site, for with its foundation in about 12 B.C. the occupation of the hill town on Mont Beuvray, 822 metres (2,672 feet) high, about 20 kilometres away to the west, comes to an end. It used to be customary to regard this abandonment of the old hill towns as a migration, ordered by the Roman state, to make sure that a possibly unruly population was brought down into the plain, where it could be less dangerous. The transfer seems to have been effected more subtly. A community already well aware of the advantages of trade might not be averse from descending to a more convenient spot, when the country became peaceful and it was no longer necessary for safety's sake to climb the steep sides of a particularly formidable hill to reach one's home.

For the rebuilding of the city, after its destruction in 272, masons were brought over from Britain, such was the shortage of skilled workers in Gaul to meet the enormous demand for reconstruction.

ALESIA. From Autun, the capital of a *civitas* which was

brought down from its hill-top, we turn to the *vicus* of Alesia, the centre of a *pagus* of the Aeduan *civitas*. It is another famous Gallic centre, and this time one where the Roman town succeeded the Celtic *oppidum* on the same site. It seems reasonable to suggest that political considerations did not play a very big part in these matters, or why should the capital of the usually friendly Aedui be moved and the capital of the Mandubii, the last centre of Gallic national resistance, be allowed to remain where it was? The real reason is much more likely to be topographical. Bibracte is very hard of access; but Alesia (418 metres) is not nearly so high or steep, and a much more suitable spot for a permanent town.

Extremely interesting excavations carried out over a long period of years have revealed a substantial amount of this town, its public buildings, its sanctuaries and its private houses, where the admixture of Roman and Celtic is notable. In the centre of the plateau the ground plans have been recovered of a three-apsed basilica, a forum on its east and temple on its west surrounded by a colonnaded court. The temple, of classical style, was probably the capitolium. To its west lies the theatre. Many other buildings, large and small, have been found. One contains a deep crypt down to which stone stairs led from a pillared hall; this, it has been suggested, was the sanctuary of Ucuetis and Bergusia, the divine couple who presided over metal-working for which Alesia was famous.

Many of the house cellars at Alesia go back to Gallic times and were incorporated in later Gallo-Roman houses. The Roman cellars have well-built stone walls and narrow windows. Many vestiges of La Tène occupation have been found on the plateau, under the Roman structures, including narrow roads, circular huts in addition to the rectangular cellar-type, and traces of metal working. Alesia got its water-supply mainly from wells, but there was one spring on the top of the hill, that sacred to Apollo Moritasgus. Other springs occur a little way down the slopes.

GERGOVIA. The third of the famous *oppida* bears out the theory that there was no enforced transplantation of Gallic cities. As far as excavations have shown, Gergovia would appear not to have been intensively occupied before the time of Caesar, and its rampart was probably raised hastily to meet the threat of his attack. After the war, some of the local population decided to remain on the site, which suggests that life in the Massif Central was not then too secure. The existing rampart was maintained, and a small Gallo-Roman settlement enjoyed a considerable degree of prosperity for nearly a century, despite the foundation of Augustonemetum in the valley below. The community petered out about the time of Nero, but the pair of little temples in the centre of the plateau continued to exist well into the second century.

PARIS, *Lutetia Parisiorum*. In 53 B.C. Caesar summoned an assembly of Gallic chiefs, a *Concilium Galliae*, to meet him at Lutetia 'a town of the Parisii'. This little town, on an island in the River Seine, comes into the history of the struggles of the following year, when the Gauls set it on fire and cut down its bridges. Another feature of this campaign is the large number of boats which Labienus managed to obtain in the neighbourhood. The Sequana was, in fact, already much in use as a great waterway, and Lutetia, on its defensible island astride an important north–south route from Belgica to Orleans, was a key point. The town was rebuilt after the war, and flourished with the growth of trade. It is appropriate that the first monument we have of a city whose renowned coat-of-arms contains a silver ship should be an altar set up by its corporation of shippers, the Nautae Parisiorum. This was found below the choir of Notre Dame. The town soon spread to the left bank of the river; most of the remains that have been found are of the flourishing city of the second century.

The main axis of Roman Paris was the road now represented by the Rue Saint Jacques, parallel to which ran another corresponding to the Boulevard Saint Michel. The Petit Pont and Notre Dame bridges had Roman predecessors. Structures in and about the Rue Soufflot proved to be a forum with temple and basilica; a small theatre was found in the Rue Racine and baths in the Rue Gay Lussac. The two monuments still above ground are the theatre-cum-amphitheatre known as the Arènes (Rue Monge) and the great building now forming part of the Cluny Museum. The latter is one of the finest of all Gallo-Roman monuments, but liable to be overlooked, standing as it does in the heart of Paris, surrounded by so many more famous structures. No other Gallo-Roman monument of the same size as this great hall has been preserved intact, but here the roof is complete, with vaults and pendentives and with consoles decorated with sculptured Seine barges (fig. 39*b*). This hall had many vicissitudes and was used as a cellar, while its roof at one time supported a garden. It contains a small *piscina*, and received an aqueduct, and the latest opinion, reinforced by the results of excavations, is that it is rightly interpreted as part of a large public bath building. Among the structures lately excavated are large cellars, with barrel vaults.

The town on the left bank was destroyed in the third century, and when Paris rose again after the troubles it was virtually confined to the Ile de la Cité, which was surrounded by a wall partly made up of the usual re-used stones, including the torn-up seats of the Arènes. At its west end, under the present Palais de Justice, the palace of the military governor was built. This is where the emperor Julian had his headquarters from 356 to 361 and where he was declared Augustus. Here was his 'dear Lutetia'. 'It occupies an island in the middle of the river; wooden bridges join it to the two banks. This river rarely fills too full, rarely runs too low; as it is in winter, so it remains in summer.'

The importance of Paris in Gallo-Roman times must not be exaggerated. Administratively it was subordinate to Sens, a state of things reflected in the ecclesiastical organization which made the archbishop of Sens the metropolitan of this part of France, so that Paris had only a bishop until the time of Louis XIII. Of the leading saints of Paris, Saint Denis and Saint Geneviève, the former appears to have lived in the third century, and the latter was a heroine of the resistance to the Huns.

BORDEAUX, *Burdigala*. This great commercial city arose a few miles above the head of the estuary of the Gironde, where it was possible to bridge the Garonne. As its name indicated, it had a Celtic predecessor. The line of the late Roman walls is known, the amphitheatre and the position of two aqueducts have been identified, but otherwise Roman Bordeaux, like Greek and Roman Marseilles, has been buried under the activities of many centuries. Large parts of an enormous and ornate temple to the Tutela of the city, its guardian goddess, still existed in the seventeenth century. Drawings have come down to us displaying the rather vulgar splendour of its colonnade surmounted by a second storey of arcades containing colossal statues.

Bordeaux, like London, grew under its own impetus; both developed because of the natural importance of their sites. Bordeaux, as much as Lyons, was a cosmopolitan city. Inscriptions recording individuals from nearly every part of the empire, and especially from the chief commercial centres, have been found. Britons and Belgae brought trade to and from their own countries. Besides these northerners there are Greeks, Africans, and others.

In its later days Bordeaux took on the more dignified character of a centre of learning. Its new walls enclosed only a small part of the early city, but still protected within their circle its chief port. Of this city Ausonius its most celebrated son, writes:

Goodly walls four-square raise lofty towers.
Where the channel of thy spring-fed stream divides the town, soon as old Ocean has filled it with his flowing tide,
Thou shalt behold a whole sea gliding onward with its fleets.

PÉRIGUEUX, *Vesunna Petrucoriorum*. There are more Roman remains in Périgueux than in other towns of Aquitania. It was a handsomely laid-out town with

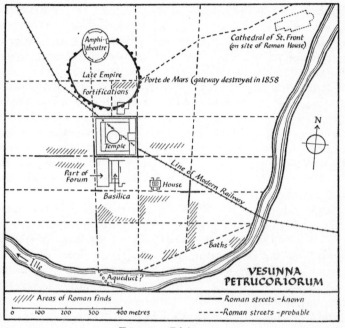

FIG. 17. Périgueux

spacious insulae. In its centre was the sanctuary to Vesunna (p. 201, fig. 45*a*), of which the tower-like *cella* still remains, and nearby were the forum and some large town houses reminiscent of those excavated at Vaison. A fine gateway of the early empire on the east side of the town was destroyed in 1858, but the amphitheatre and parts of the late Roman walls are still preserved.

BOULOGNE, *Gesoriacum*, *Bononia*. Boulogne is indissolubly bound up with Roman Britain. It was the point of departure of the Claudian invasion of the island, the head-

quarters of the British fleet, the *Classis Britannica*, and the
chief port for all official and much commercial intercourse
with Britain. In the early days of the empire it was
simply a *vicus* of the Morini, to contemporary writers the
farthest away of mankind, at least of that part of mankind
which shared the blessings of Roman rule. With the
conquest of Britain it became a vital link in imperial
communications, the terminus of two important roads,
that leading through Amiens to the centre and the south
of Gaul, and that leading through Bavai to the Rhineland.
Among the ruins which still cover the site while this is
being written there are, however, no Roman remains to
be seen. They have long since disappeared, and the
ancient topography is masked by the artificial creation of
the modern port, which fills the former estuary of the
Liane. Much may, however, be discovered during
reconstruction.

The older port was Gesoriacum, the town of the early
and middle empire, which is frequently mentioned, and
which seems to have been originally an *oppidum*. With the
growth of the population the town crept along the north
banks of the river towards the sea and up the neighbouring hillsides. On the northern heights Caligula erected
his celebrated lighthouse, probably the Tour d'Ordre
called by the English the Old Man, a Roman lighthouse
which still stood to a height of 60 metres in the sixteenth
century, when it was destroyed. Fig. 1 shows an old drawing of it. Unhappily all that is left is the foundation.

Then comes Bononia, the name which gradually
ousted that of Gesoriacum. Bononia was probably the
name of the hill suburb which is now the Haute Ville,
and which was the citadel of the late empire. Its walls
(420 × 300 metres) were found in places behind the
medieval walls.

Two other ports of the Boulogne neighbourhood which
figure in ancient authorities are Portus Itius, whence
Caesar embarked, and Portus Aepatiaci, which held a
garrison in the late empire. The former has now been

almost certainly located in the neighbourhood of St.
Omer, for in Roman times the low-lying land from Calais
to Dunkerque was a shallow bay masked by a range of
dunes, and running up to Serques, St. Omer and Watten.
Portus Aepatiaci is Isques, a little farther up the Liane
estuary from Boulogne. Here presumably a Saxon shore
fort awaits discovery.

North-eastern Gaul has many important sites. Most
of their Roman remains lie deep under medieval and
modern cities, but many of them have Gallo-Roman
museums which contain valuable sculptures and inscriptions. Such, for example, are Sens (Agedincum Seno-
num), Besançon (Vesontio) and Metz (Divodurum
Mediomatricorum). At Metz the basement of the
museum is actually within a large ancient bath building.
The ruined church of Saint-Pierre-aux-Nonnains, on the
citadel, contains substantial remains of a single-aisled
basilica with apse (39 × 18·50 metres), similar to the
celebrated basilica of Trier.

REIMS, *Durocortorum Remorum*, was the chief city of the
north in the early days, the seat of the governor of Gallia
Belgica. It has one outstanding Roman monument, the
great triple archway known as the Porte de Mars, which
was a free-standing gateway (fig. 37a). The site of the
forum, which had a *cryptoporticus*, is also known.

TRIER, *Augusta Treverorum*. This, the greatest city of
northern Gaul, lies on the Moselle, a short distance below
its confluence with the Sauer flowing from the north-
west, and the Saar from the south. The combination of
shelter, fertility and good communications had attracted
settlers before the Roman conquest and there were small
communities on both sides of the stream, south of the
position of the later city. A little group of wooden
Celtic sanctuaries grew up on the banks of the small
tributary stream, the Altbach.

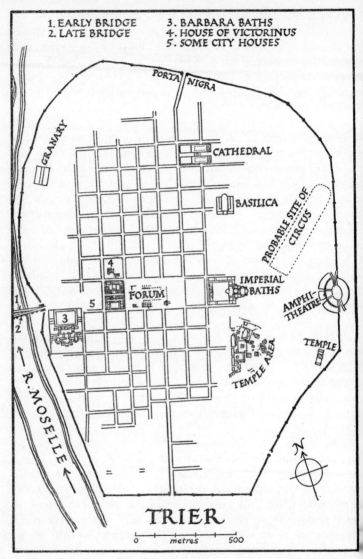

1. EARLY BRIDGE   3. BARBARA BATHS
2. LATE BRIDGE   4. HOUSE OF VICTORINUS
                   5. SOME CITY HOUSES

PORTA NIGRA

GRANARY

CATHEDRAL

BASILICA

PROBABLE SITE OF CIRCUS

4

FORUM

5

3

IMPERIAL BATHS

AMPHI-THEATRE

TEMPLE

TEMPLE AREA

R. MOSELLE

N

TRIER

0   metres   500

Fig. 18. Trier: The Claudian city lay approximately within
the area of the grid of streets

A cavalry regiment was stationed here in Augustan times, and the usual civil settlement grew up around its fort. The growing town seems to have been given the name Augusta at this time, as was the case with other tribal centres like Augusta Suessionum (Soissons) and Augusta Veromanduorum (Saint-Quentin). Its formal lay-out as a Roman colony did not come until early in the time of Claudius (before 44–45), because the streets of the new chessboard grid have been found to pass over earlier occupation layers of the Augustan–Tiberian period. So greatly did this new foundation flourish that by the middle of the century Pomponius Mela could write of it as an *urbs opulentissima*. Judging by the frequency of early finds, the quarters of the early garrison are to be sought in the neighbourhood of the Barbarathermen. The Claudian city covered about 81 hectares, and is approximately represented by the grid south of the cathedral in fig. 18. The position of the late fortifications shows how the city grew. It is to be presumed that Augusta Treverorum was given some defences, probably an earth bank and ditch, and that these were levelled at the beginning of the second century, when the city was expanding rapidly.

Trier had already made its mark industrially, and many pottery kilns south of the town show where Belgic and other wares were made. To the beginning of the second century belongs the amphitheatre, one side of which was built on the slope of the Petrisburg, the west side being raised as an artificial mound, for which some of the earth came from the vast cellar excavated under the arena. The three-fold portals at either end of the ellipse must have been particularly impressive, with a central passage leading to the arena and side passages leading to stairways, and thus to the seats. A huge public baths, known as the Barbarathermen, belongs to the same period. Substantial remains existed until the seventeenth century, and drawings have come down to us showing that it consisted of at least three storeys of rooms. The grass-grown remains of its ground floor and basements can still be inspected.

The latest Roman street surfaces lie 1·50 to 2 metres below ground level, but it has been found that the streets were relaid as many as seven or even ten times in the Roman period, which shows what a long and vigorous life the city had. There has been much speculation as to the whereabouts of the office and residence of the Procurator of Gallia Belgica and the Two Germanies. The remains of a large building running under the Basilica may possibly be this. A large house somewhat to the north of the town centre is believed to have been that of M. Piavonius Victorinus, who became emperor in 269–70, as his name occurs on a mosaic.

The late fortifications of Augusta Treverorum are dated to the early or middle third century and enclose an area of 285 hectares. The walls were 6 m. high, and were defended further by double ditches and by round towers. The Porta Nigra, the north gate, however, dates from the fourth century. A new Moselle bridge also took the place of the old one. It seems that the upper, eastern end of the town from the site of the cathedral to the imperial baths was given over to become the government quarter, with the imperial palace and offices of state. Taking them from north to south, we have, first, the Cathedral itself. Large portions of its north wall are Roman work, three courses of sandstone alternating with two of brick. Some notable discoveries have been made since 1945. First, it has been shown that the remains of a large palace lie below the cathedral. This was levelled down in order that the site should be used for an immense double church, measuring overall 124 × 109 metres, and thus larger than the basilica which Constantine erected in Rome on the Vatican hill. This twin cathedral, which had a baptistery linking its two wings, occupied the ground now covered by the Cathedral and its neighbour the Liebfrauenkirche, and also projected well to the west of the present buildings. Work on it began in 326 and it was in use in the forties at latest. When the imperial palace was broken up the painted ceilings of its halls fell to the ground. They

are Constantinian in date, and their destruction, followed
by the construction of the Cathedral, recalls the fact that
there has always been a tradition that the empress Helena
gave her palace to be turned into a church.

Big additions were made in the time of Gratian, when
the solid square structure, which is the core of the present
cathedral, was erected in the eastern part of the northern
basilica. A large tabernacle was upheld by four mono-
lithic columns of syenite brought from the Odenwald
quarries. These still stand.

A short distance south of the Cathedral one reaches the
building commonly known as the 'Basilica'; which after
various vicissitudes became a Protestant church. This
building is of brick. Its length, with its apse, is 67, its
width 27 metres. Its forehall once brought the total
length to 84 metres. The hall was 32 metres high, and
the Roman work is preserved to just below roof level.
The modern roof was destroyed in an air-raid during the
last war. This corner of Trier is a scene of desolation,
but the amazing way in which the Roman buildings have
stood fast shows that the ancient builders built better
than they realized. The Basilica was no ordinary town
hall, but was probably the Aula Palatina, the audience
hall of the palace. It was heated, paved with mosaics,
and its walls were elaborately decorated. The gilded
mosaics of some of its niches had not entirely disappeared
in recent times. Its exterior was stuccoed and had two
tiers of balconies.

The land south of the Basilica, running past the modern
museum to the imperial baths, and now mainly gardens,
contains a wealth of Roman remains awaiting the fortunate archaeologists who may one day be able to excavate
them with the care they deserve. It is more than a
guess that here lay the bulk of the imperial palace and
its offices—probably the most important late Roman site
unencumbered with later buildings still awaiting investigation. Beyond this area we come to the vast baths
which have already been described (p. 74). It may be

recalled that they seem never to have come into use as baths, and that they are a monument to the hopes of their builders which were so much beyond what fate had in store.   Beyond the baths is the site of the sacred precinct (p. 201) which in the fourth century was gradually being demolished.

The town had to be provisioned as well as garrisoned, and chances of war have brought to light a large Roman warehouse or granary (*horreum*), of the middle fourth century.   Considerable portions of the original walls remain standing, the medieval and modern work built against them having been shaken away by high explosive.

FIG. 19.   The fourth-century Granary at Trier

The building stands near the former harbour, on ground high enough to be clear of flood-water.   It covers an area of 70·30 × 53·70 metres, and consisted of two long buildings, 19 metres broad, with a courtyard between them (fig. 19).

STRASBOURG, *Argentorate*, lies on an island between the Ill and the Rhine, and was a legionary fortress throughout the Roman period, apart from a temporary break after the departure of Legion II Augusta to Britain in 43.   The fortress (area 19·5 hectares) was built on the site of a Celtic market town, and was surrounded by a large civil settlement.   Remains of buildings have been only sparsely found.   The particular interest of Roman Strasbourg lies in its wealth of smaller finds and in the large Gallo-Roman cemeteries, their grave goods and the tombstones and inscriptions, of which many were built into the late fortifications. Legion VIII Augusta was stationed here from Flavian times until the end.

The walls of the fortress were strengthened and provided with new towers in the fourth century; the towers were laced internally with a skeleton of beams. Within the walls was the extremely important headquarters of the *Comes Argentoratensis*. It is surprising that in this highly dangerous sector of Gaul no walls appear to have been provided to protect the civilian inhabitants. The authorities must have put their trust in the numerous water-courses which wound round the town and which would provide very considerable protection, and in the strength of the garrison. In times of great need the civilians could presumably crowd into the citadel. The name Strasbourg comes from Stradiburc, 'the stronghold on the paved road', under which Germanic name it passed in Merovingian times.

MAINZ, *Moguntiacum*, has considerable Roman remains, including portions of its aqueduct and its theatre and the core of a large monument, which is probably the cenotaph of Drusus referred to by Suetonius as the place where annually games were celebrated in his memory. It has a particularly rich collection of tombstones and other Roman antiquities. The civil settlement grew up naturally as an appendage to the great fortress with its two legions and their dependent auxiliaries. The fortress was set on gently rising ground a little way back from the river, and around it and between it and the port grew up various quarters, of which we can trace the Vicus Apollinaris, the Vicus Salutaris and the Vicus navaliorum. There are numerous signs of commercial buildings, there are kilns for pottery and lamps, and various corporations of traders are known. Two outstanding monuments are the Jupiter Column (p. 169), set up near the harbour in honour of Nero by two South Gaulish traders, and the arch of Dativius Victor, an archway adorned with sculptures which was raised by a rich local man about 200, probably in the entrance to a portico of some sort. The stones of this arch were used in the make-up of the later town hall, but they were rescued and the arch has been reconstructed.

The double legionary garrison was broken up after the revolt of Saturninus in the time of Domitian, but a single legion, the XXII Primigenia Pia Fidelis, was maintained until the late empire. The fortress was then given up and a new line of walls was built, encircling the now restricted town, and communicating by the restored bridge with the bridgehead fort of Castel.

COLOGNE, *Colonia Claudia Agrippinensium, Ara Ubiorum.*
Agrippa brought the friendly German tribe of the Ubii across to the left bank of the Rhine, probably in 38 B.C., and settled them in the neighbourhood of the future colony. The town is essentially a Roman foundation, though some of the Ubii may have found their way to the spot before the formal lay-out was undertaken. Among the factors influencing the choice of site was the firm ground which here runs up to the river, whereas shortly below this point the river was liable to overflow its banks; there was also a short stretch of an old river-bed which formed a very convenient harbour. The town was laid out in the time of Augustus, perhaps about 12 B.C., and the street-plan remained practically unchanged throughout the Roman period and lasted on through the Middle Ages even, to some degree, into the plan of the modern city, where the Hohestrasse still runs along the line of the main Roman north–south road.

Some time before A.D. 14 an altar to Augustus was set up, after the plan of the one at Lyons, to serve as a centre for emperor-worship for the great new province of Germany, so soon to be lost. This Ara Ubiorum, as it came to be called, was retained after the withdrawal, to function for the largely Germanic Rhineland. There were one or more legionary camps nearby, but not on the site of the city itself, and the legions were withdrawn before A.D. 30, by which time the headquarters of the Rhine fleet had been established at the Alteburg 3 kilometres upstream from the commercial harbour. In A.D. 50 a body of veterans was drafted into the community of the Ubii, which was given the title of Colonia Claudia Arae Agrippinensium, in honour of Agrippina, Claudius' niece and wife, who had been born here.

The rampart and ditch round the old city of the Ubii gave place to the new town's new walls, enclosing 96·8 hectares. These were repaired and strengthened in the later empire, probably by Gallienus or the Gallic emperors, under whom Cologne was an imperial headquarters. Standing as it did on the frontier facing the dangerous Franks, it was imperative that it should be well protected. The enormous walls of the bridgehead of Deutz, perhaps the most impressive of the fortifications on the Rhenish frontier, date from Constantine, who rebuilt the bridge (see fig. 35).

The economic importance of Cologne (see Chapter VII) is reflected in the fine collections in its museums. The city must have been very rich in public buildings, being the administrative centre of Lower Germany; inscriptions show that it was very well endowed with temples, among which was one to Mars. This dated to Augustan times, and in it was kept a sword of Julius Caesar, which was brought out and carried round the city by Vitellius when he was saluted as emperor.

VI

THE COUNTRYSIDE
AND NATURAL RESOURCES OF GAUL

THE GALLIC COUNTRYSIDE

IN the chapter on towns attention has already been drawn to the large areas of land occupied by the average tribe or *civitas*. The Celt had been essentially a dweller in the country. The landed proprietors lived on their estates, in their country houses (called *aedificia* by Caesar), surrounded by their clients and tenants. After the conquest they were attracted into the towns to some degree, and many probably maintained both town and country houses. In the heyday of the early empire the leading personages in a tribe would wish to share the honour and glory of adorning their town and taking part in its festivals; but they drew their wealth from the land, and as later on town life declined they retired more and more to their private domains, which became ever more self-sufficient, while the peasants were increasingly tied to their holdings. In a number of cases the dependent dwellings round a great villa have been excavated and we can see that long before the Middle Ages something very like a manorial system was in being. The transition from ancient Gaul to medieval France was a very gradual affair.

Only occasionally have archaeologists had the good fortune or the resources to be able to unearth the subordinate buildings in a villa complex, but the known examples are widely distributed.

The typical farmhouse of the Romano-Celtic provinces is called in Britain the corridor house, and in France the house with the *galerie-façade*. It developed from the simple 'basilical' type, the large single-room building with gable ends and with the roof supported by wooden posts. This evolution has been demonstrated in several cases in Britain and on the Continent, the classic excavation being that of the farm at Mayen (fig. 20). Mayen lies in Germania Superior, between Coblenz and Andernach, about 20 kilometres from the Rhine. The earliest structure was a large hut of the pre-Roman period, roughly square, marked by large postholes capable of taking strong timbers to support the roof, while a second series of smaller postholes outside these held the uprights for the wall, which must have been of wattle or thatch. A partition shielded the inner part of the hut from the entrance. The hearth was in the centre, and the floor of the dwelling was sunk a couple of feet below ground-level. Passing over alterations during the Celtic period, we come to the more peaceful conditions of the Roman occupation, when the owners felt that they could allow themselves something more solid, and enlarged their house. Its essential construction was still wooden, deep postholes being found for the uprights which held up the roof. The walling, however, was now of dry stone, and there are traces of interior partitions. It seems likely, however, that the beasts of the farm still shared the dwelling with their masters.

The great transformation begins some time in the first century A.D., with the construction of a corridor along the outside of the building, and, at either end of the corridor, of a projecting room. By the end of the century new walls of masonry appear, bearing the roof; there is a bath, and, in the rear, a granary. Strangely enough, this farm does not seem to have suffered in the invasions of the third century, but it underwent a thorough reconstruction at the beginning of the fourth century. It was burnt and abandoned in the invasions round about 400. Around the farm was an enclosure, containing a group of farm buildings and dwellings for the hands. There are also two small shrines, the second having been built in the fourth-century reconstruction.

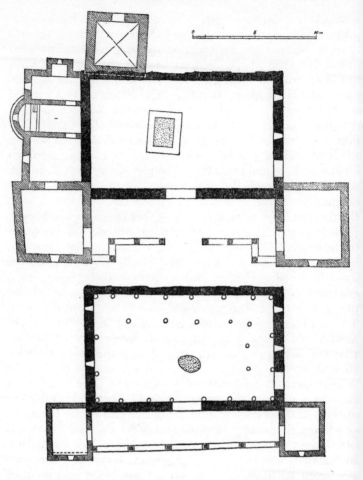

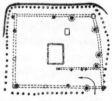

FIG. 20. The Mayen Farmhouse in
successive periods. *Below :* Celtic hut.
Middle : house of the first century A.D.
—its north-east (right-hand) end lies
over the centre of the old hut.
Above : house with additions, towards
100 A.D.

This basic plan of the corridor house is found all over Roman Gaul. Most of the houses are simply humble farms; others are chateaux on a sumptuous scale, but even among them the corridor-portico is usually a dominant feature. Many of the smaller farms of this type in the neighbourhood of the garrison towns must have been occupied by the retired soldiers who were given grants of land as their pension; such veteran holdings were a regular feature of the countryside.

In southern Gaul, however, there is, very naturally, much stronger influence from Italy, so we get a number of villas which are not corridor houses, but whose relationship to Italian town houses of the type found at Vaison is manifest. One of these peristyle villas is at Villepey-le-Reydissard, near Fréjus. A few examples are known among the elaborate country-houses of the Moselle region. An extreme case is the villa at La Grange on the Lake of Geneva, of strongly urban character, with clearly-marked *atrium* and peristyle; it is obviously only a summer residence, because there is no provision for central heating in any of the rooms.

Of our manorial establishments the first example, from the borders of Narbonensis, was excavated as long ago as 1826, and then investigated in more detail in 1895–1899. This is the famous villa of Chiragan, on the Roman road between Toulouse and Dax, a peristyle villa on a de luxe scale. It is one of the largest villas ever found in the Roman provinces (fig. 21).

The earliest, first-century farm was relatively simple; it was laid out, however, as the headquarters of a large estate, with rows of dwellings for the farm-hands. It was replaced by a much larger structure in the time of Trajan, a period in which a good deal of building went on, it will be remembered, at the neighbouring town of Saint-Bertrand-de-Comminges. The house, incorporating some of the previous structure, was built round two courts, below which a third large court, surrounded by porticoes, led to the banks of the Garonne, on which was built a small

hexagonal pavilion. About sixty years later further
additions trebled the size of the villa. A new court to the
east became the chief one, with an elaborate fountain in

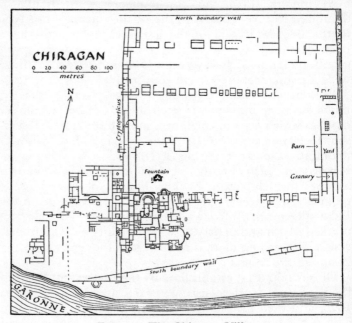

Fig. 21. The Chiragan Villa

the centre, and an entrance façade of corridor type. A
wing runs out from the east court with a *cryptoporticus*, to
facilitate communication between the chateau and the
business section.

The villa was maintained during the fourth century,
but with growing impoverishment. It ended in flames,
and as the last coins found are those of Arcadius (395–
408), the cause was probably the Vandal invasion of
408.

One of the most interesting things about this villa is the
large number of subsidiary buildings, mainly houses of the
farm workers. These buildings are regularly arranged

in three parallel lines, with others at right angles to them along the small tributary which here reaches the Garonne. In the last group is one large, solidly built structure, which is thought to be the granary of the establishment. In all there must have been over forty of these dependent buildings. The dwellings are in many cases small corridor houses. The whole establishment is enclosed by a wall, and covers an area of 16 hectares (40 acres).

Excavations in 1947–48 revealed another villa in the Haute-Garonne, at Montmaurin. This belongs to the same luxury type as that of Chiragan, and is thus a further indication of the wealth of the territory of the Convenae.

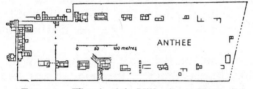

FIG. 22.   The Anthée Villa (near Namur)

Another celebrated villa, excavated during the 19th century, is that of Anthée (fig. 22). The villa lies at the head of a rectangle 12 hectares (30 acres) in area. There is an inner court separated from the main enclosure by a large gateway. In the main enclosure are about twenty buildings. The manor was self-contained, with its own smithy, its kilns for coarse pottery, and so on. The villa was large, and of corridor type. It was destroyed in the invasion of 275–276, but was afterwards rebuilt.

The more recently excavated establishments of La Vergnée (Charente-Inférieure) and of Oberentfelden (Aargau) also have their subsidiary buildings round an elongated rectangular court.

A large number of elaborate villas is known in north-eastern Gaul, especially in the Moselle region, where great palaces studded the countryside within reach of Trier. A magnificent one of corridor type stood at

Nennig, 41 km. south of Trier, along the Trier–Metz road. It was in its heyday in the second century, to the latter part of which its celebrated mosaic, which can still be seen *in situ*, belongs. Further additions were made subsequently, and it continued to be occupied under the late empire.

The 220 square-kilometre domain of the villa of Welsch-billig, near Trier, is surrounded by a wall 80 km. in length. The wall was built by the military in the time of Valentinian, and it is believed that the estate was an imperial domain, and that the villa itself may have been an imperial residence. The land enclosed is open agricultural country, so its protection had an economic as well as a political aim. The most remarkable feature of the villa was the artificial lake, planned in imitation of a circus.

At the bottom of the scale it is less easy to make a picture, for the dwellings of the poor in any age do not tend to be substantial. The stately homes of Mrs. Hemans are all about us, but many of the cottage homes of even her day have long since been condemned or fallen down; it is the same with eighteenth-century France, and still more with Roman Gaul. The poor made shift to lodge themselves as best they could, but their best did not amount to much. The village of La Roche Blanche, in whose commune stands the oppidum of Gergovia, is built at the foot of a limestone cliff in which can be seen the caves where some of its inhabitants still lived as late as the beginning of the present century. We need not doubt that such lodgments, perhaps the same ones, were used by their Gallo-Roman ancestors.

Certain old hill-villages remained in occupation during the Roman period. A number of these have been found in mountainous districts, where the huts are made of dry stone and where the roof was probably made of thatch Small communities of herdsmen and the like lived here but these villages are very difficult to date and have been the occasion for some highly controversial literature

One example which seems to belong to our period is Chastel-sur-Murat, a solitary acropolis-like hill in the Cantal, in the south of the Auvergne, a district always noted for its cattle. Here was an ideal small *oppidum*, on which was found a number of stone huts; among their débris were Gallic coins, and Gallic, Roman and post-Roman pottery.

Some of the dependent buildings of the villas described above will have been occupied by farm-labourers and other estate workers (figs. 21 and 22).

In the Vosges, in Lorraine and towards Trier there are areas where ponds or pits, which are called *mardelles*, or *fossés à loup*, or (in Normandy) *fossés à prêcheurs*, are frequent. They may occur singly or in groups, and although many of them are probably natural, others have been found to contain traces of buildings of the Iron Age or Roman periods. These structures are particularly frequent in Lorraine. Their floors are generally 2–5 metres below the present ground level, and on them have been found roof-beams on which rest smaller branches, the basis of the actual roof-covering. The regular way these fell into the *mardelle* shows that they formed part of a structure. On some of the floors hearths have been found and in and around them pieces of Roman tile and Roman pottery; in one a Roman bronze sieve was preserved.

In some places small hamlets, or groups of farm-houses or huts occur. A whole series is known along the Rhine, from Coblenz to Boppard and inland, also along the Moselle. The Coblenz group has its own sanctuaries and its cemeteries, also its smithy.

A noteworthy feature of the Gallic countryside is the little square Celtic temple sometimes accompanied by a theatre. The isolation of these temples is probably more apparent than real, for in many cases where excavation has been attempted it is clear that quite a number of habitations were often grouped round temples. There was probably a settlement round the more classical one at Champlieu in the Forest of Compiègne, and if one follows

the Roman road to Soissons through the forest one finds
on the outskirts of Pierrefonds, 11 kilometres away,
another Gallo-Roman village, which ran a little way along
either side of the road.

A few Celtic villages of the Roman period have been
observed in the northern Vosges. Their remains consist
of small fields, delimited by stone boundaries. Here and
there are signs of huts and cemeteries. These are essentially upland settlements.

In a few places in the Roman Empire it has been possible
to trace the system of land-allotment, or centuriation,
measured out by the Romans when founding a colony.
This has not been done to any great degree for Roman
Gaul, though traces have been found here and there.
The elements of the system used for Augst have been
worked out, and elsewhere in the Rhineland, especially
round Cologne, studies have been made of the relative
positions of Roman farms. Fragments of a Roman map
of the territory of the colony of Orange exist, inscribed
on stone, but are not at present easy to interpret.

The dominant feature of the countryside, as in eighteenth-century England, must have been the great estate.
The study of place-names in France, a most fruitful source
of information for the student of the Roman period, has
shown that a large class of place-names—those ending in
-ac or -at in the south, -e or -y in the north—are derived
from the names of Roman domains, for the simplest way of
recording an estate for the *fiscus* was to use the name of its
owner, generally with the suffix -acum or -acus. Thus the
names of domains called Pauliacus have been shown to
develop as follows: into Paulhac in Aquitaine, Pauliat in
Auvergne, Pouillé or Pouilly in the north. Villages exist
by the hundred in France with these suffixes, and this line
of name-derivation has been very carefully studied. It
has been found to hold good as a general rule, though it
cannot be too strongly stressed that each individual
instance requires checking by reference to early documents
such as medieval cartularies, before it can be safely cited

as an example. With this proviso, however, one cannot fail to be struck by the number of place-names ending in the suffixes mentioned above, the majority of which do in fact represent the landed estates of imperial Roman times.

The letters of Sidonius are full of references to estates with this type of name. Such are Cutiacum near Clermont, given by its proprietor to the Church, and Taionacus. We cannot trace these, but the most famous of all, Avitacum, the estate he inherited from his father-in-law, the ill-fated emperor Avitus, is identified, to the satisfaction of the philologists, and the qualified satisfaction of the topographers, with the village of Aydat, on a lake of the same name, in the hills to the south-west of Clermont-Ferrand.

The incipient feudalism of the great estates is a theme running through the story of Gaul. Before the conquest there were the nobles with their bands of war-like retainers who got the better of the weak kings—people like Gobannitio, the uncle of Vercingetorix, and clearly the opponent of the family pretensions to kingship; and Dumnorix the Aeduan. Rome did not interfere with those who were willing to come to terms, so a powerful aristocracy maintained itself throughout the Roman period, less exposed to the rapacity of greedy emperors than the Italian nobility. Nor was it swept away entirely by the Germanic invasions. The present generation in western Europe has seen two devastating wars lay waste great tracts, but has also seen how rapidly a countryside can recover from the passage of an invading army. Gaul is large and takes long to over-run without tanks. The marauders would not have time systematically to destroy all manors and farms. A horde passed by, destroying where it passed, and we need not doubt much of the gloomy tale told by writers like Ammianus Marcellinus and Salvian, but invaders had of necessity to travel by the roads and would not have time to take every by-path to every chateau, nor would they be able to enter and destroy every one they passed. So we may understand the accounts of the peaceful country life of Sidonius and his friends of the fifth century, for whom the invaders of the day seem far distant for so much of the time. Some of them, however, were already taking the precaution of fortifying their houses. Sidonius refers to Pontius Leontius, who built a wall round his villa strong enough to face a battering-ram; his friend Aper had a *montana castella*, or hill castle. Remains of such a fortified villa appear to have been found at Châteauponsac (Castrum Pontiacum) in Haute Vienne.

NATURAL PRODUCTS

1. *Agriculture.* The greatest wealth of Gaul lay in its fertile land. The ease with which Caesar's large armies could live on the country shows the abundance of its crops even before the Roman peace. Judging from ancient authors, the Gaul was an industrious and intelligent farmer, and the addition of wheels to the plough seems to have been a Celtic improvement. Throughout their history the Gallo-Romans took a lively interest in their lands, and we find Sidonius Apollinaris reproaching some of his friends for giving too much time to agriculture and not enough to literature. Gallic tombstones have preserved many agricultural scenes.

As so many ancient cities were unable to subsist on the wheat grown in their vicinity, the maintenance of the corn trade had always been one of the basic necessities of the Mediterranean world, and those Roman provinces which could export a surplus were sure of finding customers. The biggest buyer was the state, represented by special officials, *Procuratores Annonae*, whose duty it was to purchase grain and other foodstuffs for the Roman armies and for the teeming population of the capital. One of the procurators resided at Arles, for Roman Gaul had large surpluses. The plains of Gascony, the lands of the Upper Garonne and the Rhone valley were drawn on for supplies sent to Italy, while the rich cornlands of northern

and north-central Gaul were the granary for the Germanies. Wheat from imperial estates went automatically
to the official stores. The maintenance of fleets of corn-
ships and of warehouses was a primary and ever-growing
concern of the state, and the shipping corporations,
notably the *navicularii* of Arles and Narbonne, were early
accorded special recognition and favours. They had their
offices in the portico of the Corporations at Ostia, the port
which supplied Rome. The merchants might sell to
other buyers corn remaining after the needs of the state
had been met, and it seems clear that cargoes of Gallic
corn were taken to the eastern Mediterranean, there to
be exchanged for more exotic products. In the late
Empire the state more and more took over control of the
means of subsistence, and in particular of the all-important
corn supply.

Corn was mainly ground in the home on rotary querns,
but water-mills were not uncommon. A remarkable
recent discovery at the Barbegal near Arles throws fresh
light on the skill of Roman engineers. A ruin which had
long puzzled archaeologists has been recognized as a
large-scale flour-mill, worked by water-power (fig. 23)
from an aqueduct led across the hill behind it, after
crossing a valley beside the Arles city aqueduct coming
from the Alpilles. The water flowed into a large cemented
cistern, from which it poured down the hillside in two
mill-races, dropping through a series of eight chambers
arranged in steps down the hill. Wheels turned in these
sixteen compartments rotated the millstones in adjoining
chambers. After use the water ran away into the
swampy ground below. The millstones, judging by
fragments found, were 90 cm. in diameter. This large
water-mill is believed to have been a late imperial state
enterprise, and would have been able to grind enough flour
to keep 80,000 people supplied.

Other cereals besides wheat were grown—millet, oats,
barley. Barley was largely used for making beer, and
cervesarii, traders in beer, are mentioned, while Cologne

had a special barley market, a *forum hordearium*. On a Banassac cup is the motto *cervesa reple*, 'fill up with beer'.

Fruit trees, in which the Romans always took a lively interest, did splendidly in Gaul. Many of them were

FIG. 23. The Barbegal Water-Mill

introduced to Gaul by Romans. In addition, a long list can be compiled of sweet-smelling and medicinal herbs, or plants used for dyeing, which were products of the country. Among useful plants needed in Gaul, flax and hemp were widely grown. There was a factory for linen goods (*linificium*) at Vienne in the Late Empire, while the *centonarii*, who are mentioned frequently in inscriptions, traded in hemp goods—sailcloth, sacks, tarpaulins, etc.

2. *The Wine Trade.* The cultivation of the vine was introduced by Massilia, but wine from Greek lands must have been one of the earliest and most valued objects of trade with the Celts and their predecessors. During the last century of the Roman Republic viticulture expanded considerably in Italy, and the Italians gladly availed themselves of the opportunities of trade with outer Gaul beyond the new province. We have already noticed (p. 9) how one of the principal accusa-

tions against the governor Fonteius was that he had levied unjustly high tolls on the wine trade across the borders. The second testimony to its existence is the prevalence of Italian amphoras, the wine-jars of the south, on sites of the last period of Gallic independence. They are equally common on sites belonging to the period immediately after the conquest, which proves that the wine trade was not seriously interrupted by the wars.

Italian wine dominated the market for a long time, but gradually Gaul was to come into her own heritage. In Strabo's day vine cultivation was creeping across Narbonensis. By the time of Pliny we begin to hear of Gallic wines; those of Béziers and Vienne had a good reputation and Marseilles produced two types. Pliny makes a dig at the nasty concoctions of Gallia Narbonensis: he says that the inhabitants turned the making of wine into a pharmaceutical operation, colouring it and smoking it and putting in all manner of queer things—even aloes. He would not have found some of the present apéritifs surprising, though in his day, as far as we know, absinthe (*herba santonica*) was only used as a drug.

We can follow the vine on its triumphant way through Gaul and see it establishing itself on the historic slopes whence still come the world's noblest vintages. Domitian's edict restricting the cultivation of the vine does not seem to have had any lasting, or even temporary, effect. The development must have gone on quietly and steadily throughout the second century. The monuments from the Moselle showing boatloads of barrels and amphoras being rowed down the river belong to the end of the second century, and a hundred and fifty years later Ausonius waxes enthusiastic about the Moselle wine. A text of the time of Constantine mentions wines of Beaune, and Ausonius writes of the wines of his own Bordeaux. Curiously enough, the vineyards of Champagne do not figure in our records, but the Emperor Julian speaks of the vines cultivated near Paris. Evidence other than literary for export of Gallic wines comes from Monte Testaccio in

Rome, where amphora stamps from Narbonensis were found, one with the inscription *sum vetus V Beterense* (a Béziers wine, five years old). British traders are found in Bordeaux, so the claret trade has a venerable ancestry. We also know that Gallic wines reached Ireland in the sixth century, a trade that was already old, for the second-century geographer Ptolemy is aware of a number of points along the Irish coast, information of which probably came from Gallic traders.

3. *The Olive*. The chief source of fat in Mediterranean diet then as now was the olive, and the use of olive oil followed Italian troops and functionaries. Pliny and others remarked on the preference of northern folks for butter, but oil soon became important. It was used for lamps and instead of soap in the baths.

The olive was cultivated in the south, in Narbonensis. The best oil was, however, imported, and the trade in oil with the Spanish province of Baetica was specially important. In this, Narbonne naturally played a big part, and some Narbonese traders seem to have carried Baetican oil to Rome. Lyons, an important centre of the trade, has an inscription of a dealer in Spanish oil.

4. *Forest Products*. The demand for timber in the empire was heavy, and Gaul was one of the best wooded of all the provinces. The forests were to be found on the colder clayey soils, in mountainous districts or on the sandy lands of the south-west. The centre and south-east were well wooded, but the greatest of all the forests was the Ardennes, Arduinna Mons, which extended across the Eifel to the Rhine. Among the inscriptions we come across the *lignarii*, the corporations of timber-merchants.

Timber was heavily drawn on for all kinds of building, and in addition there were other formidable requirements. The fleets of the Atlantic coast and of the Mediterranean had to be kept in being, to say nothing of the innumerable river vessels. The shipyards in Arles initiated by Caesar evidently continued to function. In them worked a *architectus navalis* and *fabri navales*. Another source of heavy demand were the buildings on piles particularly abundant then as now in the Low Countries, but also not uncommon elsewhere. Add to these log roads and bridges, and it is clear that the lumber industry was kept busy (fig. 42*a*).

The fuel requirements of industries must have been considerable, and in addition the hungry maws of the endless bath-furnaces had to be fed. The baths of Gaul itself were no small item, and besides them there were the baths of Rome. There is no specific information about Gaul supplying fuel for Rome, but this fuel had to come from somewhere, and Spain and Gaul are likely sources.

Carpenters were important members of the community, and tombstones of carpenters (fig. 41*b*), showing the instruments of their trade, are frequent. At St. Germain-en-Laye we can see the whole range of the carpenter's tools, little different from those of to-day—hammer, saw, chisel, axe, adze. The Gauls excelled in carriage work; in this they followed the national bent already shown in the fine chariots buried with chieftains in the Marne region in the fourth century B.C. Gaul, perhaps Cisalpine as well as Transalpine, gave the names of a number of traps and carts, including *carpentum*—two-wheeled carriage, and *reda* —four-wheeler, to the Latin language.

Resin was an important by-product of pine forests in Alsace and elsewhere. Evidence has been found in the Rouergue up in the Causses, which in Roman times were covered with pine-woods. Here, deep pots containing melted resin have been found associated with small furnaces; the process used appears to have been a form of distillation.

5. *Livestock.* Stock-raising was of great importance. The meat supplies for the armies had to be assured (and with increasing Germanization of the army larger meat rations were needed), and also the vast quantities of hides required for leather used in military equipment. Northern and north-eastern Gaul was noted for its flocks of sheep, whence came the wool for its popular cloaks. Great

K

herds of pigs roamed the forests, and large quantities of
salted pork, including the famous hams of the Menapii
and the Sequani, were exported. The hill country in the
centre has long been a great cattle- and sheep-raising
district, and transhumance between the Cevennes and
the south goes back to very ancient times.

Cheeses were made from the milk of cows, goats and
sheep. Pliny refers to a special cheese from the land of
the Gabali as the most highly esteemed of all provincial
cheeses, but, he says, it must be eaten fresh.

The horses and mules of Gaul were also sought after,
and Gaul, like Britain, provided hunting-dogs.

Flocks of geese abounded, especially in the northern
maritime territory. The geese were prized for their
feathers and their flesh. Second only to the story of
the Capitoline geese is Pliny's yarn of how the geese
from the land of the Morini were driven all the way to
Rome, the tired birds being brought to the front of the
flock so that they might be helped along by the others
pushing from behind.

6. *Fisheries*. There are occasional references to the
fish of Gaul. Ausonius has spread himself to describe
the variety of fish in the Moselle and the fine oysters of
Bordeaux. A mysterious kind of fish sauce called *garum*
was highly prized, and Spanish *garum* was one of the most
important Gallic imports. A variant of this—*muria*—
was made in Gaul, especially at Antibes, and for this a
fish called *lupus* was used. On the neighbouring Ile-
Sainte-Marguerite there are foundations of walls which
ran some way into the sea and which are thought to be
remains of a fish-trap. A channel from the trap led into
a shallow lagoon where the fish may have been collected.

There was also the oyster, so voraciously consumed by
Roman gourmets. Oysters seem to have been gathered
with as much zeal from the Atlantic coasts in Gallo-
Roman times as now. Saintonge was rich in them and
Saintes seems to have been a centre for the trade, as
vivaria have been found in the town. Oyster shells such as

those in Strasbourg museum are not uncommon finds on Gallo-Roman sites far from the sea.

We know that there was fishing off the Atlantic coast from an inscription set up outside Roman territory at Beetgum in Friesland by enterprising Gallic fishermen. It records the payment of vows to the local goddess Hludana by some *conductores piscatus*.

7. *Minerals*. Gaul's yield in precious metals was a disappointment to the Romans. All sorts of tales were current of the fabulous treasures of Gallic tribes, but only relatively small supplies of either gold or silver were ever found. Strabo reflects the anxious interest of the Roman world in the possible output of Gaul, but Pliny, writing two generations later, regards its metals as of secondary importance, with the exception of iron.

It seems that gold-washing went on in many Pyrenaean streams during the Roman period, but the yield was poor, for the main supply was already exhausted. Tin deposits existed in the Haute-Vienne, and in them were small quantities of gold, but these again were unimportant.

Silver, associated with lead, was more common, although never to be compared with the Spanish supply. It was worked in the Pyrenees, in Alsace, Finistère and in the Hautes-Alpes, but the most important mines were those of the south-west of the Massif Central, in the lands of the Gabali and the Ruteni. Picks and Roman lamps have been found in mine-workings near Villefranche, and the most interesting find of all is the inscription from Bastide l'Evèque of an imperial overseer (*vilicus*) of the silver mines, of the time of Tiberius. This individual was, judging by his name Zmaragdus, a slave of Greek or Asiatic origin.

Lead was also produced in these mines, and there were other lead mines in the lands of the Pictones (Charente), the Mediomatrici and the Treveri. The only stamped pig of Gallic lead bears the name of the Segusiavi. British lead, however, was much more plentiful and dominated the market.

Copper was not very plentiful either, but occurred in the Pyrenees, the Massif Central, the Nièvre and the Saar. The main production of copper in the western empire was in Spain and, secondly, in Britain. Zinc was mined around Gressenich, near Aix-la-Chapelle.

Iron, however, was a major product of Gaul. It was found in nearly all areas, in easily worked deposits, so that each district could provide for itself. It is perhaps misleading to pick out localities with iron-mines for special mention, but we may note that the Petrocorii (Périgord) and Bituriges Cubi (Bourges) were renowned for their iron-mining. The iron of Lorraine was a source of wealth to the Romans as well as to the modern French. Groups of iron furnaces were often surrounded by earth banks, to keep out the curious or the hostile, or possibly to keep the personnel in, because one form of punishing criminals was to send them to the mines. The mining communities, whether belonging to iron or other mines, had a character of their own, and included many free, skilled workers, but by the nature of their occupation they were to some degree isolated from the agricultural communities around them.

The miners in the imperial domains were allowed some say in their own government, for the inscription mentioned above states that the individual in question had been elected by the *decuriones* of the *familia*, that is, the local council of the slaves, of Tiberius Caesar.

Wealthy individuals might own mines, but the cities also had theirs, with special officials to look after them. One of the sources of revenue of the Council of the Gauls was iron-mines, and we hear of a *iudex arcae ferrariarum* from Calvados. But the imperial fisc owned many mines and drew revenues from the taxation of mines in general, so it is not surprising to find a high official, a *procurator ferrariarum*, installed at Lyons.

8. *Quarries*. Numerous Gallo-Roman quarries, large and small, are known, producing both building-stone and ornamental stone. The nearness of a river, as well as

the quality of the stone, had an important bearing on the use of a quarry, as wherever possible the stones were transported by water.

The Pyrenees contain a variety of high-grade marbles, and the greatest of the marble quarries were at Saint-Béat (Haute-Garonne), where a white marble of fine quality little inferior to that of Carrara was obtained. Not far away were other quarries of black, yellow and veined marbles. The stone was taken to Saint-Bertrand-de-Comminges, and there shipped into barges on the Garonne, down which it went in large quantities to Bordeaux, where it was in great demand. From Bordeaux it went farther afield, and is found, for instance, in Normandy (Lillebonne). The chief Pyrenaean quarries are believed to have been imperial property, probably part of the *saltus Pyrenaeus* mentioned by Pliny. Other marbles, serpentines and granites were exploited in the Alps and the Massif Central.

Around the quarries, just as around the mines, dwelt specialized communities, of free men, slaves and criminals. The administration of the quarries was also similar to that of the mines—both are classed together as *metellae*. The motley groups of workers settled down, however, and have left many traces of their presence in inscriptions to the local deities whom they prudently honoured.

Towards the Rhine we enter the zone of quarries worked by the troops, who have often left inscriptions which prove their presence. Such are the sandstone quarries of Reinhardsmünster in Alsace and the limestone ones of Norroy and neighbouring sites in Lorraine, where stone was extracted by detachments from the legions of Vindonissa, Strasbourg and Mainz. The legions of Lower Germany worked in the tufa quarries of Rheinbrohl near Andernach. The greatest of these northern quarries was probably the Kreimhildenstuhl (Bad Dürkheim, in the Palatinate), which was worked from the time of Claudius until well into the third century for sandstone. The many tools found here add to the interest of the site.

The basalt-lava quarries of Niedermendig in the Eifel had been exploited for quernstones long before the Romans came to the Rhineland, and they retained their import-ance throughout the Roman period. Querns of this particular stone are found throughout Roman Germany, but they were also exported to Britain and to many places in Gaul proper (e.g. thirty millstones were found in a wreck in the Rhine near Strasbourg). They have even been found in free Germany.

9. *Salt*. It is unnecessary to stress the importance of salt, commerce in which is discernible as a major factor in the development of many prehistoric trade routes. Inland supplies were available at Salins (Franche-Comté), and in Lorraine, on the river Seille, where traces of ancient salt-works have been found. There was a Roman settlement of some importance, the *Vicus Marosallum* (sallum = salinae?) on the main Metz-Strasbourg road whose route was dictated by the amount of salt traffic. Ancient brushwood gratings for evaporating salt have also recently been discovered at Fontaines-Salées (Yonne).

Along the sea coasts salt was also collected in the lagoons of the south, as always, and along the ocean, by the *salinatores*.

VII

INDUSTRIES AND COMMERCE

THE economic history of Roman Gaul is one of the most interesting phenomena of the Roman empire. There is plenty of evidence of trade among the widespread Celtic peoples of the preceding period. Moreover, the speed of Caesar's marches and the distances he covered show the excellence of Gallic communications. The Gauls eagerly availed themselves of the commercial opportunities which incorporation in the empire brought, and they welcomed Italian goods, imitated them, and in some cases became such skilled competitors that they drove them from the market. The best-known example of this is the trade in high-grade pottery.

THE POTTERY TRADE

1. *Native Potters.* Celtic standards of pot-making were already high before the conquest, and had been stimulated by contact with Greek, Italic and Iberian products. The dominant commoner pottery of northern Gaul from the time of the conquest until the end of the first century A.D. is that known as Gallo-Belgic ware, in which Italic and Celtic elements are nicely blended. Sometimes the old La Tène forms are preserved, sometimes Italian forms are imitated; one group preserves the old grey or black ware, and is sometimes called terra nigra, another, a red ware (terra rubra) copies the Italian Arretine. The decorative elements such as wheel and comb ornaments are generally Celtic in character, but potters took to stamping their names on their pots, after the Mediterranean fashion. Many kilns have been found which

produced these wares in the country between Seine and Rhine and as far east as Alsace.

The potters were ready to adopt improved methods and willingly took over Roman forms of kiln construction. The all-conquering terra sigillata, with its bright red glaze, found these Gallo-Belgic wares serious competitors for a long time.   In the second century the Belgic potters of the Argonne themselves turned to sigillata manufacture, and their kilns remained at work right into Frankish times.

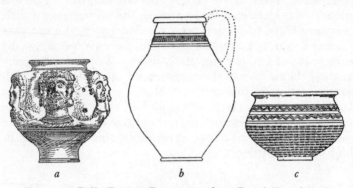

FIG. 24.   Gallo-Roman Pottery: *a*, from Bavai (⅛ real size);
b and *c*, from Gergovia (⅛)

South of the Seine we step out of Belgic Gaul into Central Gaul, which has its own grey and black wares, very similar to Gallo-Belgic pottery, but at present nothing like so much is known of their centres of production. Large quantities were found on Mont Beuvray and in the early Gallo-Roman settlement on Gergovia, belonging to the last half-century B.C.   On Gergovia the pottery is extremely varied in range and character, and has affinities both with Mont Beuvray and with Languedoc.   Fig. 24*b* shows one of its most distinctive types, a grey or grey-black jug.   There is also a large amount of a white-painted pottery which is common in the Allier valley in the time of Augustus.

2. *Imported Pottery*.   Southern Gaul had long been

familiar with Greek pottery, brought by Massiliote traders, and with the black, highly-glazed pots of south Italy called Campanian ware imported in large quantities into the Roman Province. In the last century B.C. Arezzo— ancient Arretium—in Etruria, began to develop a fine, red-glazed table-ware, modelled in part on the silver vessels of the very wealthy. The pots were made in moulds and the ornamentation on them was often of considerable merit. The potter's name was usually stamped on the side or on the base. This Arretine ware became widely popular, and was used wherever Roman armies went. Civilians also were eager purchasers, and pots known to have been made between 25 B.C. and A.D. 25 have been found in most parts of Gaul, though they are naturally rarer in the remoter northern districts. They were also bought, from Gallic traders, by the British chieftains of Camulodunum.

3. *Gallic Terra Sigillata.* It was not long, however, before the ambitions of the Gallic potters were aroused, and by A.D. 15 we find red pottery of Arretine type being made in southern Gaul, in the border districts of the Province and Gallia Comata, at Montans (Tarn), Banassac (Lozère) and La Graufesenque (Aveyron). It is probable that Italian craftsmen who had had an eye to Gallic trade had moved into Gallia Narbonensis and were induced to settle at these places and teach the Gauls, but the latter soon equalled, and in some respects even surpassed, their masters. None of the Arretine ware has the fine, hard, sealing-wax-like character of La Graufesenque ware, though, on the other hand, it should be clearly understood that the Celtic artists who prepared the moulds for the decorated pots never rivalled the beauty of the best Arretine decoration. The shapes of the commonest Gallic pots are, however, different from the prevalent forms of Arretine ware, and the Celtic ancestry of some of them can be proved. The Celtic potter was evidently making familiar shapes as a foundation on which to use his new technique and new decoration (see fig. 25).

By A.D. 50 South Gaulish terra sigillata, or Samian ware, had not only driven Arretine from Gaul but pursued it into Italian markets. A consignment of La Graufesenque pottery was found still in its crate at Pompeii where it had arrived on the eve of the catastrophe. South Gaulish pottery is also plentiful on British, Spanish, Danubian, Sardinian, Sicilian and even African sites, and Narbonne was its chief distributing centre. The products of Montans seem in the main to have gone to supply Aquitania.

Excavation at La Graufesenque (Condatomagus, close

FIG. 25.   Terra Sigillata drinking-bowl made at Banassac, with motto: GABALIBVS FELICIT[ER]

by the Aveyron town of Millau) has been fruitful. Besides the kilns themselves and numerous potters' moulds and débris, a large number of sherds was found (fig. 44a) on which the workers had scratched lists of their day-to-day output, the slaves at work, and so on, so that it is possible to form a picture of these large workshops, which almost attained the dignity of factories, with their master-potters aided by groups of slaves or apprentices.

The same process which produced La Graufesenque in due course bred rivals for it in Gaul itself. Along the valley of the Allier there were potteries which had already been important in Celtic times, and some of these began to imitate Arretine ware. By A.D. 40 terra sigillata was being produced at Lezoux (Ledosus) in Arvernian territory, 27 kilometres east of Clermont-Ferrand. It was conveniently near the Allier, so that its products could be taken in barges down that river to the Loire, and the points used for embarkation have been traced. Its central position helped its rise, and towards the end of the first century Lezoux was the dominant producer, though its products never equalled the quality of the best Graufesenque pottery. The convenience of the Loire route probably accounts for the virtual monopoly of the British market enjoyed by Lezoux during the second century, but the middle Danube countries were also excellent customers, and sherds of Lezoux pottery have been found at Antioch and Athens. Various minor wares for local consumption were also made at Lezoux, and terra-cotta ornaments for architectural decoration, including some curious capitals with heads of beasts and gods.

The economic magnet of the military zone exerted a powerful attraction, and by the turn of the century we find potters settled at Heiligenberg in Alsace and elsewhere in the north-east, manufacturing terra sigillata for the troops. The rising town of Trier also attracted potters, and terra sigillata was made here from 110 to 240, but Rheinzabern, in the Palatinate, was destined to be the greatest rival of Lezoux. This town on the banks of the Rhine possessed large deposits of good clay, and legionary brickworks had been installed here about A.D. 50. During the Flavian period, however, the frontier was advanced across the Rhine, and the legionary works were transferred to Nied, near Heddernheim. After a time ordinary potters awoke to the advantages of the site and workers from Heiligenberg established themselves on the ground left vacant by the soldiers. Soon after 130 Rheinzabern was producing, and by the middle of the century it had become a major centre supplying the armies from northern Britain to Rumania.

In the second century the number of potteries tended to multiply. Despite the great importance of Rheinzabern, Trier and Lezoux, smaller potteries sprang up at a number of places in Lorraine and the Rhineland, for it seems to have been possible to buy moulds and then make pots locally. A fall in quality followed. The finely moulded decoration becomes rarer, and potters are content with plain forms decorated with simple leaves and tendrils in barbotine, ornament applied to a pot like patterns to an iced cake. This is not unattractive and its free curves would appeal to Celtic taste. Another fashion which became apparent in the second century and lasted into the third was incised decoration, imitating the increasingly popular cut glass. The last fashion in moulded decoration was the preparation of medallions in moulds which were then applied to the pot. Rheinzabern used lions' heads in this sort of work, but otherwise did not take to it. The medallions were also made in Lezoux, and, later, in the Rhone valley, at Vienne and perhaps at Lyons.

It is misleading to dwell too much on the falling-off from some of the high standards of earlier potters. The industry was still very much alive in the early third century, as the large variety of new shapes produced in Rheinzabern shows. What killed the Rheinzabern industry were the Alemannic invasions. The incursion of 259–260 destroyed the Roman forts and settlements across the Rhine, and with them the best market for the pottery. Trouble was rife throughout Gaul; Lezoux was destroyed, and other centres of production had lost their vitality. Roads were no longer so well-kept nor so secure, and long-distance trade in things like pottery was becoming increasingly difficult. In particular the wars on the Danube must have rendered a once-lucrative market very uncertain. People also were poorer and glad to be able to buy locally.

Terra sigillata did not, however, entirely disappear. It continued to be produced in the more sheltered area of the Argonne from 270 till about 400. Pots of this final stage were decorated with rouletted patterns. This is the revival of the old ornamentation of the Belgic and allied wares. The potters of the Argonne did not work in large groups, they remained in village settlements scattered through the forest, so in the upheavals of the third century they were passed by and theirs was the only branch of the once-great industry which survived into the late Empire.

4. *Other Pottery.* Certain other wares of rather more than local interest remain to be mentioned, though we can only touch on a few of the more important or curious types.

Bavai. The Nervii show great individuality in their pottery, as in other things. In Bavai Gallo-Belgic wares were made and also a special line in *pelves*—large *mortaria* or bowls with quartz for crushing food embedded in them. Urns of the type shown in fig. 24*a* were almost certainly made at Bavai during the late first century and until the middle of the second century. Heads representing popular deities, such as the three-headed god, were made in special moulds and then applied to the pot (cf. p. 187). These circulated widely in north-eastern Gaul.

St. Rémy-en-Rollat. In the early days of the empire the imitation of Arretine, and of certain North Italian beakers, took an individual local form in the Allier valley. The mould technique was copied, and an attempt was made to reproduce the popular metal vessels of the rich, so that a number of cups on stands and with handles and decoration reminiscent of known metal prototypes have been found. The clay was soft and whitish and was covered with a shiny yellowish glaze. The glaze had nothing like the strength of the red glaze, and the St. Rémy clay seems to be more delicate than that of Lezoux, so that the potters here finished by specializing in the production of statuettes of gods and goddesses which became very popular (cf. p. 149). The glazed ware of St. Rémy, however, travelled quite far afield, and has been found in the Rhineland, and even in Colchester, as well as in various parts of Gaul, including the nearby Bourges and Roanne and the more distant Lisieux.

Hunting Beakers. Beakers with hunting scenes in barbotine, closely resembling the Castor ware so characteristic of British sites in the third century, are found in considerable numbers in north-east Gaul and the Rhineland. Similar decoration is also to be found on contemporary terra sigillata.

Black Beakers of Trier. One of the finest wares of the late empire is the series of shiny black beakers or winecups with decoration in white, yellowish (and sometimes purple) barbotine, produced at Trier, which was widely used

in the Rhineland and north-east Gaul and also reached Britain. These beakers frequently bear convivial mottoes (fig. 26). Their production dates from the late third century.

Pottery with Christian Symbols. In the fourth century there was a vogue for pottery ornamented with Christian symbols, monograms, saints, etc. This type of thing was especially popular in North Africa,

FIG. 26
Wine Cup from Trier
(4th century)

and in Gaul it is found particularly around the ports of Bordeaux, Nantes and Narbonne.

5. *Lamps.* Oil lamps were a necessary part of the Mediterranean household's equipment and were introduced to the north along with olive oil. Before that the Celts had mostly used torches or candles.

Italy was the chief lamp-producer, and the north Italian manufacturers dominated the trade with the north. During the first century lamps ornamented with mythological or other scenes predominated, but in the second century a plain type with the name of the maker stamped on its underside swept the market. These lamps are found everywhere in Gaul, and were imitated, but Italy seems to have maintained the chief hold on the market. The little lamps are so fragile that the number turned out must have been very large indeed. The severe utility of the stamped lamp is offset by other more fancy types.

6. *Terracotta Figurines.* The potter could also turn an honest penny by making clay statuettes of popular gods

and goddesses, or figurines for ornaments or toys. These little objects were made in moulds very easily. They were used as votive offerings. Temples, especially centres of pilgrimage, kept their own supplies or even had their own kilns. The white clay of Vichy and St. Rémy-en-Rollat lent itself to this manufacture, and clay Venuses from the Allier travelled far. Cologne was another big centre of production, and figures of classical-looking deities or of the local *Matronae* were made here and stamped by the maker: *C(oloniae) C(laudiae) A(rae) A(grippinensium) ipse Fabricius f(ecit)*.

A number of other stamps could be cited from other parts of Gaul, though their place of origin is not always certain. The figurines of the Gironde district seem to be recognizable by their grey or black clay.

7. *The Traders*. The above account has only taken notice of special wares. Every town, probably every hamlet and big domain, had its own small kiln for common needs, for kitchen utensils and the like, but, even so, there was a large volume of trade in pottery. *Negotiatores artis cretariae*, the essential middlemen in the formidable work of distribution, have left inscriptions in many towns; trade went as far as possible by water and barges descended the Allier from Lezoux or the Rhine from the Palatinate and Alsatian centres. A cargo of Gallic pottery from Lezoux was wrecked about A.D. 160 on the Pudding Pan Rock off Whitby. A *negotiator cretarius britannicianus* is known from Cologne; another set up an altar to the goddess Nehalennia in her temple on the island of Walcheren, in thanksgiving for the safety of his merchandise: *negotiator cretarius ob merces recte conservatas*.

In Lyons is an inscription of a Treveran who was both a wine and a pottery merchant. It seems likely that along with Moselle wine he sold the special Moselle wine table-ware, the black beakers noted above.

8. *Bricks and Tiles*. A distinctive mark of a Roman site is roof-tile: the *tegula*, a flanged rectangular brick, and the *imbrex*, the curved brick which covered the join

between two *tegulae*. Brickworks were obviously common, and in the larger ones the makers used normally to put a stamp on their products. The most important series of stamped tiles we have in Gaul are the military ones, bearing the names of their issuing units.

GLASS

The manufacture of glass became an important industry in the Hellenistic world about the last century B.C., when the art of glass-blowing was invented. For a long time Italy and the East monopolized the trade, and exported their products to Gaul, though we know from Pliny that by his time the manufacture of glass had begun in Gaul itself. The chief glass finds of the later first century are cinerary urns, which were often buried within stone containers and have therefore been preserved intact; small bottles for oils or perfumes; and there are also the vessels de luxe, beautiful bowls subtly veined with many hues.

During the second century glass became increasingly popular, and centres of manufacture multiplied. Traces of glass-working have been found in the following regions: Bourbonnais, Poitou, Vendée, Loire-Inférieure, Argonne, Eifel and above all in Cologne, which, partly because of the particularly fine quartzite sand available, soon became the leading centre of the industry. The richness of the collections in the Namur and Arlon Museums may point to local manufacture. The art of making thin-walled, clear, colourless glass had by now been mastered by the Gallic workers, and they began to experiment with various shapes and decorations. Sometimes threads of coloured glass were wound round the vessel, after the manner of icing a cake, or the glass was engraved with mythological, gladiatorial or circus scenes, or we have the more orthodox cut-glass.

A number of stamps are known, though they in no way compare in number or dating value with the stamps on pottery. One at Avenches bears the stamp *Carantus Carantodius civis Leucus*, i.e. of a member of the tribe centred on Toul. A second-century Lyons inscription mentions a Carthaginian *opifex artis vitrariae*.

The glass industry managed to resist the evils that destroyed so many activities in the latter part of the disastrous third century. The glass workers of Cologne continued to flourish throughout the fourth century and beyond. They received imperial favour, and Constantine in 337 freed *vitrarii* and *diatretarii* from all taxes, at the same time laying down that the trade must be passed down from father to son, so anxious was he to preserve this highly-skilled profession, which flourished widely throughout the empire.

The *diatretarii* just mentioned were the most skilled, and made the complicated vases in which the vessel is enclosed within an attached openwork shell of cut glass. Such vases are very rare, but there are examples surviving in Strasbourg and Cologne, and a splendid new specimen was found in a sarcophagus near Trier in 1950. The glass manufacture of Cologne is remarkable for having continued work right through into Frankish times. To oblige the growing barbarian element among the wealthy sections of the population beautiful glass imitations of Germanic drinking-horns were made. Besides the fancy patterns just enumerated there were also vast quantities of urns and bottles of a regulation type—large thick square-sided jars, flasks, etc. A characteristic product of northern Gaul from the late third century until about 380 is the bottle in the form of a barrel, stamped with the name of Frontinus or sometimes with that of one of his slaves or free workers. These are found all over northern Gaul, and are especially common in Normandy, also occurring farther south in Poitou and Autun, but the exact location of their centre or centres of manufacture is not known as yet. In the fourth century certain glassworkers carried on their industry in the Argonne.

L

METAL WORK

1. *Bronze- and Iron-work.* The Celts were expert craftsmen long before the Romans came to Gaul, and the best
examples of the continuation of this craftsmanship are
found in metal-work. Work in the old tradition was

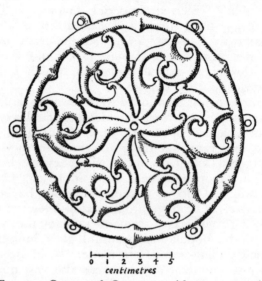

FIG. 27. Open-work Ornament with trumpet motif

carried on in Switzerland, where we find a series of first
century open-work ornaments for leather cases, sheaths
and the like, some of which bear the name of their place of
origin, Aquae Helveticae (Baden-in-Aargau) and of their
maker, Gemellianus. These have been found at Cambrai,
at places along the Rhine, and in Austria.

Open-work ornamentation always remained popular,
and about the middle of the second century there appear
on military sites along the northern frontiers a series of
brooches and harness ornaments with trumpet-shaped

motifs which recall strongly the old swollen tendril ornamentation of early Celtic art (fig. 27). Some examples have been found in Britain, but it does seem as if the centre of manufacture must have been somewhere in the Rhineland or northern Gaul. Closely allied to these are the elaborate bronze ornaments found in Pannonian graves of the second century. It has recently been suggested that these were made in the Namur region of north-eastern Gaul.

Brooches were articles of important and constant use in an age when so much of the costume consisted of draped folds for which there were no hooks and eyes or zip-fasteners. Brooch-making must have been a common routine operation of every small bronze-worker, and brooch-moulds are not uncommon finds. Certain Gallic brooches, however, had a more than local popularity, and there is one early form, the Aucissa brooch, stamped examples of which have been found as far apart as Britain and the Caucasus. The shapes of brooches have been studied very carefully, because once a type became popular it penetrated by export or imitation over wide areas.

Another craft in which Celtic feeling persists is in enamel-work. The last home of the independent Celtic enamel industry was the British Isles, but it did not disappear in Gaul, though it was modified to suit new fashions. It flourished greatly in the second century, and is thought to have had its chief centre in the Namur region of Gallia Belgica. There are a number of brooches in geometrical shapes or of stylized animals, adorned with enamel in a great variety of colours and sometimes with very delightful formal floral ornamentation (fig. 28).

Other more ambitious objects were also made, notably a series of very pleasing bowls, seal-boxes, etc. Sometimes their patterns are purely geometrical, at other times the characteristic Celtic curves are picked out in gay colours.

Bronze vessels were an important part of ancient household equipment. Gallic workers early adopted Italian types. Many of these goods were made in Lyons, and its products have been found widely distributed inside and outside the empire. In the second century a brass industry grew up in the zinc-producing area around Gressenich, near to Aix-la-Chapelle. Somewhere here, on the borders of Gallia Belgica and Lower Germany, an attractive type of brass bucket, with friezes of ornamental animals round the outside of the rims, was manufactured. These so-called Hemmoor pails have been found in Kent,

Fig. 28. Three brooches: the two above are to scale, but that on the left is c. ⅔ actual size (from H. van de Weerd: *Gallo-Romeinische Archeologie*)

in Gaul, in Roman Germany and in the barbarian north (fig. 29).

Bronze was used for a wide variety of objects, lamps, candelabra, tripods, horse-trappings, etc. Some at least of the magnificent parade helmets used by the Roman cavalry are believed to be of Gallic manufacture.

Iron tools remained much the same under the empire as before, and many forms are of course unchanged. Many tools are shown on the monuments, where we can see smiths, carpenters, shoemakers, peasants, vine-growers, and all sorts of other skilled workers with the implements of their crafts. Iron-working was in general carried out by local smiths, but in some places groups of iron-workers congregated and developed their own guilds and corporate life. Each regiment had its armoury, but also in Gaul proper there were establishments specializing in the manufacture of arms and armour, presided over by army officers. Such a one was M. Ulpius Avitus, cen-

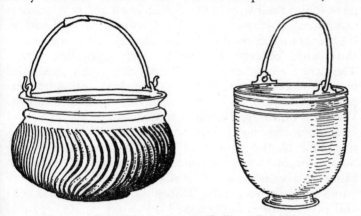

FIG. 29. Pails (¼) : *a*, bronze (Gallic or Danubian) ;
b, brass Hemmoor type

turion, in honour of whom the *opifices loricari* (breastplate-makers) of the Aedui living at Brèves near Clamecy set up an inscription.

The authorities in the late empire had to take steps to see that the military armouries were kept supplied, and here the hereditary principle was insisted on as a matter of desperate necessity. Factories for arms and armour are recorded at Autun, Trier, Amiens, Reims, Soissons and Argenton (Creuse).

2. *Goldsmiths and Silversmiths*. A rich collection of silver table-ware was the pride of all wealthy Roman house-holds, and the provincials followed suit. Such things have mostly vanished long ago in the limbo of the melting-

pot. Sometimes, however, the owners buried their treasures to hide them from marauders, but did not survive themselves to dig them up again. So there come to light from time to time rich hoards which make treasure trove a real thing. From a study of Gallic hoards we can form some idea of the quality of the silverware: of the wealth of imports which poured in, and also of the skill of the eastern craftsmen who settled in Gaul and of the native workers who learnt their art. Several fine Gallic hoards have found their way to the British Museum, so this aspect of Roman Gaul can be appreciated without leaving London.

One comes from Chaource (Aisne), and consists of thirty-nine objects, of which thirty-three are silver. They are a second-century table-service (*ministerium*), and include wine-strainer, jug, *situla* (bucket) and a pepper-pot in the form of an Ethiopian slave. A *situla* from near Vienne is of the type familiar to us in the brass buckets of Hemmoor (fig. 29). This shape seems to have been a speciality of the province. The Chaource hoard was buried about 267, with coins of Postumus. The British Museum also possesses nine silver statuettes which were found in a vineyard near Macon along with 30,000 gold and silver coins of Gallienus.

The finest Gallic hoard is that found at Berthouville in Normandy in 1830, and now in the Cabinet des Médailles in Paris. This is the temple treasure of the god Mercurius Canetonnensis and was buried by the priests in a corner of the temple portico. Its sixty-nine pieces are offerings made by worshippers in the course of the first two and a half centuries of our era and naturally vary in merit. The finest are those given by a certain Q. Domitius Tutus, whose name is inscribed on them. They include two jugs adorned with Homeric scenes of the finest Hellenistic workmanship.

Roman officers brought their table services with them on campaigns, and a silver cup was found in the siege-works at Alesia.

There must have been every inducement for enterprising Italian or Greek goldsmiths or silversmiths to settle in the chief Gallic towns. A number are known to us from inscriptions, among them the goldsmiths of Narbonne, and silversmiths of Lyons. Native craftsmen soon took up the work, and a number of silver vessels dated to the Augustan period or soon after are regarded as of Gallic workmanship. They include some of the vessels in the hoard which was found at Hildesheim near the Harz Mountains in barbarian Germany and which must be loot, but loot from a somewhat later period than the Rout of Varus to which it was at first understandably assigned.

A very interesting goblet was dug up at Lyons in 1929 and is dated to the second half of the first century. It is fashioned in the best style of the day, but the theme is Gallic, and not classical, mythology: a male figure with one torc round his neck and carrying another, a tree bearing what may conceivably be mistletoe, a wild boar, a crane and a stag (fig. 44*b*).

3. *Lead.* Finds of lead objects are also very much a matter of chance, but the quantity of lead used in Gaul must have been enormous. Gaul produced a certain amount of lead itself, but the rich British output was a valuable asset. As with us, the chief use of lead was in the making of piping. Arles Museum contains a large collection of stamped pipes, found in the Rhone, which had belonged to the siphon carrying the aqueduct across the river to Trinquetaille. It has been estimated that 10,000 to 15,000 tons of lead were employed for the siphons of the Lyons aqueducts. Lead was also used on roofs, and has been found in considerable quantity at Vaison. Lead coffins had a vogue in the third century, especially among followers of the oriental religions. Another use of lead was as tesserae for purposes like admission to the theatre and for the customs seals which have been found in quantity at Lyons.

One of the most remarkable objects for which lead was employed is the double-action force-pump found near Strasbourg.

WOOLLEN GOODS

The wool of northern Gaul was highly prized and also the textiles of the Ruteni and Santoni. Among the areas important for woollen goods is the land of the Menapii, so the famous cloth of medieval Flanders was not without its Roman counterpart. The *sagum*, the Gallic hooded cloak, was much appreciated in Rome, and the Nervii seem to have made a specially fine variety. According to Martial these Gallic cloaks were dyed in bright colours. One type of such a cloak, the *caracalla*, introduced by the son of Severus, gained him his nickname. Evidence of the wealth attained by the woollen industry is furnished by the monument at Igel near Trier, belonging to the family of the Secundinii (see p. 171). Much of the prosperity of the wool merchants was derived from supplying the army, but in the late empire, when the state had to take over the manufacture of military supplies of all sorts, official weaving establishments (*gynaecii*) were maintained at key points. We know of six in Gaul, four of them in Belgica, viz. at Reims, Tournai, Trier, Metz. The other two are at Arles and Lyons.

MISCELLANEOUS

The Gauls, with their love of bright colours, paid attention to dyes, and various herbs were cultivated for this purpose, while purple was extracted from shellfish on the Mediterranean coast. In the late empire official dyeworks were maintained at Narbonne and Toulon. Soap, made of tallow and wood-ashes, was a Gallic invention and was used for washing or bleaching hair, as well as for washing garments.

TRADERS AND IMPORTS

We have now been able to get a glimpse of the variety and activity of commercial life in Gaul, first of the eager import of all manner of southern goods, then of the development of native exports in addition to the basic one of agricultural produce. This active trade was maintained by well-organized ports on sea and river, with large fleets to serve them, and by a fine road network. From earliest times merchants and craftsmen organized themselves into corporations not unlike medieval guilds, and as the state came more and more to concern itself with commerce these became important features in an increasingly regimented society. In sea-ports like Narbonne and Arles the most imposing corporations were those of the traders by sea, the powerful *navicularii*; at river ports there were the *nautae*, the river shippers, barge owners, etc.—generally men of substance and weight in their city. Rather less august are the corporations of *utricularii*, lightermen, boatmen, etc., and the *ratiarii* who were concerned in the building and use of rafts and may have worked ferries.

The *utricularii* seem to have been distinguished by their boats or rafts made buoyant by inflated skins, very useful in the navigation of the lagoons of the south. Such boats had been used by Hannibal when he crossed the Rhone. Many inscriptions of *utricularii* have been found, particularly in Provence, and at Narbonne and up the tributaries of the Rhone (e.g. at Vaison on the Ouvèze). One interesting case is an identity disc from Cavaillon, with on one side the inscription *Colle(gium) utri(clariorum) Cab(ellensium) L(uci) Valer(ii) Succes(si)*, and on the other a little model of an inflated skin.

Heavy traffic went as far as possible by river, and the *nautae* are extremely important all over Gaul and are known on the Rhone, Saône, Seine, Durance, Ardèche, Ouvèze, Loire, Aar, Moselle, Rhine. The *nautae* were responsible for the portage of goods from one river to another, so owned wagons as well as ships and barges. A shipper from Vannes has left an inscription at Lyons showing that he belonged to the corporation of *nautae* both of the Loire and the Saône.

There were also corporations of hauliers—*helciarii*, whose painful task it was to tow barges upstream, and some attractive sculptures show them at work. Sidonius writes of the boatmen he heard singing as they towed their cargoes through Lyons.

Some attempt has already been made to show the routes followed by the main exports of Gaul. A little more must now be said of imports. Of some luxuries there is no trace, save for occasional mention in literature, but we may remember that silk garments still found their way to Gaul in the days of Sidonius Apollinaris and that barbarians as well as Roman noblemen eagerly snapped them up. The import of works of art was a very profitable business in the days of prosperity and along with this went the import of marbles of all sorts for the decoration of buildings. Much Carrara marble is known in Gaul. At Aix polychrome pavements include marble from Carrara (white), Siena (yellow) and Italian cipollino (streaky white and green) as well as local porphyry. The orchestras of the recently excavated theatre and odeum at Lyons are gaily paved with a variety of coloured marbles from Italy, Greece and Egypt. Forty different kinds of marble have been collected from Roman monuments at Trier. Numbered also among the imports were papyrus, the paper of the day, eastern textiles, spices, ivory, gems and skilled slaves.

The attempt in the late empire to keep the state alive by nationalizing its essential industries broke down under the accumulated weight of invasions and internal disorder. The communications of the empire were rendered increasingly hazardous by this unrest, and large-scale inter-provincial commerce was the first to suffer. It was, however, possible for enterprising individuals to carry on, and they turned more and more to luxury trades—to transporting valuable wares which did not take up too much space or weigh too much. The large-scale cargoes were confined more and more to meeting the needs of the public corn supply. The late-empire trade of which we know anything is therefore mainly concerned with ivories, jewellery, silks, glass, and wines.

VIII

ART

SCULPTURE

The phrase 'Roman provincial art' does not inspire. It suggests mediocrity, a slavish copying of standard models which only varies with the degree of technical incompetence of the craftsman. If we only glance at the art of Roman Gaul we can but agree that there is all too much truth in this, but when we look closer we find plenty to interest us. Under its apparent sameness there are currents and cross-currents to be detected, of great interest in the history of the province, and occasionally not without significance for the art-historian. At times we find local trends that can even aspire to the description of a 'school'; sometimes we find traces of a skill and feeling which transcend mere craftsmanship.

We may usefully begin by asking two questions. First, what is there to be found of the old Celtic art whose exuberant decoration delights us on such objects as the fourth-century B.C. Lorraine flagons in the British Museum or the helmet from Amfreville in the Louvre, and second, by what channels did Roman imperial art reach Gaul?

Celtic art is almost wholly decorative. It was derived, on the one hand from primitive geometric patterns, and on the other from the influences of Greek and Eastern art. Greek vases and Etruscan bronzes had been brought to the northern peoples as early as the sixth century B.C., and the Celts took over their decorative motifs, like palmettes and tendrils, imitated them, and then moulded them into something quite different.

In Gaul this art was at its best in the fourth and third centuries B.C., when the continental Celts had mighty princes and none could withstand them. In the last two centuries B.C., however, Gallic society became insecure and there was a distinct falling off. A civilized art of a dominant people, like the Romans, had the dice loaded in its favour, but there was, too, the general decline in inspiration and in wealth in Gaul. In one respect, however, this statement needs qualification. Indications have been coming to light with increasing frequency of late that in the south—that is, in the area under the influence of the Greek city of Massilia and its colonies—the Celtic artists were developing a new phase of their art and were beginning to turn their attention to sculpture and the representation of the human figure. A few sculptured heads are known in and on the borders of Narbonensis, where Celt, Ligurian, Iberian and Greek met. The cross-legged statues found in the Celto-Ligurian sanctuary of Roquepertuse belong to the Greek period; the bust of a warrior found at Grézan (Gard) is dated to about 150 B.C., which is also the generally accepted date for the remarkable series of sculptures found at the Saluvian oppidum of Entremont, which was subdued by Sextius in 124 B.C. These sculptures include groups of what must be representations of severed heads, a reminder of the Gallic custom reported by Posidonius, who states that the Gauls severed the heads of the vanquished and nailed them on their doors.

A magnificent statue of a Gallic warrior (now headless) dated to the beginning of the Roman period, was found at Mondragon (Vaucluse), and of the same period must be a warrior in a coat of mail from Vachères (Basses-Alpes). The skill and the will to create works of sculpture were thus not wanting among the Gauls of the south, and there are isolated instances of Celtic sculpture in the north.

With the *Pax Augusta* the flood of imperial art surged up the province of Narbonensis. Celtic art, slowly feeling its way in a medium hitherto quite foreign to the native genius, was engulfed and all but disappeared, though it was not entirely blotted out, as we shall see later. But

it could not make headway against the sheer bulk of the
new art, all the more as sculpture was reinforced with
architecture.

It is sad, but true, that art and economics are closely
combined. An artist must eat, and therefore he has to
earn his daily bread just as a labourer must. Daily
bread, and indeed cake, must have been plentiful in the
Augustan age for every man in Gaul who could chip
stone. If he had any semblance of skill in rendering
figures, then his fortune was made. But he had to supply
what his patrons demanded, and he was no longer free to
develop an art of his own.

First of all there were the official monuments and
buildings set up to commemorate the glories of the
Imperial House, whose remains to-day make a visit to
Provence one of the most rewarding journeys anybody
interested in the Roman Empire can make. The sheer
labour involved in their production excites our admira-
tion and wonder, but there is also their lavish decoration
to consider. Who carved these endless imperial statues,
trophies, mythological scenes, cornices, capitals, inscriptions? Their erection must have been closely supervised
by Italians, and we may assume that a certain number of
artisans came from Italy to the Province for the express
purpose of working on them.

The adornment of the colonies of Caesar was under
way before Augustus was secure in the saddle. The
earliest of these monuments remaining are two or three
triumphal arches, or portions thereof. Of the 'Arcus
Mirabilis', probably the first of the series, which still
stood at Arles during the Middle Ages, there are only a
few fragments now in the museum, but these show its
quality. Next in age is the arch at Saint-Rémy, outside
Glanum. The richness of its decoration can be judged
from the beautiful scroll-work, with flowers and fruits, of
its archivolts. On its south face are male and female
captives, standing bound. The most notable arch is that
of Orange, which is dated to the Caesarian age, or

immediately after. It stood outside the west gate of the colony and has three passages with fine coffered vaults. Its decoration has much in common with another arch at Pola, in Cisalpine Gaul, and some of the same artists may have been employed on both, but among the sculptors at Orange there were certainly local men. The arch has elaborate sculptures, and was originally crowned with a group of bronze statues. On the friezes are depicted battles of Gauls and Romans. The surfaces above the smaller gateways are covered with arms and armour of Celtic character. There are Celtic helmets, and ensigns, the Celtic trumpet (*carnyx*), and shields closely resembling British examples decorated with spirals, birds or animals, and some inscribed with names such as Mario, Sacrovir, Dacurdo, Boduacus. One is inscribed *Boudillus avot* (made by Boudillus), which has led to the belief that a Celtic artist worked on this part of the monument. One or two severed heads are also displayed, which may betray a Celtic hand.

The attic above is filled with naval trophies, prows, tridents, anchors, masts, etc., commemorating Caesar's victory over Massilia. Above these are two faces of an altar with implements of sacrifice, perhaps symbolizing the ceremonies of laying out the colony. On the sides of the arch are standard trophies of trees from which hang arms and armour, with captives kneeling beside them. A noteworthy technical feature of the set trophies is the deep groove cut in the stone round the figures (see p. 167).

These commemorative arches set the seal upon the conquest of Gaul by a victor who had no compunction about celebrating his victory. The erection of a trophy sprang from the ancient custom, in which the arms of the slain on a field of battle were piled up and offered to the gods. The heap might be raised round a tree on which were suspended arms and armour. In time it became customary to erect permanent memorials of great victories, and on these would be carved representations of the trophy proper, the tree and associated arms, and along with this captives would be shown. Domitius and Sextius erected trophies and temples after their victories; Pompey erected a monument *in summo Pyrenaeo*, where the coast road crosses the mountains. Of all these no trace remains.

In the hills above Monte Carlo the trophy erected by Augustus to commemorate his victories over the tribes of the Alps has long been a familiar landmark. In recent years houses of the village of La Turbie built against it have been cleared away and the monument reinforced and, as far as possible, restored. In its heyday it was a huge structure some 50 metres in height resting on a square base whose sides measured 32·50 metres. It was built round the usual core of rubble and mortar, but internal staircases led to the upper storeys. The lower storey was over 12 metres in height and bore on its west side an inscription, once copied by Pliny, of which the greater part has been recovered and replaced. This enumerates forty-four Alpine tribes subdued under the auspices of Augustus. At each end of the inscription were sculptured trophies.

Next came a series of marble-coated offsets, above which rose the circular colonnade, of twenty-four columns, 9 metres high, and above them triglyphs and metopes. The walls of the monument within the colonnade were provided with niches in which statues were set. A head of Drusus belonging to one of these has been found.

Above the colonnade came a stepped pyramidal section surmounted by a large pedestal supporting a bronze statue, a small fragment of whose drapery was found wedged high up on the ruin. The statue was probably one of Augustus, below which, on either side, were two captives. This view fits in with what is known of other great Roman monuments and also with a legend of St. Honoratus, who is said to have visited the *Tropaeum*, or Tower of the Giant, as it was called; for the Giant Apollo had raised the tower by magic and set on top of it an idol and the two demons Beelzebuth and Matafellon, in whom we may recognize Augustus and the captives. Needless to say the saint took prompt measures for their destruction.

This enormous monument was built with stone quarried near at hand and ornamented with Carrara marble. It is the most complete of all remaining Roman monuments of the type. Its present state, carefully but not over restored, is shown in fig. 45*b*.

Another Augustan trophy stood just outside the western confines of the Province, in the *Civitas* of the Convenae, at Saint-Bertrand-de-Comminges. Here the excavators had the good fortune to discover some of the statues associated with the trophy. They were set up on a large rectangular monument, 25 by 14·60 metres, in a special enclosure at the east end of the forum. In the centre was the tree-trunk bearing arms and armour and further decorated with the prow of a ship. On either side were groups of captives. The most beautiful are figures of a young girl and a youth. The head of the youth is missing, but the girl's has been preserved. She wears a torc, which makes her a symbolic figure of *Gallia capta*. This trophy is taken to represent the victories of Augustus by land and sea.

There was now a considerable Italian population in Narbonensis, but plenty of Celts remained, and the wealthy men among them hastened to acquire the outward appurtenances of Roman civilization. They purchased works of art and choice furniture and tableware from Italy and farther east, and their houses were decorated in the manner in vogue in Italy.

One factor which helped the spread of ancient art-forms was the use of copy-books with pictures of favourite models. There is ample evidence that a travelling craftsman, whether he was a tombstone artist or a mosaic-worker, took with him a series of drawings from which he worked for his clients.

There are two technical points seen on many of the sculptured monuments of the south of France. One is the method of carving the figures out of stonework already carefully dressed and coursed; this is found in the Arch and Mausoleum at Saint-Rémy, on the arch at Orange, on the monument of Biot (an early trophy, fragments of which are in the Antibes museum), and elsewhere. It is a feature of the first century B.C. and becomes rarer under Augustus.

The other feature is the deeply incised line round figures in relief. It occurs on most of the early monuments mentioned above, and on a number of humbler tombstones at Narbonne, etc. It is also known in some Ionian sculpture, and scholars have thought that here may be some old Greek mason's tradition lingering on in the far west. A recent, less romantic view is that these incisions are simply guide lines to help the less skilful workers.

It is very difficult to make definite statements about this Greek influence in the art of Gallia Narbonensis, for imperial art was strongly imbued with Hellenism and itself inevitably brought much that was Greek to Gaul. There are, however, some monuments which show that the Romano-Hellenistic art was reinforcing a Greek element already present. The theatre of Arles furnishes examples. Each storey was surmounted by an architrave with triglyphs and metopes on the outside, above which ran a frieze with scroll pattern and a cornice. A typically Roman theatre is not thus decorated, and it is plausible to think that the Roman colonists found it convenient to employ masons who were familiar with the Greek way of doing things. The fine quality of the stonework all over the old Province suggests a well-established tradition of meticulous workmanship.

Inside the theatre of Arles a collection of fine imported sculpture was lovingly gathered together by successive generations of Arelatensians. Among them stood a statue of Augustus and two altars to Apollo, equal to anything of the same type in the empire and with the grace and lightness of the very best period. Arles theatre was destined to be a treasure trove for works of art and a quarry for marble during the Middle Ages and Renaissance.

It had many not unworthy rivals. Vienne must once

M

have been a city of great magnificence, but it has been systematically plundered and many of its finest relics have been taken away, among them the crouching Venus now in the Louvre. For Vaison, as for Arles, copies of Greek masterpieces of the fifth and fourth centuries B.C. were purchased by rich patrons.

The rich cosmopolitan merchants and successful freedmen of Narbonne decorated the city with a baroque lavishness different from the more restrained and dignified taste of Arles and its neighbours. Among the fragments of Narbonne sculptures there is a superabundance of ornament, which reflects a desire to be impressive at all costs. Narbonne has produced a large and interesting series of tombstones of the first century, including some following a favourite Italian type which is carved with scenes from the daily life of the deceased. We are reminded of Trimalchio's instructions for his tomb: "Put ships in full sail on the monument, and me sitting in official robes on my official seat". Several Narbonese tombstones have reliefs of the ships which meant so much to the citizens; one ship is being loaded; among other scenes there is one showing a school. The robust but rather heavy art of Narbonne had great influence in Aquitania, and especially in Bordeaux in the fruitful soil of a similar commercial community. Bordeaux monuments show scenes of daily life of high quality, including what seems to be a dispute before a magistrate, and one of woodmen hauling a log (fig. 42a).

A large art collection was found in the enormous villa at Chiragan on the borders of Gallia Narbonensis. The great majority of the many busts of gods and emperors are of Carrara marble, though some, including a particularly lovely head of Venus, are of Parian marble from Greece and some work in the local Pyrenaean marble is to be found. A long line of owners of the villa must have taken pride in assembling the collection, for there are heads of emperors of the first three centuries.

Imperial policy and imperial bounty dowered most of

the chief towns of Gallia Comata with the usual gamut of temples, altars, triumphal arches. Most notable of all was the altar of Rome and Augustus at the Confluence, erected in 12 B.C., and thus just preceding the Ara Pacis of Rome (p. 101).

The second focal point of Roman art in Gaul was the military and romanizing area of the Rhineland. Here there is no wealth of magnificent works of art comparable with those which the south affords, but the way in which Roman influence worked and spread can be traced even more clearly.

Much of this art came direct from Italy, but there were not wanting links with Gallia Narbonensis, as is shown by the Jupiter Column of Mainz. It was set up by Q. Julius Priscus and Q. Julius Auctus, whom we may take to be Gallic merchants, in honour of Jupiter and of the emperor Nero, and the names of the sculptors, Samus and Severus, are stated. They are generally regarded as south Gauls who had come to work in the Rhineland, and there is much grace and skill in their work. The base and shaft of the 9·14 metre-high column are covered with figures of gods and goddesses, among them Jupiter, Minerva, Fortuna and Vulcan, all of them very Roman in character and treatment. The foot and thunderbolt of the bronze statue which stood on top were also found.

In the train of the great armies that were based on the Rhine from the time of Drusus came all imaginable sorts of workers, among them masons who could make tombstones of the kind with which the legionary had been familiar in his native land, and many of these are still to be seen in Rhenish museums. A common type is the full-length figure of the legionary, in his uniform, carrying his weapons. The cavalryman also had his own favourite tombstone, in which he was shown mounted on his horse, which sometimes would be galloping over the body of a fallen foe.

About the time of the Flavians the predominant fashion in tombstones came to be that of the funerary repast, with the dead person on a couch beside a table on which the meal is laid out. Sometimes other members of the family or slaves are also shown. This type remained popular to the end of the pagan empire.

The headquarters building of Mainz had crudely sculptured figures of captives chained together, and of legionaries, all far too short in proportion to their breadth. There is a somewhat more graceful and sophisticated female prisoner, but taken as a whole, these sculptures reflect a crude but powerful legionary art, in no way comparable with the lovely figures on the Jupiter Column.

It is possible to identify certain Rhenish tombstones as coming from the same workshops, and we can follow the products of these workshops into the neighbouring, more purely Gallic background, for the Gauls took to this new way of commemorating their dead, and sculptured tombstones for civilians became increasingly common. We may believe that the masons working for the legions were ready also to work for the rich Gauls, but native workers also learnt the trade. Thus in the course of the second century what may justly be described as independent schools of sculpture grew up among the Treveri and neighbouring tribes, and that at Neumagen at least produced work which can take its place among the fine arts.

The course of the development of this art can in some cases be traced. The drapery of some first-century work at Arlon seems identical with that in a group of monuments in the Rhineland, which have been ascribed to a single workshop. The stone is local, however, so it is to be presumed that an artisan from the Rhenish workshop was sent to carve the tombstone for the Gaul who ordered it.

The funerary art of north-eastern Gaul became outstandingly successful in depicting scenes from the life of the deceased, his business and his recreations. The cloth merchant tells the story of his trade, the wine merchant likes to show his barrels of wine on their way to the consumer by land or water; we are shown scenes in homes, shops, markets or schools, on the road or on the river.

This genre-sculpture is one of the most fascinating products of Roman Gaul. The phenomenon is not confined to Gaul, and it was certainly not invented there, but in no other province is this type of funeral relief so freely used or used with such gusto. It seems to fit in admirably with the great commercial activity which burst out all over the province. Here is a nation of merchants who delight in their manifold if prosaic achievements and enjoy commemorating them, and we cannot but be reminded of the merchants of the sixteenth-century Netherlands and their liking for paintings of the ordinary life of office or household. These Gallo-Roman reliefs are of the greatest interest, though generally more, it must be confessed, as historical documents than as art. Artistic merit, however, is also not lacking.

Their adoption coincides with the development of the funeral monument. The rich merchants of Belgic Gaul were not long content with the simple stele, or single narrow stone. There was already a tradition of elaborate burial-mounds among the Belgae, as the great tumuli of the first century along the Roman roads near Tirlemont and Cortil-Noirmont in Belgium show. The Roman custom of raising great mausolea therefore made an immediate appeal. Monuments of this sort offered an ideal ground for scenes from the life of the deceased; the most famous example, the Igel Column, still stands where it was erected in the early third century, a few miles outside the city of Trier. The sandstone monument 23 metres high, belonged, we learn from the inscription, to the Secundinii, a rich family of cloth merchants, and must have stood on their estate. Its central relief shows two men, with a youth between them, while other members of the family are shown in medallions behind. The rest of the sculptures depict scenes from the life of the family, interspersed with mythological themes (fig. 39a).

The pyramidal top of the monument is surmounted by a group of the rape of Ganymede, while in the gables below are the sun god, the moon goddess, Mars and Rhea

Silvia, the rape of Hylas. The attics show cloth being examined, a two-wheeled carriage passing a stone marked in leagues (cf. p. 35), tenants paying rent, and Eros and a griffin. The frieze below has a meal, tenants bringing gifts, a kitchen scene, and pack-animals carrying bales of cloth over a hill. On the base panels are a scene in a cloth shop, a loaded cart, cloth-making and bales being corded. Dolphins, Cupids, a boat being hauled upstream, complete the tale, except for mythological scenes in the chief panels of the three subsidiary sides.

Similar monuments were an outstanding feature of the land of the Treveri and the Mediomatrici. The finest sculptures we have are those of the little town of Neumagen (Noviomagus) on the Moselle, which were torn up and used in the late third century town walls. Our knowledge of the 'school' of Neumagen, as of the 'school' of Arlon, comes from the stones recovered from the fortifications.

Arlon and Neumagen had followed Rhenish fashions in the first century, but a century later they had gone their own way. The rich proprietors who liked elaborate monuments encouraged the artists. As time passed various styles succeeded one another. About the middle of the second century draperies with delicate and abundant folds were popular. A reaction from this is the more solid style which predominated from about 180 to 190 in both Neumagen and Arlon (fig. 42b). The figures of this style are strong and solid, with very few folds in their heavy garments. It includes the school scene of Neumagen and the fishing scene of Buzenol. Closely following this are the Neumagen boats of the early third century (fig. 41c). Another style of the third century is to be seen in the somewhat elongated figure of the Satyr of Arlon, or the monument to a cloth merchant called the *Pilier du Drapier*, which at times calls to mind the long, graceful lines of Gothic sculpture. It may also be seen in a series of monuments at Sens. These sculptures were originally brightened up with paint, or which traces remain here and there, such as the pale green background to one of the Neumagen banquet scenes.

These scenes of daily life are not confined to north-east Gaul. A careful study of the sepulchral monuments would reveal some other strongly-marked schools. This is notably the case in Bordeaux, where even a casual examination can detect a strong individuality in the monuments. The portrait of a bald carpenter, roughly but powerfully hewn, is but one of a rich series of tomb-stones (fig. 41*b*).

The sculptures of Sens include not only gracefully draped portrait statues, but some excellent daily life scenes, in the local stone, and elsewhere in the north-central region of France there is much fine work which would repay further study.

The pillar-like monument in Gallia Belgica has its counterpart in the tower tombs of Narbonensis and Aquitania. The finest of these is the Saint-Rémy one, but there are many other tall monuments all over Aquitania, commonly called *piles*. Unhappily they have all been reduced to their rubble cores, but museums of neighbouring towns often contain sculptures which can be ascribed to them.

It is not only in funerary sculpture that we see how in the middle of the second century Gallo-Roman life had settled down and become fused with that of the Roman world in general. Everywhere there were large, richly ornamented buildings, temples, baths and so forth, covered with lively and exuberant sculptures. Examples regarded as belonging to this period are the temple of Champlieu, the baths of Sens, the Porte Noire of Besançon. The stele of the god Cernunnos at Reims illustrates the combination of the classical and the Celtic, with the graceful classical gods, Apollo and Mercury, on either side of the antlered but amiable-looking Celtic deity. The mythology of the classical world was becoming increasingly familiar to the provincials (fig. 47*a*).

Mediterranean works of art were appreciated in the north and west as in the south. Two very different imports are the torso of an Amazon found in the Barbara baths at Trier, and an extraordinary Minerva, or, rather, Athena, found at Poitiers. The latter is a creditable copy, in Carrara marble, of an archaic Greek statue of sixth-century type, which reminds us that the ancients, like ourselves, had the works of art of many centuries to copy at will, and that the archaic had its vogue from time to time with them, as with us.

An art type found predominantly in north-eastern Gaul is the Jupiter and Giant column. On its four-sided plinth were carved figures of gods and goddesses; next usually came an eight-sided stone bearing the planetary deities of the days of the week on seven sides and an inscription to Jupiter on the eighth. From this rose a column, often carved with a fish-scale pattern, on the top of which was a group of a god on horseback upheld by a crouching monster—a giant, with serpents' or fishes' tails instead of feet. These columns seem to be an imported art form, or group of art forms, adapted to local beliefs, and their artistic ancestry can be plausibly traced back to north Italy and Etruria, where the fish-tailed monster and the galloping warrior are not uncommon themes.

As might be expected, the strongest feeling for the Celtic past is to be detected in the images of Celtic divinities thinly disguised under classical forms, or not disguised at all. Many are exceedingly crude. Three strange, neckless heads at Chorey near Beaune recently described (fig. 50b), with their fringe of hair and prominent eyes, show the persistence of the Celtic traditions, and are the more interesting because of parallel cases known in Britain at Towcester and Corbridge.

It has been suggested that Romanesque sculptors derived ideas from the surviving sculptures of the picturesque, bizarre native gods, rather than from the more sober classical gods, and that Sucellus and Cernunnos persist in the underworld of the medieval artists' imagination as they do in folklore.

The Pyrenaean valleys have a unique series of tombstones. The bust of the deceased, sometimes extremely primitive, is usually shown in an arched niche, with a background decorated with geometric ornaments rooted in the religious conceptions of the region. Allied designs are found in the south Pyrenaean valleys, and we may therefore recognize in them survivals of Iberian ideas. The ornaments include circles, semi-circles, swastikas, crosses or daisies in a circle, stars, seven-petalled roses and the like. The most lively of all these sculptures is the funeral stele of Agassac: a female figure, distantly derived from the Nereids of Narbonese sculpture, rides through a sky studded with Pyrenaean solar symbols, accompanied by gambolling sea-monsters. This stone was known locally as the *pierre blanche* and was believed to possess the power to ward off thunderstorms and hail. A more striking contrast to the decorous imperial monument in the neighbouring Saint-Bertrand-de-Comminges would be hard to imagine (fig. 48).

Sculptured sarcophagi became fashionable with the spread of inhumation during the second and third centuries. The early ones are mostly imports: the Greek east exported ready decorated sarcophagi to Rome and the west. Such are the two examples in Parian marble found at Saint-Médard-d'Eyrans near Bordeaux and now in the Louvre. The famous second-century sarcophagus of Hippolytus at Arles is claimed by some authorities to have been sculptured by Greeks in an Arlesian workshop. Whether this is so, or whether it arrived ready made, it shows the powerful external influences still coming into Gaul during the second century. Many sarcophagi were made at Arles and other Gallic centres. They tend, for subjects, to follow a limited number of standard copies and lack the variety of the daily life themes. An attractive change from the endless mythological scenes is the beautiful and simple sarcophagus of Julia Tyrania, priestess of Isis, whose musical instruments are carved on the sides: there is her lyre, her guitar with its plectrum, a syrinx, a water-organ and her music-book.

These sarcophagi are less often preserved farther north, but they do occur. A very celebrated one, perhaps third-century in date, is the so-called sarcophagus of Jovinus, at Reims. This again is a scene of Hippolytus going hunting and is in many respects similar to one in the Louvre from Italy, depicting a hunting-scene, so it is probably an import. What is particularly interesting is that this sarcophagus was never lost, but was always preserved in a church at Reims, so that its work must have been familiar to the medieval sculptors. There is another with a hunting scene from Saint-Etienne-de-Déols (Indre) which was believed to have power to cure childish ailments. It stood in a church, and a hole had been made in the floor under it, so that children could be made to crawl through it. If they did this three times and also drank a potion containing some marble dust scraped off the sarcophagus their mothers could rest assured of their recovery.

Arles was in close touch with Rome during the later empire, and its sarcophagi show very close resemblance to those of Rome. Greek imports had now dropped out and the workmanship is Italian in character, probably influenced by Italian artists who had come to Arles in the train of Constantine and his successors. We now get Christian and biblical themes, the Good Shepherd, the crossing of the Red Sea, Noah's Ark, etc. Some of the work is of very lovely quality. Fig. 50a is the head of a young and beardless Christ taken from one of the scenes of New Testament miracles on the so-called *sarcophage des arbres*. It shows what beautiful sculpture the fourth century could still produce.

The strangest of all sarcophagi, and perhaps of all funeral monuments found in Gaul, is one now in the Leyden Museum, which was dug up at Simpelveld in Limburg. It is decorated with real life scenes, which are designed not to be a monument for the passer-by to admire, but to be company for the deceased, for they are carved inside the coffin, which is perfectly plain on the outside. The sculptures show the deceased lying on her couch, surrounded by various furnishings of her house, tables, glass jars, bronze vessels, and, finally, an impression of the exterior of the house itself (fig. 49). This sarcophagus is so far unique; it dates from the late second century and contained cremated remains, not a skeleton.

Another aspect of Gallo-Roman art which is now being more closely studied is the flowering of imperial Trier in the fourth century. Among works of the period 367–381 are about seventy herms, or busts, which were recovered from the villa at Welschbillig. This strange collection includes heads of various racial types, of philosophers, etc. Some of them have the Celtic coiffure, but they are all curious, highly conventional works, reflecting an eastern trend, if we may believe the authorities on the subject (fig. 50c). The symbols employed to decorate the popular lead sarcophagi are also predominantly eastern.

BRONZES AND OTHER METAL WORK

One important art has, unavoidably, left few traces, namely the monumental bronzes which played a big part in Gallo-Roman art, as in the art of other parts of the empire. Just a few remain to give a hint of their quality. They are so well done that no apology has to be made for them, and perhaps had we more we could make greater claims for Gallo-Roman art than most of the modest achievements in sculpture allow us to advance.

Some Celtic essays in bronze figure-work of pre-Roman period are recognizable. Human and animal figures began to appear towards the end, just as in sculpture. A strange bronze mask, found at Tarbes, may well be pre-Roman; and the cauldron from Gundestrup, Denmark, with its embossed gods and warriors, is generally dated to the first century B.C. The finest of the bronzes of the Roman period is a group from Switzerland which includes the head of a young Helvetian found at Prilly. The hair combed forward in front and straight down on the rather flat back of the skull is a characteristic feature of Gallic work. This way of arranging the hair became fashionable under Trajan, but it is found earlier among the Celts, and reappears again in the fourth century, in the Celtic provinces. (See fig. 41*d*.)

The Celt excelled in modelling animals; a series of interesting and often finely-executed beasts of the Roman period exists, among which are: the three-horned bull from Martigny, Switzerland; a fine statuette of a bear with a goddess (Dea Artio), also Swiss; the images of animal gods found in a sanctuary at Neuvy-en-Sullias (Loiret) (fig. 43*b*). The third group is cruder than the Swiss models, but if a remote sanctuary like Neuvy possessed such bronzes, we may be sure that many others of far higher quality were to be found in the great centres.

There are two other works of art which chance has preserved, a fine golden bust of Marcus Aurelius found in a drain at Avenches, and the silver portrait bust found in a house at Vaison, which give further hints of the wealth of works of art which must have disappeared (fig. 41*a*).

Bronze statuettes are to be found by the score in every Gallo-Roman museum of any size. Some of them are of very fine workmanship and come from the workshops of Italy or Alexandria. Others are native products and range through all degrees of skill or lack of it. They are almost all images of deities and their native origin is to be deduced from the symbol carried by the god or some other little peculiarity which distinguishes him from the purely classical type. Thus Jupiter often carries the Gallic symbol of the wheel. Fig. 43*a*, from the temple at the source of the Seine, shows a goddess in a Seine barge.

When we come to purely ornamental bronzework Celtic art is back in its old sphere and the sure-handedness of the Celt in decorative art is at once apparent. Examples of this have been noted above (pp. 152 ff.).

PAINTING

The art of painting certainly flourished in Gaul, as elsewhere, following the fashions in Rome, but few traces remain. It was usual to cover a wall with painted plaster, and if the owner could afford it the plain surface might be decorated with elaborate patterns or with naturalistic paintings. Augst has a fine painting of two men carrying an amphora, and there are some nice pieces at Strasbourg, but the most startling specimens are the portraits of ladies of the Constantinian House recently found under the Cathedral at Trier. One is identifiable as Fausta, wife of Constantine, and another is thought to be Helena, his mother. Their coiffures and diadems are very finely rendered. The piecing together of these and other paintings from over 50,000 plaster fragments is a miracle of patience and skill.

MOSAICS

Floor mosaics do not in general deserve a place among the arts. At their best, however, they attain real beauty. Even the most ordinary ones have the personal touch of the skilled mosaicists who travelled from place to place, armed with their copy-books, plying their far-from-easy trade. Not infrequently they put their name to their work, and some of them are therefore known to have been Greeks. We can be specially grateful to Sennius Felix of Puteoli for putting his town as well as his name on the large mosaic of Apollo, Daphne and hunting-scenes which he laid at Lillebonne in Normandy: *T Sen Felix C(ivis) Puteolanus.* His African apprentice also added his name: *Amor C(ivis) K(arthaginiensis) discipulus.*

Brive Museum (Corrèze) has an imported mosaic medallion showing Pan and a sleeping nymph. It measures 48 × 31 centimetres and was executed on a large tile. The tile bears the stamp of the *Figlinae Vocconianae,* a tileworks in the neighbourhood of Rome, where it was made in the time of Commodus.

Lyons Museum owns a magnificent series of local mosaics. One has a chariot race in full cry, and in the central medallion of another is the god Orpheus playing his lute, surrounded with forty-four panels, each containing a different animal or bird. This type of mosaic with a large number of small pictures was a great favourite. The amphitheatre had a great influence on mosaic design, and it is in depiction of animals that mosaic workers excelled. One found at Saint Romain-en-Gal (Rhône) has fifty compartments and fifty different animals, including the camel. Sometimes the small pictures constitute a rustic calendar of the changing work on the farm as the months go round.

The famous mid-second-century mosaic in the Nennig villa (p. 126) has panels showing scenes from the amphitheatre, including the musicians who were evidently part of the show, complete with water-organ and trumpet.

Perhaps one of the most attractive mosaics is a fragment at Boscéaz in Switzerland. Only a portion of the border remains, but it is one to give pleasure by modern standards, with its free and elegant drawings of a country cart drawn by oxen, with trees and peasants, all freely spaced (fig. 30). Another naturalistic example is a delightful medallion of a horse, dog and trees in the Trier Museum.

When the other arts declined in the fourth century, mosaic work continued to be widely popular and to develop a new magnificence. Mosaics became gayer than ever and were now brightened with cubes of brilliant blue and green glass, and used increasingly for wall decorations. The Basilica of Trier was once richly decorated, and fragments of gilded mosaic cubes were found in some of its niches.

Sidonius lets himself go in some verses describing the glories of a church built by his friend Bishop Patiens in Lyons:

'High stands the church in splendour, extending neither to right nor left, but with towering front looking towards

the equinoctial sunrise. Within is shining light, and the
gilding of the coffered ceiling allures the sunbeams
golden as itself. The whole basilica is bright with diverse
marbles, floor vaulting and windows all adorned with
figures of most various colour, and mosaic green as a
blooming mead shows its design of sapphire cubes winding
through the ground of verdant glass.'

FIG. 30.   Mosaic at Boscéaz (Vaud, Switzerland): detail

IX

RELIGION

THE IMPERIAL CULT

On the first of August, 12 B.C., a great concourse assembled at the confluence of the Rhone and Saône to witness the consecration of the altar of Rome and Augustus, the symbol of the unity of the Celtic provinces within the empire and of their enjoyment of the *Pax Augusta* with the rest of the civilized world. Above the right bank of the Saône the new Roman city built on the old home of the god Lug looked down on the scene. The imperial Governor, Drusus himself, adopted son of Augustus, descended to the confluence to be one of the two leading figures in the ceremony. The other was the high priest of Augustus, C. Julius Vercondaridubnus, the ceremonial head of the imperial cult, chosen from among the leading Gauls. The sixty tribes of the Three Gauls had sent representatives to affirm their loyalty to the imperial house, and to join together in discussing the affairs of their provinces.

The altar was the provincial shrine, the symbolic centre of the life of the province, and the annual festival was henceforth to be a great national occasion. Many of the same people were there who would have been among the Druids at older gatherings. Gladiatorial shows and rhetorical contests took place, both greatly to the taste of the Gauls. Vercondaridubnus, the first high priest (*sacerdos*), was an Aeduan, and many of his successors are known to us from inscriptions.

Another such altar and another provincial council existed for Gallia Narbonensis, at Narbonne, but of this next to nothing is known. Yet another was the Ara

Ubiorum set up at Cologne by Drusus to be the religious centre for Greater Germany, and still maintained after the attempted conquest had failed.

The imperial cult in its early days was not a religion properly so called, but its claims grew with the years. It was the outward sign of loyalty to the empire, and much of imperial prestige was bound up with it. Its organization was from the beginning regarded as a matter of considerable importance by the emperors, and there is no doubt that as time went on it bit deeply into the social, and even the religious life of Gaul.

The cult was not, of course, confined to the provincial festivals. In every Gallo-Roman town we find dedications to the reigning emperors, to their houses and to their deified predecessors. The *duumvirs* often held the imperial priesthood (flaminate) of their city, and there was also an office reserved for freedmen or the sons of freedmen, that of the *seviri Augustales*, which gave this section of society honorific representation in the life of the city—an honour for which they had to pay, in the way of the Roman world, by heavy donations towards the well-being and pleasure of their fellow-citizens.

The worship of the emperor was also twined into the fabric of more popular religion. The emperors were thereby being accepted as essentially divine and not merely objects of official loyalty. The title Augustus was incorporated into many local cults by being used as an epithet of some other god. A very popular cult of Mercurius Augustus flourished, especially in Narbonensis, whence it spread to Switzerland and other parts. Sometimes the emperor shares the healing qualities of the other deities, as in the cases of Aesculapius Augustus, and the Augusta Acionna of a sacred spring near Orleans. At Neuvy-en-Sullias, as Augustus Rudiobus, he shares the honours with Rudiobos the horse-god. The Celts have always thought highly of horses.

More sophisticated cults were also associated with the emperor, notably those of Cybele and Mithras, whose

N

supreme rites were coupled with vows for the safety of the imperial house.

THE OLYMPIANS AND THE OLD GODS

Wherever Roman or Italian soldiers went, there went their gods. The building of Roman colonies, in which it was customary to set up a capitolium, introduced the triad, Jupiter, Juno and Minerva. For the well-to-do, Romanizing Gauls, there was snob value in accepting these gods; for simpler folk here were new deities in attractive guise, who had moreover proved their superiority over the old gods in battle. To the polytheist of the ancient world a new god was always welcome and could readily be given a place in the scheme of things. It was easy to equate the new deity with an old one, to ascribe to Mercurius, for instance, an epithet which had belonged to his Celtic forerunner. Such assimilations were a familiar feature of the Roman empire. Gradually the assimilation became very close indeed, and we find many gods with classical names who have obviously grown much closer to their Celtic counterparts than to their Mediterranean prototypes. Thus the Mars of the non-military areas of Roman Gaul is very far removed from the Latin war god which he still remains to the army. He is, for instance, often invoked as a god of healing, which is an unusual role for the Mars of Rome. Mars was much worshipped in Narbonensis, between the Pyrenees and the Garonne, and in the land of the Treveri, where, at Trier, there was the important cult of the healing god, Mars Lenus.

The Roman state did not interfere in the religious practices of its subjects so long as they did not trespass on its preserves, so there was no question of imposing Italian religion on the Gauls. The Druids, however, had to go This sinister national priesthood had been too closely linked with the practice of human sacrifice, which is such a dark thread in the story of ancient Gaul, for even the Romans to stomach them. Also the political motive of uprooting a possible focus of subsequent rebellion was probably not lacking, though it is not directly mentioned. It is noteworthy, however, that such Druids as remained in A.D. 70 were quick to spread prophecies that the fall of Rome was imminent when they heard of the burning of the Capitol.

By the time of Caesar the Celts had begun to express their religious beliefs by making images of their gods, doubtless as a result of their contact with the classical world, and one of the most remarkable proofs of this is the famous silver bowl of the first century B.C. found at Gundestrup. On this one finds a strange mythological world, including a procession accompanied by a ram-headed serpent, approaching a giant figure, clearly a god, who is immolating a human victim by plunging him head first into a great jar.

This gives us a glimpse into the dark, backward abysms of Celtic religion which lie behind the classical façade of the *interpretatio romana*. This was the religion administered by the Druids whose suppression, or at least modification, was obviously one of the benefits of Roman rule. It is a matter of great interest to try to trace its survivals into the Roman period. Though it has its blood-thirsty side, there are numbers of beneficent deities, including numerous goddesses, who were intertwined so closely with the nature of the French countryside, its customs and its crops, that happily they were not all dislodged by classical importations, and some of them linger on in old superstitions to this day.

Lucan in his *Pharsalia* pauses to tell us something of the Gallic gods: how the ferocious Teutates, Esus and Taranis were appeased by human blood. A manuscript of the poem now in Berne preserves a few words of commentary by an ancient scholar: 'Mercurius is called Teutates in the Gallic tongue, and the Gauls appease him by plunging the head of the victim in a basin of water until he suffocates.' The ceremony on the Gundestrup cauldron, noted above, illustrates this all too vividly. A second commentator upon the same MS. added another note that Mars was Teutates, and that Mercury was Esus; that Taranis was the greatest celestial deity, to whom formerly human sacrifices had been offered, though under the Romans he was content with offerings of animals.

A study of the monuments suggests that there was no clear-cut functional distinction between the Celtic divinities of Gaul, so that no rigid equation with the occupants of the Greco-Roman pantheon was possible. The ancient marginal comments of the Berne manuscript are thus not contradictory, but complementary, for Teutates is both Mercury and Mars, just as Esus is both Mercury and Mars.

We are told by Caesar that Mercury was the god most worshipped by the Gauls, and this remained true of large parts of imperial Gaul, where nearly five hundred inscriptions to Mercury are known. Over a third of these appear to invoke an indigenous god in Roman dress, and under Mercurius is hidden the personality of the great god of the Gauls, sometimes called Teutates, sometimes called Esus. Mercury was also, according to Caesar, the god who in his day had the greatest number of images, and this is also true of great areas of Roman Gaul.

Here was a great god, far more dignified than the graceful messenger of the Olympians, and sometimes indeed depicted under very strange forms (see fig. 31). He was a god who reigned from mountains and hilltops, who watched over roads and commerce, who presided over springs, and who had power over the nether world. From his great temple on the Puy-de-Dôme (1463 metres) he looked down over the tumbled heights of the Massif Central, on to the fertile Limagne, and far away to the lands of the north. Here was found a dedication on a small tablet to Mercurius Dumias. The Arverni commissioned Zenodorus, a sculptor of Nero's day, to make a colossal statue of Mercury, but where it was erected is not known. Arverni far from home also remembered their great mountain and its presiding deity, and dedications to

Mercurius Arvernorum or Arvernorix have been found in the Rhineland.

Mercurius is to be met on other hills and mountains. Montmartre is Mons Mercurius (not Mons Martis), and a temple to Mercurius stood on the Donon, one of the chief heights of the Vosges.

Reims and Soissons lie towards the centre of a region that likes to depict the strength of its great deity by giving him three heads, or, more exactly, three faces. Fig. 31 is an example of this barbaric god in the form he generally assumes on Belgic altars. It is noteworthy that on this altar, as on many others, we find the ram's head and the cock so often associated with Mercury, and we are therefore justified

FIG. 31. Three-faced god from Soissons: ht. 60 cm.

in thinking that this deity is equated with Mercury. Statues of Mercury all over Gaul frequently have ram's heads as attributes.

Another three-faced god, a standing figure this time, was found underneath the Hotel Dieu in Paris, holding the ram-headed serpent in his left hand and the purse of Mercury in his right, while at his feet is what is probably the tortoise, another attribute of Mercury.

At Mavilly (Côte d'Or), however, the serpent with the ram's head is shown on an altar dedicated to Mars.

One of the most celebrated Gallo-Roman statues is the bearded Mercury of Lezoux (fig. 46a), a pleasant, elderly peasant, totally different from the lissom Mercury of the

Romans, but clearly Mercury by his winged hat as well as by the dedication *Mercurio et Augusto sacrum*. The second commentator on the Berne MS. noted above states: 'The Gauls believe that Esus is Mercury, or at least so he is worshipped by the traders'. Lezoux was one of the chief centres of the Gallo-Roman pottery trade, and on the back of this very statue is the inscription in Celtic: *Apronius ieuru sos (in?) Esu (n?)* which is believed to mean 'Apronius made this in honour of Esus'. Esus also appears on an altar in Paris as a forester cutting down a tree, above him being inscribed the name Esus. On the other side of the altar is a bull, and above him appear branches of a tree in which perch three cranes. The same figure of a forester chopping down a tree on which are three cranes is found on one side of an altar at Trier. The central part of this altar has a figure of the classical Mercury, who is, however, wearing the Celtic torc. An inscription at Cologne records an offering of two cranes to Mercury. The relationship therefore of Mercury, Esus and the cranes may be regarded as established.

The most majestic image we have of a real old Celtic god is the bearded deity, seated cross-legged in a Buddha-like posture, found at Reims. Antlers (now nearly all gone) spring from his forehead, he wears a torc round his neck and holds a cornucopia, sack or purse, from which pours forth a stream of coins. At his feet are a stag and a bull, and on either side of him stand the purely classical figures of Apollo and Mercury. In the cornice above him is a rat. This is obviously a great primitive god of many attributes, the dispenser of benefits, the emblem of strength and fertility and guardian of the nether world, with the rat, the animal of the underworld, above his portrait.

A similar relief was found at Vendoeuvres, but this time the central antlered figure is a youth or child and the two supporting gods stand on serpents which seem to have rams' heads. From near Autun comes a statuette of an antlered, cross-legged god holding two ram-headed serpents on his knees.

In all about thirty-one examples of the cross-legged deity are known, some in stone, some being bronze statuettes, and the majority come from the territory of Gallia Lugdunensis—the old Celtica—from the tribal country of the Arverni, Aedui and Senones. Their illustrious ancestry in Celtic iconography is shown by another of the chief figures, obviously a god, on the Gundestrup cauldron. The god in question is crowned with antlers, is cross-legged, has one torc round his neck and another in his right hand, and in his left hand holds by the neck a huge ram-headed serpent. An impressive but damaged head of the antlered god is carved on an altar found beneath Notre Dame in Paris. From his antlers hang torcs. We have only his head and shoulders, so do not know his pose, but, more valuable, we have his name— Cernunnos.

We have still to consider the Celtic Taranis, and here we are on firm ground, apart from the pointer in the Berne marginal notes that he was equated with Dis Pater on the one hand, and that he was god of war and of the sky and equated with Jupiter, on the other hand. The name Taranis, or close variants of it, occurs in five inscriptions, ranging from Chester to Dalmatia, two coming from the Rhineland and one from Provence. Among these the inscription to Jupiter Tarannarus confirms the identification.

Jupiter's cult was held in great favour in the second and third centuries in north-east Gaul, where one of the most important series of Gallo-Roman sculptures is that of the Jupiter and Giant columns. The columns are crowned with a group consisting of a deity, often in military garb, riding a galloping horse, supported by a strange monster with two serpents' tails instead of legs. The warrior sometimes carries the wheel, a primitive symbol of the sun, which supports his identification with Jupiter, and the columns are commonly dedicated to Jupiter Optimus Maximus and sometimes also to Juno

Regina. These columns seem to have been particularly popular in the country, and many were erected on the great domains. The interpretation which seems best to accord with what we know of Celtic religion is that the group shows Taranis in his dual aspect, as Jupiter, sky god and warrior, and also as Dis Pater, god of the underworld, from whom, Caesar says, the Gauls claimed to be descended. In the towns the cult of Jupiter was provided for in the capitolia.

The Dis Pater identification seems also implicit in the God with a mallet who is a common figure in Gallo-Roman iconography, especially in the Rhone Valley and in the land of the Mediomatrici. His name in some cases at least was Sucellus; this god is found with his consort Nantosuelta on altars at Sarrebourg, Metz, etc., he bearing a wallet, she a dovecote, while below them is their sacred bird, the crow.

The *interpretatio romana* did not of course end with Mercury, Mars and Jupiter. Caesar himself speaks of others, notably of Apollo. Apollo was specially welcome in his guise of a healing god. We find him presiding over springs to which no known therapeutic value attaches, such as the shrine of Apollo Moritasgus in Alesia, but he was also, as Apollo Grannus, the god of Aix-la-Chapelle. Grannus seems to have been an important Celtic healing god, and Grand (Ad Grannum) in the Vosges was one of his chief sanctuaries, where he delivered oracles as well as cured diseases.

A major Celtic deity associated with Apollo was Belenus, the god of the sun and the light. Many individuals known from inscriptions were called after him. The most interesting notice of his cult in Gaul is in a poem of Ausonius which mentions that the grandfather of Attius Patera, a professor at Bordeaux, had been a priest of Belenus in Bayeux.

Hercules, too, had his Celtic equivalents. The strangest is the Hercules Ogmios of whom the writer Lucian tells us. He was depicted as an elderly god, equipped as

Hercules, but drawing after him men fastened by chains which were attached to their ears and to the tongue of the hero. Lucian says that a Gaul explained to him that this was intended to show the power of eloquence, but it is now believed that Hercules here functioned as a god of the underworld, drawing men's souls after him.

The female divinities of the Gauls retained their identity on the whole more tenaciously than the male gods. The cult of the mother goddess—the earth, which brings forth all life and to which all life returns, perhaps the most ancient of religions—flourished throughout the Roman period. Here the religions of conquerors and conquered differed little. The protective female deity is found everywhere, and expresses the same underlying principle, though her name and form vary from place to place. The Gauls often worshipped mother-goddesses in groups of three, which fits in very nicely with classical conceptions of three Fates, or three Graces, and many images of these groups are known. They show certain local features; the Matronae of the Rhineland found in the German as well as in the Celtic districts generally consist of two older goddesses on either side of a younger one, the two elders wearing huge bonnets which may belong to some local costume. They hold cornucopiae, or baskets of fruits. A relief found at Trier shows the three-headed Celtic Mercury beneath the central goddess. Elsewhere the goddesses are called Matres, or Parcae, or Junones. Their names are sometimes very strange, especially in the Rhineland, where there are Alagabiae, Berhusiahenae, Hamavehae, to name but a few (fig. 47b).

Other matres are found in Narbonensis, and it would seem that the famous site of the Saintes Maries on the Rhone delta once had a sanctuary to these goddesses, as an inscription to the Junones Augustae indicates. It is noteworthy that the Maries number three: Mary-Jacoby, Mary-Salome and Mary-Magdalene.

The matres and other goddesses outlived official paganism and took refuge in the countryside as fairies and other creatures of folk-lore. The Latin *fata* (fates) have become *fadas* in Provence, *fades* in Gascony, *fayettes* elsewhere, and are sometimes seen in the moonlight, washing the garments they have woven; they live in springs or sacred trees, and sometimes they have serpents' tails.

Three fairies appeared to a certain Raimondin as he passed the fairy fountain in Poitou described by an English chronicler as the 'well of thursty gladnesse'. He married one of the three, the fairy Melusine, and became ancestor of the famous Lusignan family. Another group of fairies called *martines* seem to derive their name from the old Matronae, but they came to be regarded, by Christian prejudice, as malevolent spirits, and are the wicked godmothers of the stories.

Goddesses also occur in pairs or singly; some are of great importance. There is Nehalennia (probably Germanic) on the island of Walcheren, who had an important sanctuary to which sailors and merchants resorted. Goddesses protected the creatures of the forest, or helped the hunter, so that their identification with Diana the huntress and moon-goddess was obvious. So the Ardennes—Silva Arduinna—were the province of Diana Arduinna, and in the once Celtic land across the Rhine we find Diana Abnoba presiding over the Black Forest. It has been observed that Diana was the longest-lived of the pagan deities and that testimonials to her influence are found in many medieval sources. From Switzerland and the north-east comes a bear goddess, Dea Artio.

We also find female consorts of gods, and it is notable that while the god has generally adopted a Latin name, the goddess retains her Celtic one, an exception being the couple Sucellus and Nantosuelta already noted; we have Mercurius and Rosmerta, Mars and Ancamna, Apollo and Sirona.

Most interesting of all Celtic goddesses is Epona, goddess of horses. She is generally shown sitting sideways on a horse, and she may be holding a key—the key of the stable, or a whip. Sometimes she has two horses with her, and very often a hound or a foal runs alongside. She is shown in fig. 46b. She is indeed the only really Celtic deity who was exported to non-Celtic parts of the empire, whither she was carried by the Gallic troopers, to whom she was particularly dear. She was worshipped at the circus, and everywhere where horses went. Juvenal satirizes a consul who used to swear by Epona.

All over the Roman world reverence was wisely paid to the spirit of the locality—the *genius loci*. The genius of a city is frequently represented as a *tutela*, a guardian goddess. The most striking of these *tutelae* come from two western cities, Périgueux, where the goddess is Vesunna, and Bordeaux, where she is simply called Tutela on the inscriptions; Ausonius, however, refers to the sacred spring in the city of 'Divona, urbis genius', so perhaps Divona was the real name of the goddess.

ANIMALS, PLANTS AND OTHER GODS

We have already noticed the bear-goddess, Dea Artio, and the goddess of horses, Epona. It seems that in some cases the animals themselves were still worshipped, judging from the striking group of bronze statues of animals found at a temple at Neuvy-en-Sullias (Loiret); they include a stag god (fig. 43b), a horse god (Rudiobos) and a wild boar god. There is also the three-horned bull's head found in Switzerland. A passage in one of the martyrologies refers to the existence of a temple to a god Baco at Chalon-sur-Saône. An inscription to Baco has also been found in the town. It has been suggested that Baco may have been a wild boar god, and thus the source of the word bacon which the dictionaries tell us comes from Old French *baco.* Coming back from seductive fancy to sober reality, we have a name for one boar god, for his image was found on the Donon with the inscription *Surburo*. Among nature gods in general there is mention of a god of the Mistral, Circius, to whom Augustus built a temple while he was in Narbonensis, and in the

Pyrenees we find tree-worship and dedications to a Deus Fagus (god beech-tree) or to the Sex Arbores (six trees).

The association of cranes with the worship of Mercury has already been noticed (p. 188). It is to be observed that cranes occur on the Arch of Orange on a Gallic shield bearing the name Catus. Lug, the god of Lugudunum, may have been a crow or raven, and Sucellus and Nantosuelta had their sacred crow.

The veneration of sacred stones is extremely ancient the world over, and Gaul with its many strange megaliths, survivals of a long-distant past, shared the cult. Stones are particularly associated with fertility rites. They were often allotted to saints in the early Christian period, to dissociate them from their previous incumbents. A menhir carved with figures of Mercury and other deities was found at Kernuz (Finistère), while a small temple appears to have been built round another at Triguères (Loiret).

ORIENTAL CULTS

The spread of the worship of oriental deities which is so marked a feature of the religious development of the second and third centuries A.D. is as noticeable in Gaul as in other parts of the empire. Their infiltration had already begun in the first century, but it was in the second century that they really gained a hold.

Isis the Egyptian was an early comer, perhaps too early to be prominent among all the Roman deities arriving with the conquerors. Her worship was popular at one time in Narbonensis, especially at Nîmes with its Egyptian link, and in Arles, and is found elsewhere, as in the dedication at Soissons to Isis of Ten Thousand Names, but it could not stand against the powerful competition of Cybele, the Great Mother of the Gods, for she was a female deity specially fitted to be made welcome in Gaul —far more so than the over-specialized, if attractive ladies of Olympus. Cybele was a goddess for whom the *interpretatio romana* could work without strain, for she was in truth, despite her strange ritual, the same as the humble mother goddesses, the matres of the crops and the springs, already since man's infancy at home in Gaul. If she made this appeal to the most ancient religious instincts of the Gauls, she also suited Roman officialdom from her long and close connection with the Roman state. So she is one of the central figures of the last consolidation of Gallo-Roman paganism, official and personal. Inscriptions to her are plentiful and show that she was established in Lyons by 160.

There was also the popular Mithras, the Unconquered Sun—Sol Invictus—a god particularly dear to military men. He is, of course, found in Gaul, but it is in the Rhineland that he seems to have been especially popular. He was established there early in the second century, and was worshipped in sunken temples, recalling the mysterious caves associated with his myths. One of these was excavated at Koenigshoffen in Alsace, and most of the remains re-erected in the Strasbourg Museum. Worshippers entered down a flight of steps which led into an entrance hall in which were basins for ceremonial ablutions. Then they stepped down again into the temple proper, with its benches running along either side. The chief object was the long formal sculpture or *typus* of the god slaying the bull, surrounded by figures of gods or animals associated with his myth, in particular the two figures Cautes and Cautopates, symbolizing respectively day and night or life and death, the one with torch held aloft, the other with torch held downwards. This handsome sculpture had been deliberately broken into fragments by the Christians, who regarded Mithras as a special enemy. Another interesting item of the temple paraphernalia was a hollow altar inside which a man could sit to emit mysterious noises or perhaps oracles at appropriate moments or where a lamp might be placed.

All these oriental cults furnished plenty of entertainment for their votaries. They provided for corporate worship, but their members had to go through various forms of initiation before being admitted; they were graded according to the stages they had passed. They thus enjoyed the psychological advantages of feeling marked off from other men. It has been abundantly shown how dear religious gatherings were to Gauls. So here was another reason why the Oriental cults should be welcome.

The worship of Isis was enlivened by music, and the rattle of the sistrum accompanied her processions. Mithras had his strange grottos, as noted above, with their cult pictures in an art as formalized as the Christian groups depicting the Crucifixion. The Great Mother had her symbols, her hierarchy—her priests and priestesses, known to her followers as Father or Mother. There were the *archigalli*, who might also be prophets and deliver oracles, and humbler ranks charged with various offices in her numerous ceremonies. Among the most colourful of these were the processions bearing the image of the goddess in her sacred carriage. The greatest glory was attained by those of the faithful who submitted to the *taurobolium*, the baptism with bull's blood, which assured them a second birth and a place in the halls of immortality. This revolting but edifying ceremony was undergone with great satisfaction by numerous Gallo-Romans who recorded the event in inscriptions. Apparently a shallow trench was dug and covered over with planks, between which gaps were left. The worshipper went down into this trench and the animal was slain above, the blood being allowed to trickle down through the holes on to him or her. It he could not afford the *taurobolium* he might have the baptism of ram's blood, the *criobolium*. Or he might like to be on the safe side and have both.

BURIAL CUSTOMS

In burial customs, as in other matters, we see the essential nearness of the Celt to the Italian. The Romans of the Republic practised, in the main, cremation, though there were always certain families who clung to an ancient tradition of inhumation. Both rites are met in

Gaul before the conquest, the Celtic tribes being given to inhumation, the Belgic to cremation. In the strong tide of early Romanization cremation tended to prevail, but the Gauls no less readily adopted the changing fashion of the third century, when inhumation became the practice.

After cremation the ashes of the deceased were placed in urns, generally of earthenware, though glass urns became popular in the second century. Beside the urn might be put a jug for drink, a comb, a coin and other offerings at will. Poorer people buried the urns direct in the earth. They might, however, be placed in wooden, tile or stone chests. Over the grave those who could afford it raised tombstones, in which every degree of elaboration is found, and some interesting local variations, for instance the stone cists of the Vosges region, which are constructed in the shape of a hut with sharply pointed gables pierced with small doors. The urn is placed inside the little house, which may be ornamented and which stood above ground level. Luxembourg Museum also has some excellent examples of house urns.

The classical type of tower-like monument derived from the mausoleum was brought to Gaul early in the Roman period, and won widespread popularity among the very wealthy (see p. 171). On the other hand, some rich men preferred to erect funerary chapels with burial vaults below, which might be elaborately painted. *Columbaria*— that is, monuments with a large number of niches, to serve as burial-places for groups of persons who could not afford their own family monuments—are found in Gaul as elsewhere.

Roman law forbade the burial of the dead within a town, so cemeteries grew up along the roads leading out of towns, and their location has often proved most valuable in determining the limits of a town.

One group is of special interest to students of Roman Britain. These are large round barrows raised along some of the main Roman roads in Gallia Belgica. Their contents show that they are the burial-places of rich

Belgae of the first century A.D., and they have produced some of the finest treasures of the Brussels Museum. They invite comparison with the barrows of Bartlow Hills and Royston, both in Belgic territory, and are clearly the survivals of some ancient custom. Very few tumuli of the Roman period are known elsewhere in Gaul. A few, however, have been noted in the Corrèze and in Lorraine.

With the third century and encroaching oriental religions, the fashion of inhumation grew. The corpse might be buried in a wooden coffin, or under a covering of tiles, leaning together roofwise and covered along their ridge by the usual *imbrices*. Another variant is the lead coffin, a mode which seems to have come in from the east. Where stone could be afforded it was used to make a massive sarcophagus, which might be plain or elaborately carved (see p. 175).

Thousands of epitaphs are known, many of them full of interest. Those of small children are often pathetic, like that of the little girl at Mainz who blossomed like the rose and straightway faded (*rosa simul floruit et statim periit*), perhaps a hackneyed phrase, but none the less expressive. A Sequanian in Lyons mourns the death of his wife who was 18 years and 8 months old—she died after five years of married life. Her epitaph ends: 'You who read this, go to the baths of Apollo and bathe, as I used to do with my wife. Would that I still could!' A lady of Auch had verses carved upon the tomb of her pet dog.

In the late empire long metrical inscriptions were much admired, and twenty-four lines of verse, carved in two columns on white marble, still extol the virtues of one Nymfius who was a grandee of Saint-Bertrand-de-Comminges in the early fifth century and held office and gave public games of great magnificence.

TEMPLES

The standard classical temple is naturally most commonly found in the larger towns. It was rectangular, and often stood high upon a podium in which there might be large storage vaults. Two very fine examples exist almost intact, the Maison Carrée at Nîmes and the first-century 'Temple of Livia' at Vienne. They are rectangular buildings, with graceful Corinthian columns, and were both probably the capitolia of their respective towns. In Avenches there still stands a tall angle column, called Le Cigognier, belonging to a temple of the second half of the second century, which was excavated in 1938–41. It was about twice the size of the Maison Carrée, measuring 40 × 26 metres, and occupied the centre of one side of a great court (106 × 90 metres), round three sides of which ran a portico. In the centre of the court was a large altar. The sites of numerous such temples of the classical type are known, but only very rarely has thorough excavation been possible.

Still more interesting is a type of temple which is found only in the Celtic provinces of the empire—a form of temple architecture evolved by the Gauls themselves from a wooden prototype. It is a simple square edifice, surrounded by a square portico, and it frequently stood within a colonnaded *temenos*.

The sides of the portico may measure not more than 10 or 12 metres, the inner 4 or 5 metres. Such little shrines have been found in large numbers in Normandy, in the forests near Rouen. The Gallo-Roman liked the company of his fellows and he liked his gods to have company too, so very many of their temples occur in twos or threes or larger groups. On the hill of Gergovia there was a pair of little Romano-Celtic temples. At Petinesca in Switzerland at least six of these temples and some subordinate shrines, as well as a dwelling-house, stood together within an enclosing wall. Sometimes circular sanctuaries may be found along with square ones.

The most elaborate of all these temple-groups known to us is the whole quarter on the banks of the Altbach, on the south side of the city of Trier, and within the circuit of the late-empire walls (fig. 32). Some seventy shrines and temples, big and little, were excavated here in the

o

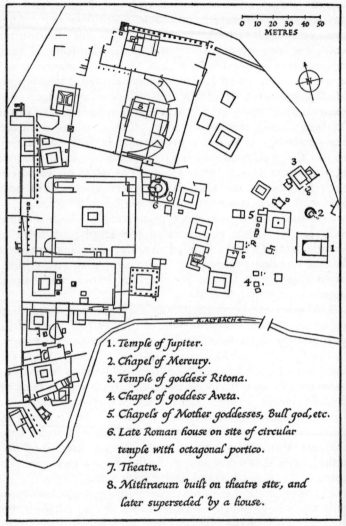

1. Temple of Jupiter.
2. Chapel of Mercury.
3. Temple of goddess Ritona.
4. Chapel of goddess Aveta.
5. Chapels of Mother goddesses, Bull god, etc.
6. Late Roman house on site of circular temple with octagonal portico.
7. Theatre.
8. Mithraeum built on theatre site, and later superseded by a house.

FIG. 32.   Trier: the Temple Quarter

1920s. They are nearly all built on the Celtic plan; most are square, though a few are circular. They cover the whole period from, and perhaps before, the Roman conquest until the fourth century. Some of them were preceded by wooden structures, of which the postholes have been found. It has, unfortunately, not been possible to preserve this unique site for visitors to see, and indeed its preservation in intelligible form would have been extremely difficult. The site demonstrates the importance of Trier as a tribal religious centre in pre-Roman days.

The simple, square, porticoed temple had a number of derivatives which show a very lively and unorthodox interest in architecture among the Gallo-Romans. One is the so-called Temple of Janus at Autun, on the right of the road as one drives in from the Morvan. The square *cella* was carried up aloft in a towering mass whose stout masonry still stands to a height of 11 metres.

One of the best of Gallo-Roman temple remains is the circular 'tower of Vesunna' at Périgueux, still standing 23 metres high (fig. 45a). Portico and *cella* stood on a podium 3·90 m. high; the niches for the beams of the portico roof are 10·70 m. above this floor. The whole was built within a handsome *temenos*. Another circular temple has lately been excavated a little way north of Bordeaux, near Talmont-sur-Gironde. Its centre is now occupied by a disused windmill. It must have been an elaborate temple and its internal diameter was 15·40 m. Its wall was very thick, and it was presumably another of these tower-temples. Remains of its elaborate ornamentation have been found, and various kinds of marbles were evidently employed.

A notable variant in our collection of shrines is the Gallo-Roman temple of Sanxay (Vienne), south-west of Poitiers. This is a small octagonal building, and was probably vaulted. It was surrounded by projecting arms with porticoes pointing directly north, south, east and west which gave the plan the shape of a Greek cross. A large porticoed court surrounded the whole structure, and there was a colonnaded passage from the *temenos* entrance to the temple itself. The central *cella* was probably carried up as a tower.

The sacred precinct of the 'Château des Cars' (Corrèze) contains besides a temple a mausoleum, which suggests some form of veneration of a dead hero or holy man.

The sanctuaries of the gods, so rich in their variety, played a big part in the social life of ancient Gaul. The elaborate precincts found round so many of them are a clear indication of the large crowds of worshippers which they expected, at any rate for their special festivals. Many of the temples were closely associated with small theatres, and here some part of the corporate manifestations of the festivals must have taken place—whether theatrical performances proper, rhetorical contests, or sports like cock-fighting or boxing. There was a theatre in the Trier temple area. Baths also often stand near the temples as at Sanxay. It is probable that, as in the Middle Ages, the religious festivals were occasions for fairs.

Many of the temples, also, were therapeutic centres. One of the best-known of the Paris expresses which steams daily southwards during the appropriate season is the one taking its load of rheumatics, cardiacs, asthmatics and other invalids to the great thermal stations of Auvergne. Whatever their destination, we can be almost certain of one thing—that the Gallo-Romans were there before them. Nearly all these spas can show masonry where one or more of their springs were used by the ancients. The 'Source César' of Royat or Vichy is shown with pride, and in some cases remains of the temples which were erected around the springs are to be seen. The spas of volcanic Auvergne are the most numerous group, but other medicinal waters were prized, as the names Aquae Sextiae (Aix-en-Provence), Aquae Bormonis (Bourbon-l'Archambault), Aquae Helveticae (Baden, Switzerland) show. One Gallic spa, probably Dax, Aquae Tarbellici, was patronized by no less a person than Augustus himself in *c.* 25 B.C. To these springs with a practical as well as a religious value the invalids of the day flocked, and there they faithfully followed the regimes of their particular cures, controlled by the local priests, instead of the doctors and the Chambre de Commerce of to-day. In the Mont Dore Établissement is a notable collection of fragments from what must have been an ornate temple, which proves the popularity and wealth of this remote mountain spring.

We know that many springs of non-medicinal character were believed to have healing qualities, just as are some to-day. Examples are frequent, and the temples erected beside them were just as magnificent as those by real medicinal waters. As they often occur in places not inhabited in later periods, there are more remains from them, including votive offerings, than from constantly used springs like those of a Vichy. The votive offerings are varied and interesting. They may simply be the images of the deities of the temple, or they may be small clay models of the parts of the body for which a cure was sought, or had been achieved.

There were few districts that could not boast of some springs or lakes of special virtue. Their descendants, the 'wishing wells', are found in France as in Britain. In a few cases we have echoes of their more dramatic functions. Gregory of Tours tells us of how the good Bishop Hilary (doubtless Hilary of Arles) travelled into the Rouergue to put down a popular pagan ceremony at Lake Helanus (the Lake of Saint-Andéol near Ad Silanum), and we get a glimpse of Gallo-Romans really enjoying themselves. 'Here was a large lake into which at a certain time a multitude of country folk threw offerings of linen cloths, cloth used in men's garments, fillets of wool, cheeses, wax models of loaves, each according to his ability, all of which to enumerate would be too long, I think. They came, however, with wagon loads of food and drink and after sacrificing the animals they fell to and feasted for three days. On the fourth day when they should disperse, a tempest with thunder and lightning anticipated

them and there was such a rainstorm with violent hail
descending, that hardly could one avoid another . . .'
Hilary converted the pagans with the aid of this timely
thunderstorm, and thereafter they presented their offerings instead at the church which he caused to be built.
The meetings at the lake did not die out, however, and
until 1868 they continued to be held on the second Sunday
in August. They were then prohibited, owing to the
bloodshed and broken heads with which they usually
ended. The local peasants still ascribe to this lake a
power of curing rheumatism.

Pilgrimages were by no means confined to sacred
springs. Certain mountains were greatly venerated,
none more so than the Puy-de-Dôme, the strange, rounded,
volcanic upcast which dominates the Auvergne. On its
summit a large temple was built in honour of the god of the
mountain—Mercurius Dumias. It was an elaborate
structure, but its central shrine has a square plan. Its
most striking remaining feature is the range of semi-
circular exedrae with stone seats where the pilgrims could
rest and admire the incomparable view.

CHRISTIANITY

The earliest undisputable evidence of Christianity in
Gaul belongs to the second half of the second century. The
new religion was propagated essentially by the orientals of
the empire, and its chief point of entry into Gaul seems to
have been Lyons, the cosmopolitan emporium where so
many easterners were to be found; Vienne, too, had an
early community.

The persecution under Marcus Aurelius has left no
record except from these two cities and possibly Marseilles, but Eusebius quotes a detailed account of the
sufferings of the martyrs, sent 'to the churches of Asia
and Phrygia' by the churches of Lyons and Vienne.
The Christian communities would seem largely to have
been recruited from persons from Asia Minor who, like
Attalus the Pergamene, figure prominently among the

martyrs, who also included Pothinus the elderly bishop and a slave-girl, Blandina. The martyrdoms took place at Lyons, and there seems to have been considerable public feeling against the Christians, probably exacerbated by the growing popularity of the cult of the Great Mother, whose worshippers were always likely to come into collision with those of the rival religion. A place like Lyons, with its large population and with the great concourses which gathered periodically for its public festivals, was one in which the authorities would view with anxiety any possible source of public disorder. The authorities ordered the Christians to keep away from public gatherings and public buildings, but it is clear that they refused to do so, with consequent breaches of the peace. The incident ended with the beheading of the Roman citizens concerned and the delivery of the others to the wild beasts in the arena, the regular form of execution of non-citizen criminals. The Christians were not further interfered with, and the Church then entered on a period of expansion. This growth was due in part to the interest excited by the steadfastness of the martyrs and in part to the vigour of the next bishop of Lyons, Irenaeus a Greek from Asia Minor who must have been born in the thirties of the century. He had made his way to the west, and was a presbyter at the time of the persecution. He is the first great figure of the Gallic Church, taking a prominent part in the controversies of the day. A number of his writings have survived, and he was probably responsible for the letter quoted by Eusebius.

The towns of the Rhone valley and neighbouring regions now began to have their communities, and their bishops. Septimius Severus dealt a shrewd blow at further development by forbidding propaganda, and the early third century seems to have been a period of quiet. Signs of the development of Christian art at this time are to be found, notably the celebrated sarcophagus of La Gayole (near Brignolles), in which Christian legends and

symbols like the fisherman and the Good Shepherd re-
place pagan stories.

The next records show renewed activity in the forties
and fifties of the century. Two very eminent saints and
martyrs, Dionysius (Denis) of Paris and Saturninus of
Toulouse, seem to belong to this period and to have died
in the persecution of Decius (250–251). Reims and Trier
had well-established communities by the end of the
century, for both cities had had four bishops by the year
314, while Bordeaux and Autun have produced third-
century Christian inscriptions.

The next setback seems to have been the executions,
carried out under Maximian, of St. Quentin in the north,
of St. Victor of Marseilles and others. Then things
settled down once more under the tolerant Constantius,
who did not share the fears of Christianity expressed by
his colleagues, and who quietly refrained from carrying
out Diocletian's edict of persecution in 303, contenting
himself with a few token demolitions of Christian buildings.

The Christian communities of Gaul prospered under
Constantine. In 314 he decided to lay the Donatist
controversy before a council of bishops of Gaul (and
Britain). The Council duly met at Arles; the Donatists
were condemned and the opportunity was taken of passing
various regulations about the status and duties of Christians under the new order of things: they were enjoined
to play their part in municipal life by becoming magistrates and they were to be allowed to become governors
and other high officials.

The Church of Gaul continued its undistinguished way
for a time, taking no special part in the Arian controversy
but remaining quietly and mildly orthodox. Like other
Gauls, the Christians were perhaps glad to rest and be
thankful after long years of warfare and disturbance, and
live a quiet life without adventures. As yet the Church
had scarcely penetrated beyond the cities. The countryside—home of the *pagani*, the pagans or *paysans*—remained

obstinately pagan, and would so remain until most of the
great landowners had joined the Church.

Trouble came with the Arian emperor Constantius,
who exerted sufficient pressure on the bishops to persuade
them to condemn orthodoxy at the second Council of
Arles in 355. He was not, however, destined to succeed,
for the second great Gallic churchman, the first of Gallo-
Roman blood, Hilary of Poitiers, was just entering upon
his bishopric. Hilary had been born of pagan family in
Poitiers, and had received the excellent education in both
the Latin and Greek languages then available in Gaul.
He had been converted to Christianity and had risen
rapidly in the Church. He was above all a fighter, and
plunged with a will into the controversy on the side of
orthodoxy. He called the bishops together and made
them recant their pronouncements of the Arles Council.
Constantius replied by calling another Council at Béziers
(356), at which his deputy Julian presided, and this
Council did the imperial bidding and drove Hilary into
exile. Hilary departed to Phrygia, but made himself
such a burden to the imperial authority that he was
ordered back to Gaul, as a lesser evil, in 360. After
writing a virulent pamphlet against the emperor, he went
home, where he continued to write and organize. He had
a faithful friend and ally in his pupil Martin, a Pannonian
who had formerly been a soldier and who, with his
approval, founded a community of ascetics at Ligugé
(Locoteiacus), close to Poitiers. This rudimentary monastery was the first in Gaul.

In 372, four years after Hilary's death, the people of
Tours sought Martin out in his retreat, and insisted that he
become their bishop. He agreed, and one of his earliest
acts was the foundation of another monastery at Mar-
moutier near Tours, a community more in the nature of a
seminary than a monastery, for, as Sulpicius Severus
said, 'what church is there that does not want to receive
its priest from the monastery of Martin?'

The emperor Valentinian, preoccupied above all in

securing Gaul from the barbarian menace, troubled little
with religious matters. Under him the pagans enjoyed
their last period of toleration. He was a Christian, but
had no hand in ecclesiastical disputes, expecting Christian
and pagan to live in peace, and Christians to settle their
own differences. He did not intervene in the affairs of
Arians or non-Arians, and had a restraining influence on
the passions of the day. His son Gratian thought otherwise, and was a convinced Catholic, determined to combat
paganism and Arianism. This determination he marked
by the edict of 382, which deprived the pagan religions of
most of their former rights.

The old religions were now being subjected to official
strangulation just as the new had found vigorous leadership and means of training its own priests. Up to now
Gallic Christianity had been confined to the towns: all
the evidence points strongly to this. The country folk—
the majority of the population—were faithful to their old
gods, and continued to use their old temples. There were,
in fact, no rural Christian centres to take their places.
Now was Martin's chance, and he took it with both hands.
Out into the country he went, with his followers, preach-
ing the gospel, and arousing an enthusiasm which in many
places brought him willing co-operators in the destruction
of the heathen shrines. His friend and biographer,
Sulpicius Severus, has preserved the stories of some of
these encounters: at Leprosus, in the diocese of Bruges,
the destruction of 'a very rich temple, its altars and
images'; sanctuaries at rural markets, as Cisomagus and
Turnomagus 'a column of immense size with an idol on
top of it' (one assumes that this may have been a column
of Jupiter and the Giant). Sometimes Martin found
himself in the middle of a fight with outraged *pagani*, and
there seems to be some suspicion that he may have taken
along with him on these occasions a few troops, lent by the
delighted Gratian. He had the genius, moreover, to
follow up his victories by erecting churches where he
destroyed temples, so that his new converts should not

feel a vacuum after the first enthusiasm subsided. Gregory of Tours records a number of Tourainian parishes founded by Martin. It is noteworthy that the coin series in excavated pagan temples of this area are in no case later than Gratian. This has been observed also in the temples of Normandy, in which region a specially vigorous prelate, Victrice of Rouen, is recorded as a contemporary of Martin.

Many examples are known of statues of gods and temple sculptures badly, and obviously deliberately, mutilated. The destruction is sometimes so systematic that it seems obvious that here must be the work of a religious opponent rather than of a casual barbarian. To take two recently observed cases: a colossal statue of Apollo from a shrine at Entrain-sur-Nohain (Nièvre) was thrown face first into a marsh; similarly, at Fontaines-Salées (Yonne) a mutilated bas-relief from the temple was found cast into the former bed of the neighbouring stream. This cannot have happened by accident.

There is something very rough and ready about St. Martin's evangelization of the countryside: he made short work of his opponents and gave them no quarter. This, however, does not give a complete picture of him. He could succeed in the more difficult task of firing the enthusiasm of the learned and the wealthy, and in dealing with the authorities he was remarkable for probity and good sense. The real charity of his spirit is evident in his attitude towards the Priscillianists, a heretical group inspired by some violent Spanish clergy. The emperor Maximus condemned and executed them, but Martin protested vigorously against this persecution.

Martin was among the first to introduce the practice of asceticism into the Gallic Church. The vogue for this had grown up in the deserts of the East and had spread rapidly through the empire, and numerous men and women in Gaul followed suit. It was as yet little regulated, and practitioners could mortify their flesh according to their fancy. Martin and his little group of associates leading simple lives were very different from some of the monks who began to roam the country and pester the faithful for alms. The climate of Gaul did not lend itself to the extravagances of the pillar saints and other eccentrics of the East, but the bishops were not too friendly to a movement which often tended to undermine their authority, and they encouraged the development of a more regular monastic life, which became the practice in the early fifth century, and was signalized by the foundation of the first regular monasteries of Gaul, at Marseilles, and at Lérins on the Ile Saint-Honorat.

As we enter the fifth century the Gallic Church has attained full stature and is to provide an integrating force in the decaying civil structure of the day. Roman Gaul lives on during the century, but the leadership of the country, practical as well as moral, is increasingly in the hands of its bishops. The bishops are now of very different calibre from the rather obscure worthies of a century earlier. The aristocratic and educated classes of Gaul were now taking an interest in the Christian religion, and members of leading senatorial families long used to high office were beginning to enter the episcopate. The same great landowning groups with whom Rome had come to terms in the time of the conquest were now beginning to play a prominent part in laying the foundations of a new age. Many of these bishops were filled with a love of the classics, and the old secular learning was not allowed entirely to disappear. The population of a diocese welcomed a great noble like Sidonius Apollinaris as its bishop, for in the manifold tribulations of the times such a man was an effective protector. Not only would he minister to the spiritual needs of his people, but he could dispense justice and organize food supplies in times of need. A notable case is Archbishop Patiens of Lyons, a man of vast wealth, who sent foodstuffs at his own expense into many stricken towns. So in the fifth century we find a number of eminent bishops in Gaul filling the gaps left in municipal life by the decay of the authority of the empire. Their inherited ability and habit of rule were put to the service of Gaul, and in times of peril they stayed at their posts. The great estates in the country and the bishoprics in the towns were the chief institutions which eased the transition to the Middle Ages.

X

GAUL IN THE LATER EMPIRE

AFTER the disorders of the previous half-century it was necessary for Diocletian both to tighten up control of the provinces and to reduce the power of each individual general. This aim was attained by the complete separation of civil and military offices and the reduction in size of their territory; so the empire emerges from the reorganization with sub-divided provinces and a greatly increased number of officials. There were now seventeen provinces of Gaul, shared between the two dioceses of Viennensis in the south and Galliae in the north (fig. 33). This multiplication of officials added to the burdens of the tax-payer, and yet without a strong organization the empire could not hold together.

Diocletian felt, however, that to rule the whole vast empire was beyond one man's powers, and in 286 he associated with himself as a second Augustus the able soldier Maximian, to whom he assigned the western half of the empire.

To share still further the burdens of supreme rule, and to secure, as he hoped, a peaceful system of succession, Diocletian in 293 appointed two junior emperors or Caesars. Maximian now made Milan his capital, while Constantius, his Caesar, ruled from Trier. Gaul was fortunate in coming within the province of Constantius for he is one of the great figures in its history. He made the Diocletianic system work, and brought peace to the province. He first had on his hands a war with the daring governor Carausius, who had established himself in Britain, earning some right to do so by the signal ability with which as Diocletian's deputy he had repelled the

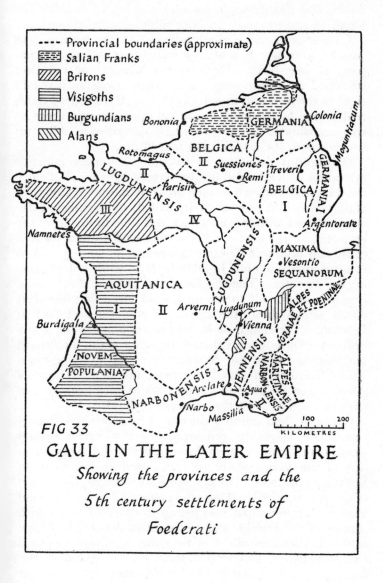

FIG 33
GAUL IN THE LATER EMPIRE
Showing the provinces and the
5th century settlements of
Foederati

Saxon and Frankish pirates who had begun to infest the Channel and its coasts on both sides.

Carausius is the earliest admiral of the narrow seas who lives for us. It is usually stated that he was a Menapian of low birth. He was the admiral of the fleet stationed at Gesoriacum, and when Constantius laid siege to the port and took it (293), Carausius retired to his real source of strength, the island opposite; but there he was assassinated by an ambitious subordinate, Allectus, under whom the last act was played out.

Constantius prepared to invade the island—a major operation which he did not undertake lightly. Not since the days of Claudius had such an army mustered along the Gallic coast. When he finally sailed, the weather, as so often, played an important part, this time in favour of the invaders, for the fleet of Allectus was held up by a fog and could not intercept Constantius before he landed. Constantius moved against London by land while a fleet came up the Thames. The success of this combined operation is preserved for all to see on a gold medallion found at Arras, which shows the arrival of emperor and fleet at London. The return of Britain to her place in the newly ordered empire was a valuable thing for Gaul, for Britain had not shared in the devastation of the third century. The Channel had saved her from the depredations of Aleman and Frank, and she appears to have been able in various ways to assist the recovery of Gaul.

Carausius had pointed the way to various new departures. He might be removed, but the Saxon pirates would come again, so from this time proceeds the organization of the Saxon Shore (p. 219), well known to us in Britain by its great fortresses like Richborough, but a part of the province of the Dux who commanded the Channel Fleet. Carausius had also begun to come to terms with certain of the Franks, and Constantius decided to follow suit. He became allied with some relatively peaceful Frankish tribes, and settled them on the island of the Batavians, now Holland—land which their ancestors had ravaged so utterly that it was now denuded of population. Thus the Salian Franks came into history as the allies of Rome, and though they might encroach upon the empire, their encroachments were legalized by Julian (see p. 219), and for over a century they were open to influences of Roman civilization to a degree not found among many other barbarians.

With the plundering Alemanni there could be no good relations, and Constantius had from time to time to deal with marauding bands of them near the frontier—as in 298, when he had to drive them off near the city of the Lingones. Prisoners captured in these expeditions replenished the labour supply in the empire, and Franks, Frisii and Alemanni tilled the fields from which so many of the Gallic peasants had disappeared.

This influx of barbarians has been condemned as one of the major woes of the age by many nineteenth century and modern writers, but it was in the circumstances a sensible and indeed inevitable development, as far at any rate as the western empire was concerned. The depopulation of the empire had become serious, and no recovery was possible without a revival of its agriculture. This was furthered by the recruitment of barbarians, the displaced persons of the day.

THE DEFENCES OF THE LATE EMPIRE

The maintenance of an imperial court was a heavy charge upon the finances of Gaul. Yet a heavier burden was the essential expenditure on defence. While the emperors were still engaged in driving off the invaders and quelling internal disturbances they were faced with three long-term problems: they had to devise a means of protecting the towns, or what was left of them; they had to provide secure communications along the main arteries of the province; they had not only to drive the enemy out, they must keep him out. The solution to the first problem was two-fold, fortifications and garrisons; to the second, fortified posts and numerous signal towers;

P

to the third, a chain of more forts and signal towers along the best available natural frontier line.

The Rhine was now once again the frontier, from Lake Constance to the land of the Salian Franks. On the north-west and west the coasts had to be guarded against Saxon and Frankish pirates. The system is essentially one of defence in depth, as indeed the old system had been to a lesser degree, though now the whole land, and not just its fringe, was a fortified zone. The frontier was well guarded, with its own troops, the *Riparienses*, in a chain of fortified towns; but although at one or two key points, like Strasbourg, garrisons of legionary calibre were maintained, the main striking force, the *Comitatenses*, were kept far inland near the Emperor, ready to proceed to any threatened point. All main roads and road junctions were provided with fortified posts, and the whole country was a network of strongholds. Gaul could not afford to revert to the comparatively defenceless, peaceful cities of the previous century.

The signal-tower was the essential link holding the whole system together—vital in an age without telephones or radio—and more than ever important now that so many of the troops were stationed far from the frontier. Such towers were equally important along the main lines of communication and on high points, and a number have been found in the Vosges, in Roman Germany and in Belgium. The towers along the Yorkshire coast are a close parallel, and others must await discovery along the French coast. A fortlet on Alderney, known as the Nunnery (40 m. sq.) is probably a station of this type. So the red glare on Skiddaw had its counterpart in the Roman Empire, and it was this signalling system which enabled the emperor Julian to move so rapidly to counter the Alemannic host in 357 before it attempted to leave the plain of Alsace.

　1. *The North-Eastern Frontier.* The sector of frontier line most interesting to the archaeologist is the stretch along the Rhine from Stein on Lake Constance to Basle,

where there are watch-towers at regular intervals, just like the familiar signal-stations of the German frontier of the middle empire or the turrets of Hadrian's Wall (fig. 34). The towers are generally 1200 to 1500 metres apart (i.e. roughly a Roman mile) and are from 4 to 16 metres square. On one tower an inscription was found stating that it was set up in 371 by Legion VIII.

At intervals there were forts. One of these was Castrum Rauracense, on the bank of the Rhine about a quarter of a mile north of the former colony at Augst. It was protected by thick walls, which still stand on the west and

Fig. 34. The fourth-century Frontier from Basle to Constance

south, strengthened at intervals by polygonal towers projecting outwards. The area of the fort was about 3½ hectares (fig. 35). The bridge was maintained for a time, and on the opposite side was a small bridgehead.

Zurzach, a camp of very irregular shape, deserves attention for its curious plan. There are two forts on the south bank belonging to the late period, the earlier very irregular one perhaps designed to include already existing buildings, and showing many signs of subsequent strengthening. At a later period a second, more regular and smaller fort was built, and the two were joined by a wall on the landward side. This wall covered the approach to the bridge, and it is suspected that there may have been a bridgehead opposite, as at Augst.

The Romans, as usual, adapted their designs to the needs of the day. Where they built on unencumbered

P 2

ground their work could have all the old regularity.   This
is especially noteworthy in a little group of small *castella* of
Diocletianic or even earlier times, of which Irgenhausen
(fig. 35), is a good example.   Alzei on a road into the

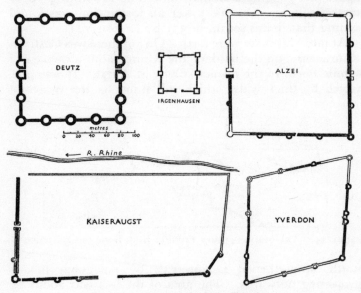

FIG. 35.   Forts of the later Empire

interior in the Palatinate, is also very regular, but it has
round towers.   Andernach is an example of a *castrum* on
the banks of the middle Rhine.   It is defended by many
circular towers, and is very irregular in shape, the lay-out
of its walls being dependent on a pre-existing Roman
town.

2. *The Northern Frontier.* The northern frontier is less
easily definable.   The Roman settlements on the Lower
Rhine had been virtually wiped out in the invasions of
256 and subsequent years.   One such was Nijmegen,
which was burnt down and plundered by the Franks
about 260.

Into the deserted country of the Netherlands and northern Belgium, the former country of the Batavi and the Menapii, filtered the Salian Franks, and they seem to have been settled there in considerable numbers when in 358 their delegates went before Julian near Tongres. The result of their conclave was that Julian conceded them right of settlement in the lands they already occupied, and thus purchased an effective shield for the northernmost part of Gaul. The Salian Franks honoured their bargain, and gave no trouble to the empire till its final disintegration. The linguistic boundary between the Flemish and the French tongues coincides roughly with that of the land of the Salians—always, be it remembered, less heavily Romanized than the territory immediately to its south.

There is, however, the intermediate period, 276–360, to think of. What provision was made for the fortification of the north? A claim has been made that the old Cologne–Bavai–Boulogne road was the northern frontier of the late empire, and this may have been so for some time before 360. Its long-established importance, however, as the key road uniting the British and Rhenish armies is enough to account for the line of fortified posts along it at a time when all trunk roads were being provided with garrisons. After the arrangement with the Salian Franks, in any case, this line lost most of its importance as a defensible frontier. Julian reoccupied some of the ports, such as Utrecht, along the lower Rhine, probably to protect ships from Britain bringing supplies to his armies.

3. *The Coast Defences.* The coasts of Belgica, like those of south-east Britain, now bore the ominous name of the Saxon shore. In Gaul it is divided into two sections, a northern one under the *Dux* of Belgica Secunda and a southern one under the *Dux Tractus Armoricani et Nervicani.*

Unlike the Saxon Shore of Britain, the fortifications of the Saxon Shore of Gaul remain virtually unknown.

The three stations which are specifically mentioned as under the command of the *Dux Belgica Secunda* are—

(*a*) Marcis, now identified with Mardyck, which is connected with Cassel by a very ancient road.

(*b*) Quartensi sive Hornensi, headquarters of the *Praefectus classis Sambricae*. Tiles of this fleet have been found at Etaples. Sambricae probably means the river Somme (Samara) at whose estuary is Cap Hornu with which Hornensi is now usually identified.

(*c*) Portus Aepatiaci, seat of the *Tribunus militum Nerviorum*, probably at Isques in the estuary of the Liane, a little above Boulogne. This identification has the satisfactory result of explaining why Boulogne is not mentioned as a Saxon Shore stronghold, as we should expect of a port which continued to be of great importance in the Late as in the Early Empire. Portus Aepatiaci would be the naval port and arsenal of the Boulogne harbour, while the ordinary citizens retired within the contemporary *castrum* of Bononia.

Under the *Dux Tractus Armoricani et Nervicani* garrisons are specified for Blabia (Blaye), Venetis (Vannes), Osismiis (Carhaix), Manatias (? Namnetibus, Nantes), Aleti (Alet, near Saint-Servan), Constantia (Coutances), Roto-magus (Rouen), Abrincatis (Avranches) and a mysterious Grannona which may be Port-en-Bessin, a convenient port for Bayeux.

In these many stations we know little more than the walls of Rouen (500 × 375 m., 19 hectares) and Nantes (500 × 350 m., 18 hectares). Their rectangular lay-out is very like that of the majority of our Saxon Shore forts, though their area is much greater. The fortlet on Alderney (above, p. 216) is doubtless an example of the signalling stations which were part of the system.

4. *The Interior*. Turning in from the frontiers, we find that all towns of any size are part and parcel of the imperial defence system. The old road stations also were of vital importance, both in the maintenance of

communications and in the storage and guarding of the taxes paid in kind for the armies. Such was Tournus by the Saône on the great road to the north. From the *Acta Sanctorum* we hear of a *horreum castrense*, that is, a fortified store depot, at this point, which was doubtless protected by the late empire fortifications (area 1½ hectares), of which portions still remain.

The *castellum* of Junkerath (Icorigium) is also interesting. This circular fort of 1½ hectares, with exceptionally stout walls 3·65 to 3·85 m. in thickness, bestrides the Trier–Cologne road to protect an older *mansio*, some of whose foundations, however, it cuts across. The buildings to be seen on the plan are thought to be stables or granaries. Here is, in fact, a *mansio* of the imperial post, which would in case of need shelter the local population. Ausonius refers to fortified posts in the Moselle region used as granaries.

5. *The Towns*. The vast majority of Roman town walls now to be seen in France and the other parts of Gaul belong to the period of reconstruction after the disasters of the third century and continued in use as fortifications during the Middle Ages. It is no exaggeration to say that the towns of early medieval France were shaped and fortified by the Gallo-Romans. They can be sorted roughly into two groups, one in which the walls are generally constructed as an irregular circle or oval round the centre of the earlier town, the other in which the walls are laid out deliberately in the familiar rectangular pattern of the military camp. Their geographical distribution seems to be fairly haphazard, unless the regularity of the plans of Boulogne, Rouen, Nantes and Bordeaux can be regarded as part of a single scheme, and not enough is known about their comparative dates to embark on generalization. It is likely that many of the more irregularly planned walls may have been embarked on earliest, in the immediate reaction to the first wave of invasion. The most important distinction, however, seems to be simply the chance factor of size. The largest of the *castrum* type is Bordeaux (31 hectares), whereas from

the 50-hectare Poitiers upwards all the encircling walls of the large towns are irregular in shape—circular, semi-circular or oval. There are many small towns of the 10-hectare class with circular perimeters, but no large towns with rectangular outline.

In both groups material from the destroyed cemeteries and buildings of the damaged towns is freely used. The remnants of earlier masonry are so regularly and systematically used in the foundations of the new walls that we have to recognize in this a system encouraged, if not from the beginning enjoined, by a central over-riding authority. The sculptures which had adorned proud buildings now in ruins were immured in the foundations of the last defences of the towns of Gaul as of the rest of the Empire. A striking case is the small fort of Neumagen, built in the time of Constantine to guard the Trier–Mainz road. Into its foundations were swept the works of art of nearly two centuries—the funerary monuments of a once-flourishing community which have revealed to their discoverers a new chapter in Roman provincial art (see p. 172). So the new fortifications arose, at what cost to the builders who piled in the débris of their once-cherished monuments can only be imagined. It would seem that Postumus made a beginning with rebuilding after the early burst of invasions. Probus also has received much credit for his work of reconstruction. The task was continued by Maximian and by Constantius and his son. The strengthening of fortifications remained a recurrent problem during the remaining years of the empire, and it is interesting to find references in the Roman collection of laws known as the Theodosian Code to the re-use of stones from old buildings. It is expressly stated in a law of Honorius that the stones and sculptures from dismantled temples may be used in town walls, but some attempt is also made to prevent the disappearance of real works of art.

The walls are built on massive foundations, for which the remains of old monuments, columns, bas-reliefs, etc., were carefully dressed and laid together without mortar.

The walls above the foundations vary from 2·50 to 3 or more metres in thickness, with an extremely strong concrete-and-rubble core. The facing is still of small ashlar blocks, but a regular feature is the brick bonding courses, running right through face and core, a common proportion being seven courses of ashlar and then three of bricks. This *opus mixtum* is characteristic of the late empire, but had already made its appearance in many buildings of the second century. Another technique is the insertion of layers of large blocks of stone at intervals in the small ashlar, seen at Dijon.

Towers have become more important than ever—they are, in fact, what we should call bastions (fig. 51*a*). Those at the angles of the walls in particular are very massive structures. The towers are found closer together than those of earlier fortifications.

The gates were protected by large towers like those round the walls. Sometimes the gates of the earlier fortifications were included in the later system, as at Nîmes and Autun. The finest of the late empire gateways, perhaps the most famous Roman ruin north of the Alps, is the Porta Nigra at Trier, which dates from Constantine. It is closely related in type to the Porte d'Auguste of Nîmes, but has only two entrances instead of four. In every other respect it is larger, and it has two storeys of arcading above the level of the ramparts. The projecting towers are rounded in front, but rectangular in plan in the rear. There was a portcullis and a large internal court of 17·50 × 7·70 metres, dominated by two tiers of internal galleries. Despite its great military strength, the gateway was adorned with pilasters, so that it was an ornament as well as a protection to the northern capital (fig. 51*b*).

Postern gates are not unknown in the early empire (examples are known at Fréjus and Arles), but they are a regular feature of the fortifications of the late empire, and occur at Sens, Le Mans, Tours and elsewhere.

Our information as to whether or not these fortifications were provided with ditches is very scanty. There was,

however, a ditch in front of the wall of Trier, and a ditch
was observed at Le Mans. Further research may well
produce more examples.

One of the best-preserved examples of a late Roman
fortified town is Le Mans (Sarthe). Portions of the
ancient walls and massive circular towers are still to be
seen (fig. 51a); there were about thirty of these, 25–30
metres apart, projecting from the wall. The gateways
have, however, disappeared. Some of the towers still
retain their conical medieval roofing, which gives a very
good idea of how they must have looked in the fourth
century, as can be gathered from medallions of the Roman
period. Another fine example of late Roman fortification,
within easy reach of Paris, is the little town of Senlis.

The areas enclosed by the new walls were in nearly every
case far smaller than those of the earlier towns. The inhabitants living outside the defences would have to crowd
into them in case of need. The previous wall-circuit was
often abandoned, or only one corner of it was preserved as
part of the new fortifications. Such cases are Tongres in
the north, Autun in the centre and Nîmes in the south.
Sometimes the new walls were laid out to include the
strong walls of the amphitheatre as part of the defensive
system. This was done at Trier, Metz and Périgueux.
At Arles the theatre was incorporated in the defences.
An extreme case of contraction is Bavai, where the late
castellum merely encloses the earlier forum and where
indeed it would seem that the town had virtually ceased
to exist except as a small police post.

LIFE IN THE LATE EMPIRE

Despite this vast system of grim fortifications, despite
the ruins now rapidly being covered by ivy and willow
herb, life went on, and, what is more, there were plenty
who found it pleasant and who brought to it all their
native gusto.

Trier enjoyed its new status as capital of the west, and
around it rose magnificent villas belonging to the great

men of the court—luxury dwellings which give no hint
that their owners felt any peril hanging over them,
despite the nearness of the frontier. The catastrophic
third century with the progressive impoverishment of the
empire meant, however, growing distress among the
middle and lower classes and the poor folk. There is
now an ever-increasing gap between the great senatorial
families which managed to cling to their wealth and the
lower orders. The reorganization of life must have been
a nightmare business for the state. There was depopulation, and enough men could not be found to till the fields;
so, as we have seen, barbarians were brought in, and are
found planted all over the countryside.

It is difficult to get a balanced view of the society of the
late empire, because the sources we have present such
widely differing pictures. We cannot pick and choose
between the comfortable literary circle of Ausonius, the
harassed municipal magistrates, the toiling serfs and the
bands of brigands. We have to admit them all into the
story and try to understand why they could all exist
together. The state of affairs is one which we of the
middle twentieth century need not find very difficult to
imagine. The constant wars of the third century had
brought economic ruin in their wake, and though Diocletian and his successors endeavoured to remedy this,
their success was only partial. In a poverty-stricken land
the demands of the state were great as never before.
The periods of peace were never long enough for the
wounds to heal throughout the empire. To use current
phraseology, the ever-recurrent and painfully necessary
rearmament programmes inflicted burdens on the economy
of the empire, which its reduced and impoverished
population was unable to bear. Despite the restoration of
a reputable coinage by Diocletian and Constantine, the
monetary system had had too great a shock to recover
properly. It was found more satisfactory to impose some
of the taxes in kind, and many officials drew considerable
parts of their salaries thus, which they felt to be a safer

method in days of inflation. From the point of view of
the state it was imperative that the army and the city of
Rome be fed. The exactions in farm produce for this
purpose might be met in a good year, but after a bad
harvest things might go ill with the farmer.

Even so, the broad lands of Gaul continued to produce
their wonted riches, and there was a great measure of
recovery in the sixty years of peace which followed the
rise of Constantius Chlorus to the purple. Nowhere in the
empire was there greater peace, and even prosperity, than
in Gaul south and west of the Loire during these tranquil
years: there were burdens to be borne, to hold the
empire together, but Gaul does seem to have achieved
some sort of equilibrium. The south-west also escaped
the miseries of the great invasions of the mid-fourth
century, for the Alemannic hordes did not penetrate
beyond Sens and Autun, though the civil war caused by
the revolt of Magnentius affected the centre. From 365
until 405 there was again peace, though deterioration in
prosperity now becomes more apparent. This period
nevertheless includes not only the ministry of St. Martin
and leisure for all manner of theological experiments and
controversies, but also the brilliant court of Trier and the
last blossoming under Roman rule of the Moselle valley,
which is to be set between 365 and the end of the century.
Happily for Gaul, most of the civil wars of the period were
fought elsewhere, though there was the growing menace
from the barbarians across the Rhine.

The most remarkable evidence of well-being in this
period is that to be culled from the writings of Ausonius,
the eminent don from Bordeaux, who in middle age was
called to become tutor of Gratian, son of the emperor
Valentinian. Previously he had taught in Bordeaux, and
his circle of friends is essentially an educated well-to-do
middle-class one. He tells us much of his friends and
relations and we gather that they were peaceful citizens,
comfortably off, content with their lot and proud of their
city. He tells us of his father, a physician by profession,

of his uncle who taught rhetoric at Toulouse, and of the women of the family, some of whom were, he hints, severe and strait-laced, but all of whom took an interest in literature, though mostly of the religious kind. One aunt of his refused to marry, but studied medicine instead. Ausonius was born about 310, and grew up in an age when society was gradually turning over from paganism to Christianity. The change-over seems to have occurred painlessly in his family, and in the course of his career he must have deemed it expedient to conform, but in reality religion troubled him little, and his real love was for the great literature of the past and for the beauties of his native land. There is little sign that he felt he was living in a decaying world, and yet from his position at the court of Valentinian, and from the great offices to which he was promoted under Gratian, he had ample opportunity of realizing the dangers besetting the empire. The murder of his friend and pupil Gratian did for a time cast a cloud over him. Perhaps, however, like ourselves, he hoped for the best and rejoiced, while he could, in the blessings he had. He retired in ripe old age to Bordeaux, and died peacefully about 390.

Bordeaux was, of course, in an unusually fortunate position in this period, sheltered for many years by its remoteness from barbarian incursions. Round it grew famous vineyards, and the commerce of the day dealt in just such objects of luxury as vintage wines. Trade with Britain was still maintained. It was also a University town, which must have brought some profit, even if small, to its citizens. Here, if anywhere, the decay of the age was arrested, and it would seem that Bordeaux, despite its shrunken area, retained some of its old prosperity right into the era of the more primitive but not entirely oppressive Visigothic government. This began with Wallia's settlement in Aquitania in 419, after the marauding Saxons had begun to find their way down to the south-western coasts.

Letters flourished in other towns besides Bordeaux in the

fourth century, which shows that what we may call the professional classes managed to keep their heads above water. Toulouse has already been mentioned, and Trier was a centre of learning. The huge expansion of the civil service after Diocletian also eased matters for a time by providing many openings for young men of the middle classes.

Ausonius is by no means the only man of letters of the fourth century in Gaul who is known to us. Many others appear in his own works and among his own correspondents. There is his pupil, Paulinus of Nola, born about 353, who was fired by religious enthusiasms quite foreign to the ideas of Ausonius; he gave up his Aquitanian estates and retired to live a hermit's life in Italy, from where, however, he conducted a lively correspondence with his old friends in Gaul. Still more remarkable is the correspondence carried on by people in Gaul with Saint Jerome during his retirement in Bethlehem (386–420). Among Jerome's correspondents are some of the learned ladies of Bordeaux, and one of them, Hedibia, is especially notable for her interest in textual criticism. One point to be noticed in all this is the apparent ease with which these letters reached their destination, which suggests that despite the periodical outbreaks of brigandage and other troubles, the Roman system of communications still functioned remarkably well.

Among the major problems of the later empire was shortage of man-power. The land had to be tilled and its products had to reach the army and Rome, but there were never enough men to do the job, save in very favoured regions. So we find the state, in self-defence, assuming the 'direction' of industry, as we should say. This extreme form of 'direction', however, compelled a man to stay in his own job and did not move him from one job to another. All work of any importance now became hereditary. The cultivator was compelled to till the soil as his father had before him. The once-proud *navicularii* were bound by law to the calling their ancestors must once have gladly adopted, and their engagement in ventures outside the prescribed one of conveying food to Rome was heavily restricted. All trades of any importance were now hereditary, since they had ceased to attract recruits by the hope of reasonable profits.

Perhaps the hardest case of all was that of the *curiales*, the local municipal officers, of whose sad state, even in Gaul, evidence comes in as the fourth century wears to its close. The chief evidence for Gaul is to be obtained from rescripts in the Theodosian Code addressed to the governors and other great officials; there are also some trenchant comments in the writings of Salvian, a Gallic Jeremiah, who wrote of the evils of the first half of the fifth century.

For long the municipal magistrates had been subject to the pernicious system which made them personally responsible for the taxes in their *civitas*. This might not matter in an era of prosperity, but in a time of declining wealth of every sort it brought ruin, and the unlucky local magistrate found himself between the upper and the nether millstones. The Government demanded payments he could not make, and when he sought to collect the money or the goods he was reviled as a tyrant. Salvian describes the *curiales* as tyrants. How different from Ausonius' description of his father's career: 'Vasates was my birthplace, but Burdigala my home. I was a senator in the council of both towns. Not wealthy nor yet needy, I lived thriftily yet not meanly'.

Tax-evasion was the most highly cultivated art of the times, and its most finished practitioners were the very rich. Though many high-principled public servants are found among the Gallo-Roman nobles, some of the leading senatorial families of the late fourth and fifth centuries cut a sorry figure when it comes to a patriotic willingness to shoulder financial burdens, and as they had great initial privileges, they could evade their responsibilities the more successfully. They had the paramount advantage of not being liable for municipal service. The wealthier *curiales* got out while they could, and crept into the senatorial order, legally, or illegally. Others, less fortunate, were glad to leave the relics of their property and take refuge on the estate of some local magnate for whom they could do useful work in return for protection. The only real wealth was in the land, and the only persons enjoying real security were these rich landowners. Even the richest had their troubles, however, for their acres, too, had to yield up some produce to the state, and the masters had to find the cultivators. But a great landowner could lay up stores from good years to carry him over the lean years and, as he was strong enough to protect his *coloni* from military service, or robbery, or official violence, he found it easier to maintain a staff than did the small man.

These rich men unscrupulously added to their fortunes and property from the misfortunes of others, but the protection they gave was the only measure of security many an unhappy citizen, driven to beggary, could find, and so they were not without their usefulness. Though they might in time be dispossessed, the Frankish or Visigothic interloper would maintain the estate. The *coloni* might degenerate still farther into villeinage, but at any rate their means of livelihood was reasonably secure: they were too valuable to their masters to be allowed utterly to starve.

Coming to the peasants, their greatest need was peace and good seasons. It is hard to believe that their life was one of unrelieved gloom, or that they, the producers of food, could not usually manage to hide enough away from the tax-gatherer to maintain existence, but there were few incentives to do more work than bare necessity demanded. The neighbouring farm might often be tilled by a German husbandman, especially after the invasions of 355 and 408. A community of interest would early tend to bring the two together, and when the Gallo-Roman discovered that in the territories occupied by Visigoths and other *foederati* there was less oppression, he often sought refuge there himself.

It became, indeed, an era of flight and flux, an era when to be honest became more and more difficult, and all forms of dishonesty, cruelty and oppression were rampant. And so we come to one of the greatest scourges of latter-day Roman Gaul, the robbers or Bagaudae. As in similar circumstances and similar ages, miserable men betook themselves to the greenwood. The Bagaudae were compounded of discontented soldiers, run-away slaves, peasants driven from their homes by barbarian devastation or the exactions of the tax-gatherer, all ruined folk who had nothing to lose.

Disorder of this sort became a major problem after civil wars. The first serious outbreak was that of Maternus in the time of Commodus (186) with his 'body of deserters who were then ravaging Gaul in great numbers'. Brigandage reached alarming proportions under Severus, resulting from the civil war and punishments meted out thereafter. Deserters made these bands peculiarly dangerous, and the numbers of the outlaws were swollen by run-away slaves, about whom we find this dictum in Dio. 'Carry this message to your masters: feed your slaves, so that they may not turn to brigandage'. Tertullian states, 'Military stations are distributed through all the provinces for tracking robbers'. The conditions breeding such disorders were multiplied a hundredfold during the third century, and culminated in the formidable outbreak of 284, which Maximian had to tackle. Now for the first time the outlaws banded themselves together and adopted the name Bagaudae, a Celtic word meaning the valiant. Their chief zone of operations was the Loire, but they wandered over the country, the only protection against them being the new town walls initiated by Probus. They went to some trouble to organize themselves as a fighting force. They saluted their leaders as 'emperors', and Maximian had two of these to face, Aelianus and Amandus, leading their armed peasant infantry and their cavalry of mounted shepherds.

Maximian's job was in fact the clean-up of the countryside, and the organization of certain regional forces such as a cohort in the troublesome land of Savoy, must go back to this time. The prosperity of Gaul in the succeeding half-century shows how well Maximian had done his work. But he could not root out the Bagaudae completely, their remnants melted away and hid in the mountains and forests. From every writer of the next two hundred years references to the activities of the brigands may be culled. Even the peaceful Ausonius notices them. Ammianus, writing of the time of Valentinian, says that Gaul was pullulating with bandits who watched the main roads and attacked without hesitation all likely to furnish rich booty. Among their numerous victims was Constantianus, the *tribunus stabuli*, a kinsman of the emperor. We find them operating in the Alps in 365 and again in 407, when there was also a new outbreak in the forests of the Loire.

Among the Bagaudae were men who fled rather than endure military service and barbarians who escaped from their work on the land, along with Gallo-Roman peasants, and who gave useful help to the invaders when the Germans swept into Gaul. A force of British newcomers in Armorica was engaged to hold the Visigoths in check and, being left without sufficient pay, took to plundering on their own, and enticing people's slaves away.

We hear of brigands in the letter of Sidonius to the Bishop of Troyes about an unfortunate woman who had been carried off and whose family had been endeavouring for some years to trace her.

One of the most amazing earlier tales of brigandage is that of the short-lived pretender Proculus, who was invested with the purple at Lyons in 280. He came from Albenga in the Alps behind Genoa and was a member of a well-known and well-born family, which had practised brigandage for generations and which was 'very rich in cattle and slaves and all that they had carried away'. He won renown by fighting the Alemanni 'in the manner of the brigands'. It is interesting to find the Ligurians reverting to type.

305–475 A.D.

In 305 had come the abdication of Diocletian and Maximian, and Constantius became Augustus. Constantius died a year later at York. His son Constantine was at hand to step into his shoes, and to supplant the Caesar of the West by being hailed as Augustus. The interests of this numerous and vigorous family were not to be passed over to maintain the system of Diocletian.

For the first three years of his reign Constantine maintained the traditions of his father. He ruled in Gaul, watched the frontier and conducted forays across the Rhine. At first he showed special favour to the cult of Apollo, and is said to have visited the temple of Apollo Grannus at Grand and to have had a vision of the god. But the inevitable conflict with his rivals could not be long postponed, and in 311 the army of Gaul invaded Italy. Constantine was not, however, leaving his frontier inadequately guarded, and discipline had now been restored to an admirable degree in the army of the west, so that he had his forces completely under control, and men marvelled at their good behaviour as they passed south through many tempting cities which they left untouched.

There followed in 312 the battle of the Milvian bridge, preceded by the more celebrated vision, this time ascribed to the Christian god: the same year the Edict of Milan proclaimed religious toleration throughout the empire— making general a state of things already introduced into Gaul by the liberal-minded Constantius.

In 314 Constantine was back again in Gaul. He had to deal with unrest on the frontier and to attend the Council of Bishops at Arles. His stay at Arles was an important landmark in the history of that city. It enjoyed many privileges, while the northern rival, Trier, temporarily lost some of its political lustre. Lyons and Narbonne had now definitely fallen behind in importance.

These imperial visits of the late empire must have been tremendous occasions, because every emperor since

Diocletian had adopted the state and ceremony of the Persian monarchs, and was accompanied wherever he went by a vast concourse of officials and courtiers, by his treasure and its guards, and by his army. The array in and around Arles in 314 recalls a medieval gathering—the camp of an Edward III, or a Saladin, or a Field of the Cloth of Gold. Constantine was, however, becoming more and more involved in the East, and his personal story ceases to be of special interest to students of Gaul.

In 337 his thirty years' reign, prophesied by Apollo, came to an end, shortly after he had been baptised a Christian. The Roman world had to face a fantastic scheme of division designed to please the family feeling of the deceased emperor. The empire was divided between his three surviving sons as Augusti and two of his nephews as Caesars, but the Augusti made short work of their cousins, and we are left with Constantine II, Constantius and Constans, Constantine receiving Gaul and its associated provinces. Three years later he attempted conclusions with his brother Constantius and invaded Italy, where he met his end (340).

Under the unattractive Constantius the peace which Gaul was so greatly enjoying continued, but half-way through the century this happy state of things was shattered by the usurpation of Magnentius, who set himself up as emperor at Autun. A civil war ensued, which, unlike those of the previous century, was won by the legitimate emperor. The Alemanni, taking advantage of the conflict, poured into Gaul. At this juncture Constantius called upon his kinsman, the as yet untried scholar Julian, to take over the Gallic command, and Julian, a young man of twenty-five, full of misgivings, made his way in December over the Alps from Milan to Vienne, meeting bad news at every stage of his journey. After attending the Council of Béziers, he journeyed to Reims, by way of Autun, Auxerre, Troyes and Châlons, menaced as he went by marauding bands of Germans. A series of great campaigns followed, in which he suffered many perils. At last in

Fig. 36.   The City of Arles (see page 90).   *Greff*

FIG. 37a.   The Porte de Mars at Reims (p. 71).   *Les Éditions d'Art*

FIG. 37b.   The Theatre and Odeum at Lyons (p. 80).   *E. Pernet*

FIG. 38.   Trier: the east end of the Imperial Baths (p. 74).   *Landesmuseum, Trier*

Fig. 39a. Monument of the Secundinii at Igel (p. 171). *Landesmuseum, Trier*

Fig. 39b. The Baths of Cluny: the spring of the vault is decorated with a sculptured barge

FIG. 40.   The Metz Aqueduct (p. 84).   *E. Prillot*

FIG. 41a. Silver Bust of a citizen of Vaison: ht. 28 cm. (p. 76). *J. Sautel*

FIG. 41b. Bordeaux Carpenter: ht. 64 c (p. 173). *R. Lassus*

FIG. 41c. Neumagen Steersman: ht. c. 20 cm. (p. 172). *Landesmuseum, Trier*

FIG. 41d. Helvetian Youth: ht. 27 c (p. 178). *Berne Museum*

FIG. 42a. Woodmen of Bordeaux: ht. 97 cm. (p. 168). *R. Lassus*

FIG. 42b. Banking Scene from Neumagen: ht. 56 cm. (p. 172).
Landesmuseum, Trier

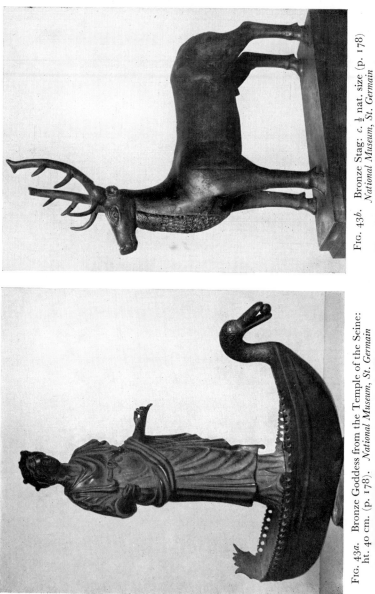

Fig. 43b. Bronze Stag: c. ½ nat. size (p. 178)
National Museum, St. Germain

Fig. 43a. Bronze Goddess from the Temple of the Seine:
ht. 40 cm. (p. 178). National Museum, St. Germain

Autagis Cintux		XXC
Tudos decametos luxtos		
Verecundo[s]	canastri S =	D
eti	pedalis	CX
eti	canastri = =	D
Albanos	panias	MXXX
Albinos	vinari	D
Summacos	catili	MMCDLX
Felix Scota	catili	V̄CC
Tritos Privatos	paraxi[di]	V̄DL
Deprosagi[los]	paraxidi	MMDC
Masuetos	acitabli	ĪXD

Fig. 44a. Graffito from La Graufesenque
(p. 144). *L. Balsan*

Fig. 44b. Silver Cup from Lyons: ht. 6·5 cm. (p. 157). *Lyons Museum*

FIG. 45a. Tower of the Temple at Périgueux (p. 201)
L. Chatagneau

FIG. 45b. The Trophy of Augustus at La Turbie (p. 165)
Combier Macon

FIG. 46a. The Mercury of Lezoux: ht. 1·50 m. (p. 187)

FIG. 46b. The Goddess Epona from near Gannat: ht. 29 cm. (p. 193). Both from *National Museum, St. Germain*

FIG. 47b. The Matronae Aufaniae from Bonn:
ht. 1·32 m. (p. 191). *Bonn Museum*

FIG. 47a. Cernunnos of Reims: ht. 1·25 m. (p. 173)
Reims Museum

MATRONIS
AVFANIABVS
QVETHVS·SEVERVS
QVAESTOR·C·C·A·A
VOTVM·SOLVIT·LM
MACRINO·ET·CELSO·COS

Fig. 48. The Stele of Agassac: ht. 67 cm. (p. 175). *M. Labrousse*

FIG. 49. The Simpelveld Sarcophagus (p. 177). *Leyden Museum*

Fig. 50a. Head of Christ on Sarcophagus at Arles, 4th century (p. 176)
J. Latour

Fig. 50b. A Celtic Deity from Chorey, 1st cent.: ht. 75 cm. (p. 174) *E. Thevenot*

Fig. 50c. Two Herms from Welschbillig near Trier, 4th century: ht. *c.* 40 cm. (p. 177). *Landesmuseum, Trier*

FIG. 51b. Trier: exterior of the Porta Nigra (p. 223)
Landesmuseum, Trier

FIG. 51a. A Tower of the Le Mans Town Wall
(p. 224). *P. Cordonnier*

357 he defeated Chnodomar in a pitched battle near Strasbourg. His victorious career continued, and he crossed the Rhine triumphantly. He followed this up by clearing the lower Rhine and sweeping the seas, thus enabling supplies from Britain to be brought up the river. And he continued his salutary work by his care of the frontier and the erection of fortifications.

For his capital he chose Paris, now no longer the proud town of the Rive Gauche, but the fortress of the Cité. In 360 he was declared Augustus here by his troops, against his will. The death of Constantius, however, saved the empire from civil war, but bequeathed to Julian the Persian War which was to take him away from Gaul to meet his death. In his absence the barbarians remained quiet, but when news of his death arrived the Saxons and Alemanni returned once more.

Gaul was fortunate in finding another emperor who worked just as faithfully as had Julian, the harsh but conscientious Valentinian, one of the greatest of the Roman soldier-Emperors. Valentinian did not attempt to rule the whole empire. Leaving the Danube and East to his brother Valens, he concentrated on the most threatened area, the Rhine. His able general Jovinus dealt faithfully with the Alemanni (365) and returned to a triumph at Paris. Valentinian moved to Amiens, to cope with the coastal and British problems, and while at Amiens his son Gratian was proclaimed Augustus with appropriate pomp.

Valentinian then made his headquarters at Trier, from where he reigned for eight years, the years of Trier's greatest glory, and carried out his major work, the re-establishment of a line of fortifications from the sea to the upper Rhine, thereby completing the work begun by earlier emperors.

For about ten years after the death of Valentinian (375) the peace of Gaul was maintained, but terrible things were happening elsewhere, for the Huns had appeared west of the Caspian Sea and in 375 had destroyed the Gothic

Q

kingdom on the Dnieper. Willy-nilly the great Germanic tribal groups, Visigoths, Ostrogoths, Vandals and numerous lesser peoples, were flung against the empire. It was now no longer a case of adventurer bands raiding for plunder, but of whole peoples desperately seeking a home.

The emperor Valens was killed in 378 trying to stem the tide, but his successor was forced to recognize a *fait accompli* and admit the Goths into the empire as *foederati*. This meant that the newcomers were given land to settle on, under their own kings, and living under their own laws, but in return they were to fight for Rome. The empire thereby received its final saturation of barbarians, and its own citizens were now completely divorced from the fighting forces. Their task remained the heavy one of paying taxes.

Gaul as yet was unaffected. Trouble came from the other side, with another British usurper, Maximus, who denuded the island of troops and defeated and slew Gratian, Valentinian's son and successor, at Lyons, in 385. In 388 Maximus drew his troops off to the Danube provinces, where Theodosius defeated and slew him. The army of Gaul was gradually being dispersed.

At the beginning of the fifth century the centre of history is Italy, where for ten years Alaric and his Visigoths ravaged the country and Stilicho, the great German general, now effective head of the state, called for still more troops from Gaul and the remnant from Britain. So only a garrison of Frankish warriors was left on the Rhine when in December 406 a host of Vandals, Alans and Lugi crossed the river at Mainz. They could not be stayed, but wandered about Gaul destroying as they went, before, in 409, they crossed into Spain. In their wake phantom emperors disputed the empire and besieged one another in decaying cities. The Burgundians meanwhile crossed the Rhine and began to settle down in Alsace. In 411–412 Honorius rid Italy of the Visigoths by agreeing to their settlement as *foederati* in Narbonensis, so yet another Germanic host entered Gaul—this time via

Italy. They seized Narbonne, Toulouse and Bordeaux, but followed the Vandals into Spain in 417.

In 418 it looked as if Roman Gaul was reviving, and to strengthen this recovery Honorius renewed the old assembly of the Gauls, which now, however, was to be held at Arles, and which in fact only included the provinces of the diocese of Viennensis. He also brought back the Visigoths in 418, this time to Aquitania Secunda, where they were definitely settled, with Bordeaux as their capital, and were given the task of driving off the Saxon pirates who infested the coasts.

This peaceful arrangement was illusory, and the twenties and thirties of the century were full of conflict. The burden of these struggles was borne by the famous general Aëtius, and his successful fights with the Burgundians are remembered in the Niebelungenlied. In 445 Aëtius settled the remainder of the Burgundians in Savoy, not as *foederati* but as *hospites*. A German chief, his family and his followers was settled in each large domain, whose owner was compelled to give up two-thirds of his arable land and one-third of his slaves, and share in common his woods and his pastures. It meant that at least some of their possessions were preserved for the Gallo-Romans.

In this troubled epoch was passed the childhood of the man whom we justly regard as the last of the Gallo-Romans—Sidonius Apollinaris, a member of an aristocratic family, who was born about 432 in Lyons. With Visigoths in Aquitania, Bagaudae on the Loire, Britons entering and harrying Armorica (440–441), Burgundians in Savoy, Alemanni in Alsace and Franks long established on the lower Rhine and in Flanders, little of the old province remained to the empire. Aëtius and his officers were trying to cope with the situation, and to their efforts is due the comparative peace of Sidonius' youth. The forties were, however, years of doom, and it is interesting to reflect what little effect they seem to have had on his consciousness.

In 437 Litorius quelled the Bagaudae, under their chief Tibatto, and then had to hasten south to defend Narbonne from the Visigoths. Aëtius and Majorian also endeavoured to contain the southward advance of the Franks, while from the east a greater peril threatened, for in 435 Attila had become king of the Huns. Fifteen years later he was approaching the west. In 451 at the head of a miscellaneous force of Huns and East Germans he crossed the Rhine, apparently aiming to destroy the Visigoths as the only important force likely to protect the western empire. His passage across Gaul was surprisingly slow, and gave Aëtius time to rouse the heterogeneous elements of Gaul. Battle was joined at the Campus Mauriacus, west of Troyes. By a narrow margin the west won, and Attila retired to Pannonia. Sidonius, although of military age, and other young nobles like him, show no signs of having been disturbed in this hour of supreme peril. Aëtius did not long survive his victory, but Gaul now enjoyed twenty years of comparative quiet, and it is to this curious Indian Summer that much of the career of Sidonius belongs.

After the death of Valentinian no man seemed capable of holding the imperial sceptre in the west. One of the short-lived emperors of the time was the Arvernian magnate Avitus, father-in-law of Sidonius. Avitus had already served the empire well, taking part in the wars of Aëtius, and proving a useful diplomat in dealings with the Visigoths, especially in the crisis of 451. With the backing of Theodoric II and his Visigoths, Avitus was declared emperor by a gathering of Gallo-Roman nobles at Beaucaire (Ugernum). Though accepted in Rome, he only lasted a year, before he was assassinated through a plot between his old companion-at-arms, the Italian Majorian, and a barbarian captain, Ricimer.

Majorian visited Gaul on his way to Spain, which he used as a base against the Vandals. He did not have the fortune he deserved, and had to return to Italy, where he was murdered (461). He was the last Western emperor worth the name, and the last Roman emperor to set foot on Gallic soil. Aegidius, Majorian's general, remained at his post in Gaul. He, and his son Syagrius after him, tried to maintain what was left of northern Gaul, in the country between Somme, Meuse and Loire, with Soissons as their chief base.

A new Visigothic king Euric made no secret of his intention of conquering in his own right. He began by the conquest of the Berry, not without encouragement from certain Gallo-Roman nobles. Then he worked south and took Arles. The Massif Central remained, the last citadel of Roman Gaul, save for the tattered domain of Syagrius, and Euric now turned his attention to Auvergne, where, in 469, Sidonius had been made bishop of Clermont.

This agreeable *dilettante* now showed his real worth. In successive years he held Clermont against the Visigoths, stoutly backed up by his brother-in-law Ecdicius, in whom we see a latter-day Vercassivellaunus. Ecdicius raised a band of horsemen on his own estates and galloped down to Clermont to harry the invaders. So the end of Roman Gaul is not an unworthy one, but the struggle was in vain, for in 475 Aquitania, including Auvergne, was surrendered to the Visigoths by the emperor Julius Nepos, in an effort to save Provence which proved illusory, for Euric forthwith occupied it also.

Roman Gaul thus ended where it had begun, in the south, but the Arverni, leaders of the last fight for Rome as once they had been of the last fight against Rome, have the last word—spoken by their bishop:—'Our enslavement was made the price of the security of others—the enslavement of the Arverni—men who called themselves brothers of the Romans'.

Seven years later Syagrius was driven from the town of Soissons, where he had maintained himself, unrecognized by Rome, mistrusted by the Franks, and where he now barred the road to fortune of King Clovis. The land was awaiting Charlemagne and Hugh Capet.

BIBLIOGRAPHY

A few of the principal works are given below. The literature is vast, but comprehensive bibliographical material is included in many of the books noted. This list is intended to serve two purposes, first, that of an introduction, and second, to show the sources of information drawn upon for particular points in the text.

ANCIENT SOURCES

The province and various periods of its history are treated most fully by: Caesar (*Gallic War*); Strabo (*Geography*, especially Book IV); Pliny (*Natural History*, especially Books III and IV); Tacitus (*Annals* and *Histories*); Dio Cassius (*History*, to A.D. 229); Ausonius (*Poems* and *Letters*); Ammianus Marcellinus (*History*, A.D. 353–378); Sidonius Apollinaris (*Letters*, especially the translation, with notes, by O. M. Dalton, 1915).

GENERAL WORKS

C. Jullian. *Histoire de la Gaule*. Paris. 8 vols. completed 1926, the foundation of any work on Roman Gaul; A. Grenier. *Archéologie gallo-romaine*. 2 vols. 1931 and 1934, the continuation of J. Déchelette's *Manuel d'archéologie préhistorique, celtique et gallo-romaine;* E. Espérandieu. *Recueil des bas-reliefs, statues et bustes de la Gaule romaine*. 12 vols., from 1907, with an additional volume for *La Germanie romaine*. This is being added to by new supplements prepared by R. Lantier. Inscriptions of Roman Gaul are in volumes III, XII and XIII of the *Corpus Inscriptionum Latinarum*, and in Dessau, *Inscriptiones Latinae Selectae*. A. Blanchet. *Carte Archéologique de la Gaule romaine (Forma Orbis Romani)*. Only a few Departments are so far represented. *Tabula Imperii Romani*. Sheet M32, *Mainz*. Ed. P. Goessler. 1940. Map of Roman Germany and part of Gallia Belgica.

Single volumes on Gaul are E. Thévenot's little book *Les Gallo-Romains*, 1948, (*Que sais-je* series, No. 314) and F. Lot's *La Gaule*, 1947, which is by an expert in the late empire and the early medieval period. There are also chapters, maps and bibliographies in the *Cambridge Ancient History*. Some regional works may be noted, but see also bibliographies to chapters below:—F. Stähelin. *Die Schweiz in römischer Zeit*. 3rd Edn. 1948. R. Forrer. *L'Alsace romaine*. 1935. K. Schumacher. *Siedelungs- und Kulturgeschichte der Rheinlande*, ii. *Die römische Periode*. 1923. *Germania Romana. Ein Bilder-Atlas*. 2nd Edn. 1924. F. Cumont. *Comment la Belgique fut romanisée*. 2nd Edn. 1919. J. Breuer. *La Belgique romaine*. 1946. S. J. De Laët. 'La Gaule Septentrionale à l'epoque romaine' *Bull. Inst. historique belge de Rome*. 1950–51. A. W. Byvanck. *Nederland in den Romeinschen Tijd*. 2 vols. 1945. A. Albenque. *Les Rutènes*. 1948.

Masterly résumés of the progress of Gallo-Roman archæology since the First World War have been given by R. Lantier: 'Ausgrabungen und neue Funde in Frankreich, 1915–1930', *Berichte der Röm.-Germanische Kommission*, XX; 'Roman Gaul, 1940–1944', *Journal of Roman Studies*, 1946, and regularly in the *Revue Archéologique* and *Gallia*.

Visitors to Paris can go to the Musée des Antiquités Nationales at Saint-Germain-en-Laye, where, in the gloomy old chateau, there is a splendid

BIBLIOGRAPHY 241

collection illustrating all aspects of Roman Gaul. See R. Lantier, *Guide Illustré du Musée des Antiquités Nationales*, 1948.

PERIODICALS

In general the most important and easily accessible are: *Gallia*, Fouilles et Monuments archéologiques en France métropolitaine (first appeared in 1943); *Revue Archéologique; Revue des Études anciennes; L'Antiquité Classique; Bonner Jahrbücher; Germania; Berichte der Römisch-Germanische Kommission*.

BIBLIOGRAPHIES TO CHAPTERS

CHAPTER I. A. Grenier. *Les Gaulois*. 1945; P. Jacobsthal and E. Neuffer. 'Gallia Graeca'. *Préhistoire*, 1933; T. Rice Holmes. *Caesar's Conquest of Gaul*. 2nd Edn. 1911; Napoléon III. *Histoire de Jules César*. 2 vols. and *Atlas*. 1865; *Pro Alésia*. Periodical with record of work at Alise-Sainte-Reine; notes on M. Gorce's excavations in Caesar's camp at Gergovia are given in E. Desforges and P. Balme, *Gergovie, Haut-Lieu de France*. 1943; G. Matherat. 'La Technique des Retranchements de César d'après l'enseignement des Fouilles de Nointel', *Gallia*. I. 1943, see also his article in *Rev. Archéologique*, 1936; R. Syme. 'The Origin of Cornelius Gallus'. *Classical Quarterly*. 1938.

CHAPTER II. For roads and camps see Grenier, *Manuel;* for an English account of the frontier of Germany see O. Brogan. 'The Roman Limes in Germany.' *Archæological Journal*. 1936.

CHAPTER III. A Momigliano. *Claudius*. 1934 (with the emperor's speech on Gaul); G. Dottin. *La Langue gauloise*. 1920; T. Haarhoff. *Schools of Gaul*. 1920; F. Brunot. *Histoire de la Langue française*. I. 1905.

CHAPTERS IV AND V. A. Blanchet. *Les Enceintes romaines de la Gaule*. 1907; N. J. De Witt. *Urbanization and the Franchise in Roman Gaul*. 1940; R. G. Goodchild. 'The Origins of the Romano-British Forum.' *Antiquity*. 1940; J. Sautel. *Le Théâtre de Vaison et les Théâtres romains de la Vallée du Rhône*. 1946; K. M. Kenyon. 'The Roman Theatre at Verulamium.' *Archaeologia*. 1935. (With distribution-map of 'cockpit-theatres'.); A Blanchet. *Recherches sur les Aqueducs et les Cloâques de la Gaule romaine*. 1923; E. Espérandieu. *Le Pont du Gard*. 2nd Edn. 1934; E. Samesreuther. 'Römischer Wasserleitungen in den Rheinlanden.' *Berichte*. 1936.

For the work on towns see Grenier's *Manuel*, and, more recently, *Gallia*. **Augst:** R. Laur-Belart. *Führer durch Augusta Raurica*. 2nd Edn. 1948. **Saint-Blaise:** H. Rolland. *Fouilles de Saint-Blaise*. 1951. **Narbonne:** P. Hélèna. *Les Origines de Narbonne*. 1937. **Arles:** R. E. M. Wheeler. 'The Roman Town Walls of Arles.' *Journal of Roman Studies*, 1926; F. Benoît in *Comptes Rendus de l'Académie des Inscriptions*, 1941, p. 97; *Les Monuments Historiques de La France*, IV. 1939. **Nîmes:** R. Naumann, *Der Quellbezirk von Nîmes*, 1937. A. Bon. 'La Fontaine de Nîmes.' *Rev. Ét. Anc.* 1940. **Glanum:** H. Rolland. *Fouilles de Glanum (Saint-Rémy de Provence)*. 1946. **Orange:** I. A. Richmond. 'Commemorative Arches and City Gates in the Augustan Age.' *Journ. Rom. Studies*. 1933; I. A. Richmond and C. E. Stevens. 'The Land-Register of *Arausio*.' *Ibid*. 1942. **Vaison:** J. Sautel. *Vaison dans l'Antiquité*. 3 vols. 1942; *La Maison d'un riche Gallo-Romain à Vaison au temps de l'Empire*. 1945. **Lyons:** P. Wuilleumier. *Fouilles de Fourvières à Lyon*. 1951; P. Wuilleumier and A. Audin. 'Les voies axiales de Lugdunum.' *Gallia*. 1943. **Autun:** E. Thévenot. *Autun. Cité romaine et chrétienne*. 1932. **Gergovia:** J. J. Hatt, M. Labrousse and others, *Gallia* II, V, VI; Desforges and Balme, *Gergovia, Haut-Lieu de France* (an account of the various excavations on the plateau and in the neighbourhood); O. Brogan and E. Desforges, ' Gergovia ', *Archaeological Journal*, 1940 (the work of 1934–37; though the theory that the walls abutting on the rampart were ramps to enable the defenders to mount the defences, is no longer upheld by O. Brogan, its author).

Paris: P. M. Duval. ' Proues de navires de Paris.' *Gallia*. 1947. **Metz:** M. Toussaint. *Metz à l'époque gallo-romaine.* 1948. **Boulogne:** Grenier. ' Deux Ports Romains du Pas-de-Calais. Portus Itius et Portus Aepatiacus.' *C.R. Acad. des Inscr.* 1944 (based on work of Vannérus); J. Heurgon. ' Les Problèmes de Boulogne.' *Rev. Ét. Anc.* 1948. **Trier:** W. von Massow. *Das römische Trier.* 1944; H. Koethe. ' Neue Daten zur Geschichte des römischen Trier.' *Germania.* 1936; H. Eiden. ' Untersuchungen an den spätrömischen Horrea von St. Irminen in Trier '; *Trierer Zeitschrift.* 1949; W. Reusch and H. Mylius. ' Zur Fragen der einschiffigen römischen Apsiden-Grossbauten im Moselraum.' *Ibid.*; W. Reusch. ' Die Aussengalerien der sog. Basilika in Trier.' *Ibid.*; T. K. Kempf. ' Die vorläufigen Ergebnisse der Ausgrabungen auf dem Gelände des Trierer Domes.' *Germania.* 1951. **Cologne:** H. Schmitz. *Stadt und Imperium. Köln in römischer Zeit.* 1948. F. Fremersdorf, *Neue Beiträge zur Topographie des römischen Köln.* 1950.

CHAPTERS VI AND VII

Villas: Grenier, *Manuel*; R. de Maeyer. *De Romeinsche Villa's in België.* 1937 (French summary and good distribution map); J. Steinhausen. ' Die Langmaner bei Trier.' *Trierer Zeitschrift.* 1936; La Vergnée villa: *Rev. Archéologique* 1940; Oberentfelden: Stähelin, *op. cit.*; Montmaurin: G. Fouet and M. Labrousse. ' Découvertes Archéologiques en Nébouzan.' *Gallia.* 1949. **Chastel-sur-Murat:** Pagès-Allary in *Bull. Soc. Préhistorique de France*, 1908, 1909. C. E. Stevens. ' Un Etablissement celtique à la Croix du Hengstberg.' *Rev. Archéologique.* 1937. A. Dauzat. *La Toponymie française.* 1946. **Economic Life:** A. Grenier. *La Gaule romaine*, in vol. III of *An Economic Survey of Ancient Rome* (Ed. Tenney Frank). 1937. Indispensable for economic history; L. C. West. *Roman Gaul. The Objects of Trade.* 1935; F. Oswald and T. D. Pryce. *An Introduction to the Study of Terra Sigillata.* 1920.

Some recent works. **Water-mills:** F. Benoit. *Comptes Rendus de l'Acad. des Inscriptions.* 1938. C. L. Sagui. ' La Meunerie de Barbegal.' *Isis.* 1948. **Pottery:** J. B. Ward Perkins. ' The Pottery of Gergovia in relation to that of other sites in Central and South-Western France.' *Arch. Journ.* 1940. G. Chenet. *La Céramique gallo-romaine d'Argonne du IVme siècle et la terre sigillée décorée à la molette.* 1941. **Glass:** F. Fremersdorf. *Römischer Gläser aus Köln.* 2nd Edn. 1939. **Metal work:** A. Alföldi. ' Chars Funéraires Bacchiques dans les Provinces Occidentales.' *L'Antiquité Classique.* 1939. P. Wuilleumier. ' Le Goblet en Argent de Lyon.' *Rev. Archéologique.* 1936. **Wine:** S. Loeschke. *Denkmäler vom Weinbau aus der Zeit der Römerherrschaft an Mosel, Saar und Ruwer.* 1933.

CHAPTER VIII. Espérandieu's great collection is the basis, and there are many special studies on art. J. Formigé. *Le Trophée des Alpes (La Turbie).* 1949; for Trophy at Saint-Bertrand-des-Comminges, see C. Picard in *Comptes Rendus de l'Acad. des Inscriptions*, 1942. E. Thévenot. ' Sculptures inédites de Chorey.' *Gallia.* 1947; M. E. Mariën. ' Les Monuments funéraires de l'Arlon romaine.' *Inst. Archéologique de Luxembourg.* 1945; W. von Massow. *Die Grabmäler von Neumagen.* 1932; H. Koethe. ' La Sculpture romaine au pays des Trévires.' *Rev. Arch.* 1937; J. J. Hatt.

La Tombe gallo-romaine. 1951; A. Blanchet. *Inventaire des Mosaiques de la Gaule romaine.* 1909; for the Brive *emblema*, M. Labrousse in *Mélanges*, 1940; F. Fremersdorf. ' Das neugefundene Kölner Dionysos-Mosaik.' *Germania.* 1941; W. Déonna. *L'Art romain en Suisse.* 1942.

CHAPTER IX. For the description of Celtic survivals in Gallo-Roman religion P. Lambrechts' book, *Contribution à l'Étude des Divinités Celtiques*, has been closely followed; for Cernunnos, cf. P. P. Bober in *American Journal of Archaeology.* 1951; A. Grenier. 'Hercule et les Théatres gallo-romains.' *Rev. Ét. Anc.* 1940; T. D. Kendrick. *The Druids.* 1927; and, in regard to their suppression, Hugh Last in *Journal of Roman Studies*, 1949. **Celtic Temples:** H. Koethe. ' Ein Menhir als Tempelkultbild.' *Germania.* 1932; Koethe, ' Die Keltischen Rund- und Vielecktempel der Kaiserzeit.' *Berichte*, 1933; J. Formigé. ' Le Sanctuaire de Sanxay.' *Gallia.* 1944; S. Loeschke. *Die Erforschung des Tempelbezirkes im Altbachtale zu Trier.* 1928, and his subsequent, more detailed accounts (1938 and 1942). **Christianity:** E. Mâle. *La Fin du Paganisme en Gaule*, et les plus anciennes basiliques chrétiennes. 1950. The tales about the lake and the fairies come respectively from Albenque's *Rutènes* and H. Dontenville's *La Mythologie française.* 1948.

CHAPTER X. **Defences:** A. Blanchet. *Les Enceintes* (see Chap IV); Stähelin, *op. cit.* (see General Works); F. L. Ganshof. *Étude sur le Développement des Villes entre Loire et Rhin au Moyen Age.* 1943; E. Anthès. ' Spätrömische Kastelle und Feste Städte im Rhein und Donaugebiet.' *Bericht.* 1917; W. Schleiermacher. ' Der obergermanische Limes und spätrömische Wehranlagen am Rhein.' *Bericht.* 1951; J. Vannérus. ' Le Limes et les fortifications gallo-romaines de Belgique, enquête toponomyque.' *Acad. roy. de Belg. Mém.* 1943; G. Faider-Feytmans. ' La Frontière du Nord de la Gaule Sous le Bas-Empire.' 1948. **General:** N. H. Baynes. ' The Decline of the Roman Power in Western Europe.' *Journ. of Roman Studies.* 1944; S. Dill. *Roman Society in the Last Century of the Western Empire.* 2nd Edn. 1899; C. E. Stevens. *Sidonius Apollinaris.* 1933.

INDEX

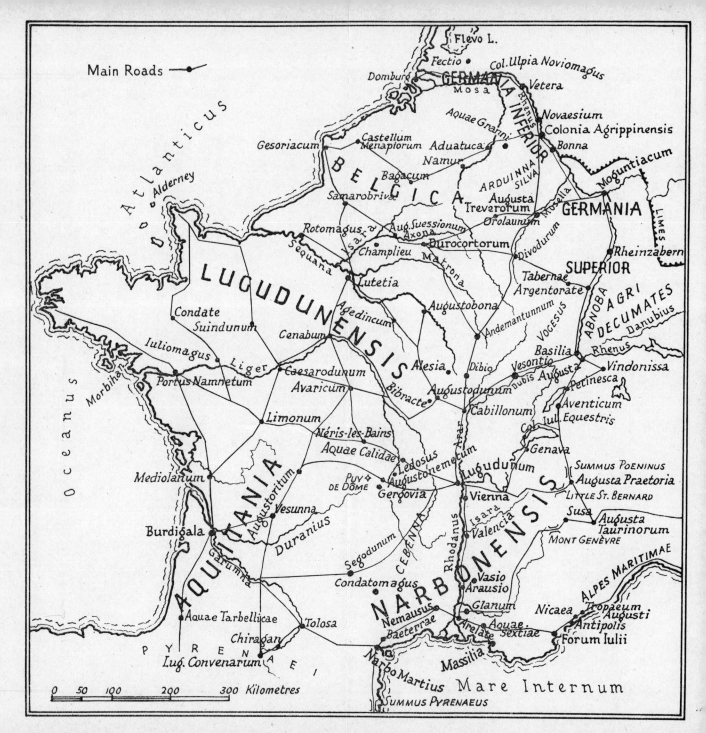

Main Roads •————•

Oceanus Atlanticus

Flevo L.
Fectio
Domburg
Col. Ulpia Noviomagus
Vetera
Mosa
GERMANIA INFERIOR
Novaesium
Aquae Granni
Colonia Agrippinensis
Gesoriacum
Castellum Menapiorum
Aduatuca
Bonna
Namur
Moguntiacum
BELGICA
Bagacum
ARDUINNA SILVA
Alderney
Samarobriva
Augusta Treverorum
GERMANIA
Rotomagus
Aug. Suessionum
Orolaunum
Mosella
Sequana
Axona
Durocortorum
Divodurum
Rheinzabern
Champlieu
Matrona
SUPERIOR
Lutetia
Tabernae
Argentorate
ABNOBA
LUGUDUNENSIS
Agedincum
Augustobona
Andemantunnum
VOGESUS
AGRI DECUMATES
Condate
Suindunum
Cenabum
Danubius
Iuliomagus
Liger
Caesarodunum
Alesia
Dibio
Vesontio
Basilia
Rhenus
Avaricum
Bibracte
dubis Augusta
Vindonissa
Portus Namnetum
Augustodunum
Petinesca
Morbihan
Limonum
Néris-les-Bains
Cabillonum
Aventicum
Col. Iul. Equestris
Aquae Calidae
Ledosus
Augustonemetum
Lugudunum
Genava
Mediolanum
Puy de Dôme
Summus Poeninus
Augustoritum
Gergovia
Vienna
Augusta Praetoria
Vesunna
AQUITANIA
Isara
Little St. Bernard
Burdigala
Duranius
Valencia
Susa
Augusta Taurinorum
Garumna
Segodunum
CEBENNA
Rhodanus
Mont Genèvre
Condatomagus
Vasio
Arausio
ALPES MARITIMAE
Nemausus
Glanum
Nicaea
Tropaeum Augusti
Aquae Tarbellicae
Tolosa
NARBONENSIS
Baeterrae
Aquae Sextiae
Antipolis
Chiragan
Arelate
Forum Iulii
PYRENAEI
Lug. Convenarum
Narbo Martius
Massilia
Mare Internum
SUMMUS PYRENAEUS

0 50 100 200 300 Kilometres